Pax Syriana

Modern Intellectual and Political History of the Middle East
Mehrzad Boroujerdi, *Series Editor*

Pax Syriana

Elite Politics in Postwar Lebanon

Rola el-Husseini

With a Foreword by Ryan Crocker

SŪU

Syracuse University Press

First Edition 2012

12 13 14 15 16 17   6 5 4 3 2 1

∞ The paper used in this publication meets the minimum requirements
of the American National Standard for Information Sciences—Permanence
of Paper for Printed Library Materials, ANSI Z39.48-1992.

For a listing of books published and distributed by Syracuse University Press,
visit our website at SyracuseUniversityPress.syr.edu.

ISBN: 978-0-8156-3304-4

Library of Congress Cataloging-in-Publication Data
El-Husseini, Rola.
  Pax Syriana : elite politics in postwar Lebanon / Rola el-Husseini ; with a
Foreword by Ryan Crocker. — First edition.
      pages cm. — (Modern intellectual and political history of the Middle East)
  Includes bibliographical references and index.
  ISBN 978-0-8156-3304-4 (cloth : alkaline paper) 1. Lebanon—Politics and
government—1990– 2. Lebanon—Politics and government—1975–1990.
3. Lebanon—History—Civil War, 1975–1990—Peace. 4. Lebanon—Foreign
relations—Treaties. 5. Ta'if Agreement (1989) 6. Elite (Social sciences)—
Political activity—Lebanon—History—20th century. 7. Elite (Social sciences)—
Political activity—Lebanon—History—21st century. 8. Lebanon—Foreign
relations—Syria. 9. Syria—Foreign relations—Lebanon. 10. Hizballah
(Lebanon) I. Title.
  DS87.54.E44 2012
  956.9204'4—dc23   2012034802

Manufactured in the United States of America

To my parents

Rola el-Husseini is a research assistant professor at the Middle Eastern and Middle Eastern American Center, City University of New York–Graduate Center. She has previously held positions at Texas A&M University and Yale University. Her publications have appeared in *Comparative Studies of South Asia, Africa, and the Middle East;* the *Middle East Journal; Orient;* and the *Third World Quarterly.*

Contents

Foreword

Since the start of the civil war in 1975, Lebanon has had an enormous impact on the region and the international community. A series of foreign powers have intervened militarily—the United States, France, Britain, Italy, Israel, and Syria. Sometimes they have come as peacekeepers, sometimes as invaders. Sometimes it is hard to tell the difference. All have departed, many with heavy losses and none with core objectives accomplished, with the partial exception of Syria. Lebanon also hosted a bewildering variety of militia groups, from every Lebanese sect and political faction, virtually the entire Palestinian guerrilla movement, and now one of the most formidable nonstate forces in the world, Hezbollah, which enjoys support from both Syria and Iran.

So Lebanon matters, and it will continue to matter. We ignore it or misunderstand it (which we commonly do) at our grave peril. In this sense, Dr. el-Husseini has done us an enormous service with her groundbreaking book. It is the first to cover the so-called postwar period with scholarly rigor. Her focus on elites is key to an understanding of the complex political landscape of Lebanon. Events and actions can unfold with bewildering rapidity; the dominance of elites is a constant. Her construct of looking at Lebanon as two republics, the first created by the National Pact of 1943 and the second through the Ta'if Agreement of 1989 is extremely useful to the scholar, the practitioner, and the lay reader. Her analysis of Hezbollah draws on sources within the movement and sheds important new light on an organization that is as complicated as it is lethal. And her examination of the Syrian role in Lebanon is more nuanced, detailed, and accurate than anything I have read elsewhere.

I served twice in Lebanon, as political counselor at the American Embassy from 1981 to 1984 and as ambassador from 1990 to 1993. As a practitioner I would have given a great deal for a comprehensive, well-researched, and balanced guide to Lebanon's chaotic politics. Thanks to Rola el-Husseini, now we have it.

Ryan Crocker
Former US Ambassador to Lebanon
(1990–1993) and Syria (1998–2001)

Acknowledgments

This book took a decade to come to fruition. Originally a dissertation written in French and defended in 2003, it was substantially revised and updated for publication. This work would not have been possible without the help and support of many people—mentors, colleagues, friends, and family. I am indebted to many people for their support, feedback, and guidance throughout the research and writing phase of the dissertation and then the book.

I am especially grateful to all the Lebanese politicians, academics, and journalists who agreed to meet with me in Lebanon. I am honored to have had the opportunity to meet Basil Fuleihan, Gebran Tueni, and Samir Qassir before their untimely deaths. Joseph Alagha and Lara Deeb were two scholars I had the pleasure of meeting while doing fieldwork, and I was delighted to get the chance to read their wonderful books on the Shi'i community.

Thank you to my friends in Paris, Aliki Angelidou, Adele Thorens, Michela Trisconi, and especially my childhood friend Khaled el-Khatib, for their moral support. I also extend special thanks to the members of the "Arab Elites" team at the Stiftung Wissenschaft und Politik in Berlin, especially to Iris Glosemeyer and Saloua Zerhouni. Their comments and feedback were crucial in shaping my thinking on the book, and their friendship made my three years in Berlin much richer. Volker Perthes, who took me on board the Arab Elites team and effectively served as my dissertation adviser, will always have my gratitude and affection. I am also indebted to Ellen Lust, who encouraged me to apply to a postdoctoral position at Yale University. Her friendship in New Haven and that of Hala K. Nassar were lifesavers.

Colleagues and friends in Texas also provided advice and a listening ear when needed. I would particularly like to thank Ryan C. Crocker and Michael C. Desch for their encouragement and mentorship. Harry Berger and Giovanna del Negro, Christopher Menzel and Tazim Jamal, Zulema Valdez and Andrew Yinger, Cara Wallis and John Zollinger, and Rhonda Struminger and Gil Rosenthal entertained me in their homes and provided much-needed solace at times. Ulrike Gretzel and Amanda Stronza were great girlfriends and essential social support.

I am also especially thankful for the work Jesse L. Rester put into copyediting this manuscript. His comments and suggestions were always helpful. Mary Selden Evans, the former Middle East editor at Syracuse University Press, deserves my gratitude for her belief in the importance of this project. Others at Syracuse University Press have also been crucial for the completion of this book. After Mary's retirement, Kelly Balenske was wonderfully supportive and helpful, and Marcia Hough was always responsive to my queries about the production schedule of the book.

I am deeply appreciative for the encouragement of Mehrzad Boroujerdi and Augustus R. Norton and their comments on sections of this book. Many others, too numerous to name, were instrumental in the writing of this book. I am deeply thankful.

This book would not have been possible without the love and encouragement of my family, especially my mother's support. She taught me the value of an education for a woman and pushed me to excel and to be resilient in the face of adversity. I would not be where I am without her. I also thank my husband, Wesley R. Dean, for his unflagging support of my academic work. He read many versions of this book and always gave valuable feedback. I would not have completed this book without his occasional prods to "go write your book."

Note on Transliteration

A simplified form of the *International Journal of Middle East Studies* style has been used for transliteration from Arabic throughout the text. No diacritical marks have been used with the exception of the hamza (') and the ayn ('). Lebanese names have been written in the most common form found in the Lebanese press in English (for example, Aoun instead of 'Awn, Geagea instead of Ja'ja', Gemayel instead of Jumayyil, Siniora instead of Sanyura). Names of places have been kept in their common English form: Beirut instead of Bayrut, Tripoli instead of Tarablus, and Sidon instead of Saida.

Introduction

The recent political history of Lebanon has been defined by the legacy of war. In addition to repeated external invasions and the ongoing presence of foreign troops of diverse nationalities, the Lebanese people have endured the scars of a bitterly contested civil war that began in the spring of 1975 and continued unabated for the next fifteen years. Political normality began to be restored only in the closing months of 1989, in the wake of negotiations brokered by Saudi Arabia under the auspices of the larger international community. Representatives of various Lebanese factions convened in the Saudi Arabian city of Ta'if to hammer out a compromise that eventually put an end to active hostilities. The document produced by these negotiations, which came to be known as the Ta'if Agreement, reestablished the same general form of government that had been in place before the civil war—a system in which political representation is apportioned on the basis of religion. In this system of confessional power sharing, an informally designated number of parliamentary seats and ministerial positions are allocated to each of the country's diverse religious communities: Sunni Muslims, Shi'i Muslims, Maronite Christians, and Druze, to name just a few of the largest constituencies.[1] Confessionalism has been a feature of Lebanese politics since the country gained its independence in 1943, and this political structure was further institutionalized by the Ta'if Agreement. The seeming intractability of the confessional system, combined with the legacy of ongoing sectarian tension, leads to an important question: does structural confessionalism act to mitigate sectarian tensions in Lebanon by promoting the sharing of power, or does the political structure merely express and exacerbate these tensions by forcing all political interests into sectarian contours?

The Ta'if Agreement also had the notable effect of consolidating the long-standing influence of the Syrian government in Lebanese politics. Syrian influence was deeply embedded in Lebanon at the end of the civil war, and owing to Syria's alignment with Saudi Arabia and Western powers during the 1990–91 Gulf War, the international powers allowed Syria to have a free hand in Lebanon. Syria's ruling regime forced the rebellious general Michel Aoun out of Lebanon's presidential palace and made Lebanon into a satellite state through a series of agreements that linked the two countries in fields ranging from security to education. Syrian political hegemony and a Syrian military presence would prove to be the rule in Lebanon throughout the 1990s. It was only after the turn of the millennium that criticism against the Syrian presence began to be publicly voiced in Lebanon, culminating in the "Cedar Revolution" of 2005,[2] which forced a withdrawal of Syrian troops, and the legislative elections of 2009, which heralded the rise of a new generation of independent Lebanese political elites. Only time will tell whether Syrian oversight was a necessary feature of the political stability that Lebanon experienced after the Ta'if Agreement. Since March 2011, Syria has been rocked by antiregime demonstrations calling for Assad's removal from power. These demonstrations have been received by the Syrian regime with force. On March 27, 2012, the United Nations estimated the number of deaths to be nine thousand. The outcome of the turmoil in Syria and its impact on Lebanon will be telling regarding the importance of Syria on Lebanon's stability.

Although much has been written about the history of Lebanese politics and especially about the tragedy of the civil war, scholars have not yet turned their attention to a systematic analysis of the evolution of the Lebanese political scene in the years after the Ta'if Agreement.[3] In this book I provide such an analysis, based on fieldwork and interviews that I conducted between 2001 and 2006, as well as on my critical readings of news broadcasts, position papers, memoirs, party platforms, and other primary sources. My approach to understanding the Lebanese political scene is focused on the examination of the small cadre of individuals whom sociologists and political scientists call the "political elite."[4] This label refers to people who exercise power in society or who can be said to have a personal influence on national decision making. It includes a range of public and nonpublic figures, from high-ranking government officials and military officers, to leaders of professional associations and business and industry representatives, to the heads of politically influential families, and to people who are highly placed in media organizations, interest groups, and religious communities. These individuals are both influential upon and implicated within the political discourse of the nation.

Studying politics through the lens of the political elite is in some ways a limited mode of analysis. Approaching politics through elite cultures runs the risk of minimizing the agency of nonelite individuals. Nevertheless, this approach provides a very direct line to understanding the shifting features of political power and of national political discourses. Significant changes in the composition of the political elite, such as those that I will describe in this study, can be understood as indicative of broader changes in Lebanese society. Approaching politics through the lens of the elite is particularly effective in Lebanon owing to the historical importance of *zuʿama*, community leaders who are perceived as intercessors for their clients or followers. In this tradition, political agency is understood to be primarily about cultivating one's place within a hierarchy of personal relationships, rather than advocating for an overarching ideology or legislative platform. The clients of a *zaʿim* (the singular of *zuʿama*) vote for their leader's person, not for a political program. In many cases, the leader may not even *have* a political platform, beyond an established ability to further the interests of clients.

Describing the prewar political system, Lebanese sociologist Samir Khalaf argued that this historical concept of personal leadership, along with an electoral system that allocated political posts according to sectarian quotas, resulted in a situation in which individual Lebanese elites were able to wield an influence extending far beyond that of their personal electoral bases. By constructing alliances with other *zuʿama*, representing other segments of Lebanese society, certain leaders were able to build extensive patronage networks and to establish long-standing family dynasties.[5] The personal relationships among Lebanese elites, more than any particular set of ideological schisms, have long been the axis around which Lebanese politics has revolved. As of this writing, there seems to have been little change in this culture of political patronage. A study of personal histories and of the fortunes of individual power is therefore particularly relevant to understanding the trajectory of Lebanese political discourse. Who belongs to the Lebanese political elite in the postwar period? How do these elites maintain their power? What kind of discourses do they hold? How are new elites recruited, and what new bases of political power are emerging?

Fieldwork and Methodology

My analysis is based on fieldwork conducted in Lebanon during September and October 2001, April and May 2002, April and May 2003, and January 2006. I conducted fifty-six semistructured interviews with established and emerging members of the political elite, in addition to twenty-two informal discussions with journalists, academics, and other observers of the Lebanese political scene. All of the individuals whom I interviewed were male (in keeping with the general absence of women from Lebanese politics, which is discussed in chapter 6). More than half of my interviewees were then parliamentarians. Others were later elected into office. The sample also includes nine cabinet ministers (from various post-2000 cabinets), one former prime minister, and three retired military officers.

My approach to conducting research on the Lebanese elite was to use the reputational method, in which the individuals chosen for study are people who are widely described as having the ability to influence the political system. This approach allows the researcher to look beyond the merely formal conduits of power. It has a great advantage over more limited studies of officeholders, and it is perhaps the most effective way to obtain information about elite cultures.[6] There remains a concern, however, that the sample obtained may not be perfectly representative of the sources of political influence. It is difficult for any researcher to gain access to a country's core elite, and this task seemed especially difficult for a Lebanese national who wanted to study Lebanese politicians. I often found that I had to overcome a sense of fear or mistrust in order to obtain interviews. I believe that these attitudes most likely stemmed from the interviewees' concerns that a Lebanese researcher might be motivated by a specific political agenda.[7] It was also impossible for me to interview active military officers, as they are not allowed to speak to researchers or journalists, although I compensated for this by speaking with former military officers who are still close to the institution. Perhaps the most significant lacuna is that my sample did not include interviews with members of the clergy. In spite of these limitations, the sample of elite Lebanese with whom I conducted interviews is relatively balanced in terms of age, education, profession, political outlook, and religious affiliation.

The majority of the interviews took place in the capital, Beirut, in a private setting in the homes or offices of the interviewees. These settings helped to minimize distractions and to establish a degree of trust between the researcher and the interviewees. In addition, anonymity was promised to these informants, especially concerning their opinions on sensitive issues. Direct references to the interviewees are thus avoided in this book. Most of the interviews were taped, but were then transcribed by the author to preserve the confidentiality of the information. Since the recording of conversations can sometimes lead to a decrease in sincerity,[8] informants who did not wish to be taped were interviewed without the recorder. These conditions helped to ensure that the interviewees could relate direct and informal perspectives on the Lebanese political scene while remaining largely unconstrained by the requirements of their positions.

The choice to use a qualitative methodology was determined by the nature of the research. A population as limited and exclusive as the political elite cannot be studied with questionnaires or surveys. Instead, to gain an understanding of the attitudes and life trajectories of Lebanese elites, I began with the classic technique of reading the local press, the speeches of politicians, and memoirs and biographies.[9] Of course, the basic facts gathered in this research needed to be corroborated and fleshed out, and it was therefore necessary to combine the study of printed material with personal interviews. This is a research process that poses distinct practical, methodological, and analytical difficulties—Jean Lacouture has described interviews using the terms *inter-seduction* and *counter-seduction*.[10] Nevertheless, when interviews are conducted by an astute and critical researcher, they remain one of the best means available for apprehending the attitudes and intentions of elites.[11] These subjective attributes cannot be easily quantified and are most appropriately studied through a personal approach.

The interviews were organized according to a semistructured format, an approach that is commonly used by researchers who are working with elites and one that is ideal for studying material that needs in-depth interpretation.[12] The same questions, with minor variations, were asked of all interviewees. However, flexibility was allowed in the direction of the conversation after the questions had been asked. The questions can be divided into four main groups: questions about the life and political trajectory of the interviewee; questions about the positions and attitudes of the interviewee vis-à-vis themes deemed to be of national and strategic interest, such as the future of the confessional system and Syrian-Lebanese relations; questions about the interviewee's perceptions of postwar elites, including their attributes, attitudes, and behaviors; and finally, questions about the future of Lebanon and of the future roles of Lebanese elites. To avoid potential drawbacks, I cross-referenced information between interviews and asked the same questions to each interviewee in more than one way, in an attempt to prod interviewees who were being evasive.

My fieldwork leads me to conclude that the postwar Lebanese elite can be divided into three main groups, which I will call state elites, strategic elites, and emerging elites. The first group, state elites, consists of those individuals who first came to power during the violence of the civil war and then found a place in the political system in the 1990s. Today these elites are at the zenith (or slightly past the zenith) of their careers, and they tend to occupy important positions in governmental institutions. The second group, strategic elites, is composed of individuals who emerged onto the political scene because of special circumstances or unusual talents. These unelected elites frequently operate from the shadows, as éminences grises who influence better-known politicians, though in some cases they can also be outspoken opinion makers who promote national agendas on the public stage. In Lebanon these unelected elites include military commanders, religious leaders, and important journalists.

The third group, emerging elites, is mainly composed of young, aspiring politicians who are ready to accede to positions of political responsibility when the occasion presents itself.

For analytical purposes, the interviewees can also be categorized into three groups according to age. Those individuals over sixty years of age were socialized in the pre–civil war Lebanese society, and they were heavily influenced (in one way or another) by the Pan-Arabist ideology that swept the region during the 1950s and 1960s. Those interviewees from forty-five to sixty years of age are of the generation that fell into sectarian conflict and participated actively in the civil war. Finally, those persons from thirty to forty-five years of age were socialized during the height of the violence and tended to exhibit weariness with conflict and a distrust of sectarian dogma. (I discuss these generational differences in more detail in chapter 6.)

Argument and Outline of the Book

My central argument in this book is that the Ta'if Agreement and the other accords that followed it ushered in an era of systematic Syrian control in Lebanon, leading to temporary stability but not to an actual reconciliation of the political tensions that led to civil war. In the period between 1991 and 2005, the Syrian influence was felt strongly throughout Lebanon, but most especially in the area of elite recruitment. Many new political players who were willing to work with Syria emerged on the scene. Former warlords who "turned over a new leaf" were allowed to enter politics after the 1991 general amnesty, and religious leaders played an increasingly important role in the political process. Businessmen also came to play a greater role in the government, demonstrating a growing importance of financial capital in the political arena. There was an inherent optimism in the creation of a viable civic government after years of violence; however, it soon became apparent that the new political elites who came together in the postwar framework were not arriving with new attitudes or behaviors.

Like their predecessors, these postwar elites seemed to be focused almost exclusively on maintaining their influence, staying in office, and establishing sectarian political dynasties. Furthermore, as the Pax Syriana continued, the postwar elites slowly merged with traditional political players. Long-standing dynasties that had played a crucial role throughout twentieth-century Lebanese history were inexorably incorporated into the postwar political scene, and it seemed that the new regime was not in fact substantially different from what had come before. The Pax Syriana also involved an insidious intrusion of military and security apparatuses into Lebanon's political life, and for many the cost of this kind of security was too high. The drastic change that occurred during the Cedar Revolution and Syrian withdrawal was a shock to this system. The elections of 2005 involved a very high degree of elite circulation, as the coalitions held together by Syrian influence collapsed and elites who relied on Syrian support were purged from office. In the wake of the Syrian withdrawal, Lebanon entered a period of new possibilities—and renewed risks.

I have organized my analysis of the postwar Lebanese elite into seven chapters. Chapter 1 is a description of the formal structure of the Lebanese political system as it was initially formulated in the National Pact of 1943 and as it was modified and reestablished in the Ta'if Agreement. In this chapter I also provide background information on important prewar political actors and the history of Syrian involvement in Lebanon. Chapter 2 explains why an understanding of the formal governmental structures is not sufficient to identify the actual political relationships through which power flows in Lebanon. In this chapter I elaborate on the concepts of "elite settlements" and "elite factionalization," and I make an argument for the value of interpreting Lebanese politics through an examination of elite interactions.

From chapter 3 onward, I begin to flesh out the detailed histories of political factions and elite actors in Lebanon. In chapter 3 I turn to a discussion of specific Lebanese political parties, explaining their function within the political system and their failure to act as vehicles for elite recruitment. The principal Lebanese parties (the Kata'eb, the Lebanese Forces [LF], the Progressive Socialist Party [PSP], and Hezbollah) are discussed in some detail, as are the individual leaders of these parties. Chapter 4 describes the composition of the state elite. I examine the various social and professional groups from which these individuals are drawn and provide biographical sketches of important postwar presidents, prime ministers, and parliamentarians. This chapter also includes an analysis of the social mechanisms by which these state elites maintain their political influence and a discussion of the problem of financial corruption among Lebanese politicians. In chapter 5 I discuss the role of strategic elites in postwar Lebanese politics. The individuals discussed in this chapter include military leaders, members of the clergy, and prominent journalists. I examine the strong and diverse influences of these nonstate actors on the country's political discourse and national decision making.

Chapter 6 examines the features of Lebanon's emerging elites and discusses the prospects for change in the political culture. I describe the unfortunate continuation of the patronage-based system and the absence of women from positions of influence. I also discuss the means by which new elites are recruited into the political system and provide some examples of this process. Finally, in chapter 7 I examine the discourse of Lebanese political elites, focusing on two central questions of national interest: the viability of the confessional system and Lebanese-Syrian relations. I conclude by discussing the sectarian backdrop of Lebanese national identity and posing questions about the political future of the country.

Pax Syriana

1

The Lebanese Political System

The Elite Pacts of 1943 and 1989

Arend Lijphart, focusing on the period between 1943 and 1975, has described this relatively stable time in Lebanese history as a successful "consociational" democracy.[1] Consociationalism refers to a political situation in which a variety of groups, none of which are large enough to constitute a majority, are able to achieve social stability by means of a pact among the elites of the various groups. In the application of this term as developed by Lijphart, elites from the various factions negotiate power-sharing arrangements among themselves and thereby regulate political life in a divided society. Lijphart's analysis of the First Lebanese Republic is also applicable to the country's situation in more recent years. In order to put an end to the country's civil war in 1989, the ruling elites in Lebanon once again united around issues of shared strategic interest, such as the presence of Syrian troops in Lebanon, which all elite factions supported as an aid to peace and stability—at least until the Cedar Revolution of 2005. In response to the chaos and destruction of the civil war, the various Lebanese elites came to share an acute fear of a disintegration of the system and the return of anarchy. In the postwar period, therefore, they largely agreed to postpone their differences in order to promote stability.

Lijphart and others have suggested that Lebanon became a "consociational democracy" after its independence in 1943. Looking at the postwar years of Syrian hegemony (1989–2005), I am forced to agree with Tamirace Fakhoury-Muehlbacher in saying that although this political system had consociational features, it cannot fully be considered a consociational *democracy*.[2] Indeed, the same power-sharing arrangements that

1

made stability possible in an ethnically and culturally fragmented nation have also tended to impair the full development of democracy.[3] I will argue that the transition to democracy was thwarted by the nature of this political system, in which elites simply reorganized their power-sharing arrangements after each political upheaval, and also by the tendency of the consociational arrangements to rely on the stabilizing influence of external powers.

Marie-Joëlle Zahar has noted that "Lebanon's experiment with power sharing dates back to 1861" (the end of the sectarian war in Mount Lebanon between Druze and Maronites) and that "power sharing has brought long periods of peace, but this has depended on external protectors."[4] In the nineteenth century, the protector of the peace was the Ottoman Empire; through the early twentieth century, the role was played by France. My view is that the authoritarian regime in Syria came to be a similar arbiter of the peace between the end of the civil war in 1989 and the Cedar Revolution of 2005. Because Lebanon's power-sharing institutions have relied on external proctors, they have consistently thwarted the country's transition to democracy. Lebanese elites renegotiated the terms of their power-sharing agreements after each civil war; however, each renegotiated settlement was only slightly different from the preceding one.

In this chapter I explain the two primary power-sharing agreements established by Lebanese elites since the nation's independence: the National Pact of 1943 and the Ta'if Agreement of 1989. Each of these pacts led to an associated period of stability—the First and Second Lebanese Republics. I also address the issue of democracy in these republics and explain the role that Syria played as guarantor of the Ta'if Agreement in the Second Republic.

The Political System and the First Republic

Consociational Democracy

Writing in the late 1960s, Lijphart defined consociational political systems as "government by elite cartel designed to turn a democracy with a fragmented political culture into a stable democracy."[5] He identified four primary characteristics of such systems: the government is composed of a coalition of leaders that represent the various factions of the plural society, these leaders have a mutual veto over the other leaders' decisions, political factions are represented proportionally, and each political faction retains a high degree of autonomy.[6] Lijphart identified the First Lebanese Republic as a clear example of "consociational democracy" and argued that it was a successful system: "On the whole, consociational democracy in Lebanon must be judged to have performed satisfactorily for more than thirty years. Its main weakness was the inflexible institutionalization of consociational principles. [However,] . . . compared with the frequent revolutionary upheavals to which other Middle Eastern countries have been prone, and in spite of the flaws in its consociational institutions, the Lebanese consociational regime established a remarkable—although obviously far from perfect—record of democratic stability."[7]

Notably, Lijphart's interpretation focuses on political elites as systemic agents of change. In his model, the role of elites is perceived as crucial in attenuating or exacerbating sectarian conflicts. According to Lijphart, in order to promote stability the leaders of the diverse political factions must make active interventions and must be willing to transcend sectarian divisions and accommodate the demands of other elites. Their ability to do so depends on a commitment to stability and a desire to avoid the negative consequences of political fragmentation.[8] Lijphart's consociational model offers a useful theoretical perspective for the examination of power sharing in divided societies such as Lebanon. Scholars have largely agreed with Lijphart's assessment of the Lebanese political system and have acknowledged that the First Lebanese Republic was a perfect example of his consociational model.[9] To examine the reality of this political system in more detail, I will begin by discussing the creation and conditions of the First Republic.

The National Pact and the Founding of the First Republic

The founding act of modern Lebanon was the National Pact of 1943. The pact was an unwritten gentlemen's agreement between representatives of what were at the time the two main Lebanese communities, the Maronites and the Sunnis. This arrangement, alongside the earlier French-sponsored constitution of 1926, regulated political life in the independent Lebanese Republic from 1943 until the breakdown that led to civil war in 1975. The National Pact was the product of intense negotiations between the notables, parliamentarians, and *zu'ama* (local leaders) of the two communities. The discussions were initiated by bankers and merchants, from Greek Catholic and Greek Orthodox backgrounds, who had a vested interest in seeing better cooperation between Muslims and Christians. The resulting coalition among members of different elite groups was based on negotiation and compromise, rather than on the dictates of a majority. The governmental arrangements of this elite pact went beyond the basic outlines of the constitution to ensure that representatives of each important faction would share in the organization of power. For example, it was (informally) established that the Lebanese president would always come from the Maronite Christian community, the position of prime minister would always be held by a Sunni Muslim, and the position of Speaker of the parliament would always be held by a Shi'i Muslim.[10] Further principles of this arrangement were that Muslims accepted the independence of Lebanon and did not try to seek its unification with Syria, while Christians forswore French protection. Lebanon was recognized by other Arab states as an independent and sovereign nation with a special relationship to the West, while Christians acknowledged that Lebanon had an "Arab character" and was "part of the Arab world."[11]

The complex governmental structure established in the constitution of 1926 ultimately became a locus of tension in the First Republic, particularly because of the "two-headedness" of this system. As noted above, the government included a dual executive. The president was elected for a six-year term by the members of the Lebanese Parliament. He was the official head of the executive and had wide powers to nominate and dismiss cabinet ministers (Article 53), to dissolve the parliament if necessary (Article 55), to send back laws to the parliament for a second discussion (Article 57), and even to promulgate laws considered "urgent" if the parliament had not voted on them after a certain amount of time (Article

58). The president did not have to answer for his actions during his presidential term unless he violated the constitution or was accused of high treason (Article 60). Two constitutional amendments in 1927 and 1929 strongly reinforced these presidential powers.[12]

The second head of state was the prime minister, who was the leader of the executive cabinet. Although officially appointed by the president, the prime minister was in practice the representative of different political interests and of a different community, the Sunnis. The powers of the prime minister in the First Republic, as described in Articles 64–68 of the constitution, involved the management of affairs of state, the development of policy, and the implementation of laws. Lebanese legal scholar Bassem Jisr has demonstrated that in practice, the cabinet provided a counterweight to presidential powers, as the system acted to "limit the use of these powers by making all the actions of the president subject to the approbation of the government and to the ratification of the minister in charge of that particular portfolio."[13] In practice, therefore, executive power rested on accommodations made between the interests of the president and the interests of the prime minister.

In regard to legislative power, the parliament of the First Republic was composed of a single chamber, the name of which is literally rendered as the "Chamber of Deputies." The number of deputies elected to parliament was always dividable by eleven (at different times, the members numbered forty-four, seventy-seven, and ninety-nine), and for every five Muslim deputies, there were always six Christian deputies. Further confessional divisions were generally agreed upon so that the various subcommunities of the Muslim and Christian populations, such as the Druze and the Greek Orthodox, each maintained some degree of representation. Although the parliament had great power in official terms, in practice it was relatively inefficient because its members made efforts to avoid any public debate of thorny issues. Instead, the workings of the parliament tended to fall into the hands of small political cartels or individuals who attempted to control the direction of legislative power behind the scenes. The executive cabinet did not have similar constraints as those of the parliament, since the deliberations of the ministers were kept secret. In practice, therefore, most confrontations and negotiations regarding governmental policy took place behind closed doors in cabinet sessions, circumventing the parliament altogether.[14]

Debates and intrigue regarding the prerogatives of the president and his relationship with the prime minister and other members of government kept the Lebanese political milieu quite busy in the years after independence. The complex, "two-headed" nature of the Lebanese state became a locus of sectarian struggles and other political quarrels, eventually leading up to the dissolution of the pact and the outbreak of civil war in 1975. Lebanese political scientist Farid el-Khazen has made two important observations about the realpolitik of the National Pact of 1943 and the First Lebanese Republic. First, el-Khazen has shown that the pact was created not only in negotiation among the internal Lebanese factions, but also as an accommodation to the positions of external powers. The arrangement would not have been possible without pressures supplied both by Arab nations (principally Syria and Egypt) and by Western nations (principally France and Britain). Each of these external powers had interests that would be better served by a cohesive Lebanese nation after 1943. Second, el-Khazen has shown that the National Pact was based on the faulty assumption that the internally and externally cooperative position of the elites would be supported at the grassroots level. The failure of this cross-confessional support to materialize led to the eventual collapse of the First Republic.[15] These two observations, which are confirmed in my analysis, bring into question Lijphart's celebration of the consociational political system in Lebanon. They indicate that the system was neither as democratic nor as internally stable as Lijphart believed.

Elite Cartels

It can be argued that between 1943 and 1975, Lebanon was consecutively controlled by five different elite cartels.[16] In 1943 the first elite coalition was established by the Maronite Bishara al-Khoury and the Sunni Riad al-Solh. They organized a cabinet and a parliament that, in accordance with the outlines of the National Pact, incorporated the five largest Lebanese communities. Al-Khoury, who became the first president of independent

Lebanon in 1943, owed his political success to the practice of confessional balancing that was initiated during the French mandate. Indeed, al-Khoury began with very little traditional political capital in the form of a local power base or family tradition. He was born in a small village near Baabda, studied at the Jesuit College in Beirut, and then went to France, where he earned a law degree from the University of Paris. Upon returning to Lebanon, he was promoted quickly through the ranks of the Lebanese administration under the French mandate. In 1919 he was appointed to the Ministry of Justice, in 1920 he became secretary of the regional government of Mount Lebanon, in 1922 he was appointed as the head of the nation's Court of Appeals, and then in 1926, at the age of thirty-six, he was appointed as minister of the interior. This meteoric rise in the ranks of the French-controlled administration was indicative of the strong bias on the part of the French for promoting local Maronites.

In contrast, the other architect of the first elite coalition, the Sunni Riad al-Solh, came from a prominent Beirut family. Born in 1894, al-Solh was a shrewd and charismatic politician, a popular figure in Lebanon with a particular talent for mobilizing popular support. He was educated at Christian schools (Lazarist High School, where he was a contemporary of Bishara al-Khoury, and the Faculty of French Law at the University of St. Joseph in Beirut). As a youth, al-Solh joined the Arab nationalist movement, and after the collapse of the Ottoman Empire he rejected French control over Lebanon, opposing the separation of Greater Lebanon from Syria as an independent political entity. He was sentenced to death in absentia in August 1920 on the charge of anti-French activity; however, his sentence was later commuted to imprisonment and then to exile. Al-Solh lived in Egypt and Switzerland before moving back to Lebanon in 1924. He was exiled again, soon after his return, for his participation in the Syrian revolt of 1925; however, he was permitted to return to Lebanon once more in 1929. In 1932 he married into a prominent Syrian family from Aleppo—his wife's cousin Sa'adallah al-Jabiri would later become Syria's prime minister. This marriage cemented close ties with the Syrian leadership.

Starting in the early 1930s, al-Solh enacted an about-face, turning from a fierce rejection of the Lebanese state to a desire to become a part of it. He ran for legislative office in a bid to enter the political elite, but the French blocked him from becoming a parliamentarian. After the 1943 elections that brought al-Khoury to the presidency, al-Solh was appointed prime minister. It had become clear by that time that change was on the way; the parliamentary elections had resulted in a majority for those who wanted to put an end to the French mandate.[17] On September 19, 1943, al-Khoury and al-Solh met and agreed on what came to be known as the National Pact, and on October 8, 1943, the principles of this pact were made public when al-Solh presented his cabinet, the first of independent Lebanon. Al-Solh would go on to serve at the head of several postindependence cabinets between 1943 and 1951. By that date a rift had developed between al-Khoury and al-Solh, encouraged by the president's brother Salim, who regarded al-Solh as an obstacle to the Maronites' political power.[18] A few months after leaving office, al-Solh was assassinated in Amman, Jordan, by a member of the Syrian Socialist Nationalist Party. The Lebanese press accused the Syrian leadership of being behind the assassination, as did some of the politicians of the day in their memoirs.[19] Al-Solh's death also seemed to spell the beginning of the end for al-Khoury. It undermined the balance achieved by the National Pact, as power shifted notably toward the president (who showed no inclination to reestablish the balance). Al-Khoury's career ended in September 1952 when he was forced to tender his resignation as president after large demonstrations protesting corruption in his administration.

A second elite cartel was constituted in 1952 by incoming president Camille Chamoun, who renewed the commitments of the National Pact to solidify his cross-confessional standing. Like al-Khoury, Chamoun was born to a professional rather than a traditionally political family and had trained as a lawyer before entering politics. His political talent, rather than an elite background or family connections, is what brought him into power. Chamoun's attempts to reestablish the political consensus in Lebanon were only partially successful, however, as his pro-Western stance and his desire to consolidate presidential power led to increasing resistance among Muslims. The political network of the new prime minister, Hussein al-Oweini, was comparatively weak, and without a governmental leader of al-Solh's status, Sunnis felt that their influence was markedly decreased. Regional tension was also on the rise in the late 1950s, owing to an expansion of Arab nationalism centered on the new Egyptian leader, Gamal Abdel Nasser, and the opposing "Eisenhower Doctrine" of the United States that (among other things) sought to limit Nasser's influence. Chamoun's embrace of the Eisenhower Doctrine and his refusal to make even token gestures toward Nasser provided Lebanese Sunnis with the right opportunity to reassert their power. In the eyes of many, Chamoun had reallied Lebanon with Western powers and thus had broken the consensus of the National Pact.

To make matters worse, Chamoun then attempted to seek reelection by means of a constitutional amendment. He also sought to organize support directly from the Maronite community, bypassing not only Muslim elites but also other Christian leaders. This strategy led, more than anything, to the cohesion of an anti-Chamoun opposition that included diverse Muslims factions as well as some Christian leaders. In May 1958, the assassination of a journalist who was at odds with the Chamoun administration led to riots in Tripoli, followed by uprisings in Beirut and Sidon. Soon, the country became divided into numerous warring factions, with major battles occurring between government and opposition forces from May 9 through May 18. Various political figures attempted to seek a compromise, but a self-brokered solution did not seem likely at the time. Chamoun had often hinted of an American intervention to defend his administration, and on July 15, 1958, in an unexpected move, US Marines landed on the beaches of Beirut in a "peacekeeping" mission to support the pro-Western government. This landing, known as Operation Blue Bat, was the first application of the Eisenhower Doctrine. Lebanese reactions were predictably mixed—Maronites welcomed the move, while Muslims viewed it with suspicion. However, the American intervention was short-lived, lasting only three months, and did not lead to the results that Chamoun was expecting. The Americans did not support his bid for reelection and instead encouraged him to leave office.

The events of 1958 ended Chamoun's cartel, and a third elite coalition soon arose under newly elected president Fouad Shehab. Born to an aristocratic family that ruled Mount Lebanon in the eighteenth century, Shehab entered the military academy in 1926, graduating with the rank of lieutenant in 1932. He then rose through the military ranks to become the first commander of the Lebanese Armed Forces (LAF) after the country's independence. During the 1958 crisis, Shehab wisely refused to let the army interfere because he suspected that to do so would be to risk its disintegration. Similar judiciousness emerged in his governmental policy, which came to be known as "Shehabism" or "al-Nahj" (the Path). Shehab tried to make changes in the Lebanese system to resolve the underlying fragility of the Lebanese polity. His coalition affirmed Lebanon as an Arab country, encouraged secularism as a first step toward national unity, and discouraged political extremism. The number of parliamentary deputies was increased from sixty-six to ninety-nine in order to maximize political participation. In this new configuration, however, Shehab often went behind the backs of other governmental leaders, calling into action his shadow or parallel government of military officers and loyal civilians. In order to execute his ambitious program, Shehab made generous use of the institution that he knew best: the army (see chapter 5). Many felt that his top-down program was moving too quickly and that it did not fully respect Lebanon's deep-seated sectarian and political cleavages. Ultimately, Shehab's ambitious strategy failed to find lasting support among Lebanese elites.

Aware of the existence of a large opposition group within the parliament, Shehab decided not to renew his mandate in 1964. After a difficult search, the Chamber of Deputies found a new candidate in Charles Helou, who proved to be acceptable to each of the principal factions. Born in 1912, Helou was the scion of a powerful Maronite family from Baabda. He made his first foray into politics as one of the founders of the fascist-leaning Kata'eb (Phalangist) Party, but he later parted ways with this group and came under the influence of Michel Chiha, the founder of anti-Arab "Lebanonism."[20] The fourth elite cartel created by President Helou bore a strong resemblance to Shehab's cartel. However, Helou did not have the support of the army, nor did he have Shehab's charisma, strength, and prestige. His mandate quickly disintegrated amid the growing pressures of the Arab-Israeli conflict and in the wake of the regional Six-Day War of 1967. Helou's inability to maintain his elite coalition was revealed by the ratification of the Cairo Agreement in 1969; this accord was reached between Palestinian leader Yassir Arafat and Lebanese Army commanders, and it basically granted the Palestine Liberation Organization (PLO) the right to launch operations against Israel from southern Lebanon. The Cairo Agreement was considered by the Christian Lebanese and by some Muslims to be a betrayal of Lebanese sovereignty.

After the collapse of the fourth elite cartel, Suleiman Frangieh emerged as another compromise presidential candidate. Frangieh was the son of the northern Lebanese political leader Qabalan Frangieh. He was elected in 1960, 1964, and 1968 to the parliament as a representative of the Zgharta district. In 1970 he was elected as Lebanon's president (by a margin of one vote), at the head of yet another coalition of elites. Frangieh had a reputation for toughness that was apparently based on his involvement in a gun battle in his hometown during the 1950s. Nonetheless, like Helou before him, Frangieh was unable to constrain the growing presence of militia factions in Lebanon. The president, as well as his prime minister, Taqi al-Din al-Solh, a relative of Riad al-Solh, attempted to stabilize the country by increasing the representation of new and various factions in the government, but these efforts did not prevent the eruption of civil war in 1975.

The Civil War

The Lebanese civil war marks the ultimate point of failure of the consociational model of the First Republic. The breakdown of the state can be analyzed as a product of both external and internal pressures.[21] External pressures emerged in the broad instability throughout the region and the simmering Arab-Israeli conflict. The presence of the PLO in Lebanese territory, combined with the repercussions of inter-Arab rivalries, weighed heavily on an already fragile political system. Many scholars attribute the failure of the consociational society of the First Republic almost exclusively to these external factors.[22] In addition, however, the refusal of traditional elites to incorporate emerging groups into their cartels undermined the political system from within. By the time of the civil war, the endogamous nature of elite recruitment had created a feeling of dissatisfaction among emerging elites.[23] The collapse of the political system was at least partially due to the inability of the entrenched elites to confront new ideological and socioeconomic challenges.

On the sectarian side, the refusal of Maronite elites to abandon some of their privileges in concession to other communities led consistently to the collapse of cartels and to the end of cooperation between elite groups. In the National Pact, the creation and maintenance of elite coalitions were seen as Maronite responsibilities, in accordance with the agreement that the president would be elected from the Maronite community. However, the presidents of the First Republic became more obsessed with staying in power than with the desire to serve their country, or even to serve their sectarian community. They often did not distinguish between their personal interests and the interests of the country. Presidents al-Khoury and Chamoun in particular tried to increase the powers of the presidency and therefore the Maronite influence on the institutions of the state. For more than three decades, the Maronite elites exceeded the mandate that was given to them in the National Pact, thwarting the stability of coalitions and contributing to the eventual eruption of the civil war.

From 1975 to 1989, anarchy reigned in Lebanon as the state lost control of many of its institutions and its monopoly on violence. New leaders emerged from various sectarian groups in response to these circumstances. Elites who had been locked out of the established political cartels encouraged the violence and the formation of militias and profited tremendously from the breakdown in social order.[24] Their newfound power was acknowledged in the Ta'if Agreement of 1989 that ended the civil war, and a number of these individuals managed to recycle themselves into successful politicians in postwar Lebanon.

The Creation of the Second Republic

The Ta'if Agreement

The Ta'if Agreement, signed in the eponymous city in 1989, consecrated a revised formula of power sharing. The consociational system was not abandoned in favor of a nonsectarian formula. The text of the Ta'if Agreement affirmed the national unity of Lebanon, but it also acknowledged the tradition of confessional representation as the organizing principle of Lebanese political society. It noted that Lebanon is a founding member of both the League of Arab States and the United Nations—Joseph Maila has explained that this point was "a way for some to stress that Lebanon is Arab and for others to underline the fact that it is independent."[25] The document also listed a number of foundational principles, including a commitment to democracy, parliamentarianism, and public liberties, such as religious freedom. It emphasized the destabilizing effect of economic disparity and the need for development in poor and peripheral regions of the country. Finally, it rejected any plans for creating homogenous confessional areas within the country or for the resettlement of Palestinians in Lebanon.

The Ta'if Agreement also contained a more explicit series of political reforms. The National Pact's formula of distributing power among the main heads of state was retained and further codified—the president of the republic remained a position reserved for a Maronite, the position of prime minister was reserved for a Sunni, and the Speaker of parliament remained a Shi'i. However, the relation of power among these positions was shifted away from the president to create a more balanced arrangement (these changes were confirmed in a constitutional amendment adopted in September 1990). The prime minister in particular was given more explicit powers than had been spelled out in the constitution of 1926. The agreement created an official designation for the cabinet, now called the Council of Ministers, an organization that had existed only in an ad hoc manner during the First Republic. In addition to providing more power to the Sunni constituency, this formula allowed the main political actors of peripheral communities to obtain representation by being nominated to a position in the Council of Ministers.

The power of the Shi'i community—which was underrepresented in the previous agreement—was also greatly reinforced, as the Second Republic was designed to be a more explicitly parliamentarian regime.[26] The president's power to dissolve the parliament was revoked, and the term of office of the Speaker of parliament (now given the title "president of the chamber") was extended to four years. This expanded term gave the head of the parliament greater independence, authority, and freedom to maneuver. A significant impetus for these changes was the attempt by Lebanese general Michel Aoun to dissolve the parliament in 1989, while the deputies were meeting in Ta'if.[27] The agreement of 1989 was designed to make such a dissolution of parliament very difficult, if not impossible. As with the changes to the Council of Ministers, changes in the parliament were also made with an eye for inclusivity in regard to communities that were representationally deprived under the First Republic. As part of these changes, the number of parliamentarians was increased from 99 to 128,[28] and the distribution of parliamentary seats was changed from the First Republic's 6-to-5 ratio in favor of Christians to an equal parity between Muslim and Christian representatives. It is important to note that this new distribution of representation probably still does not reflect the demographic reality of the nation, as most observers agree that the Muslim population is significantly larger than the Christian population.[29]

Further provisions in the Ta'if Agreement allowed for the creation of a Lebanese senate after the first nonsectarian elections, whenever such elections might become possible. The provisions for the establishment of a senate were a minor concession to the Druze community, which since the 1980s has conceived of this new branch of government as a potentially Druze-controlled institution that would confirm the Druze as the fourth-most-powerful constituency in the Lebanese Republic. On a broader level, however, this reference to an eventual abolition of the confessional quota system, and therefore of the distribution of powers based on sectarian affiliation, was one of the most forward-looking aspects of the Ta'if Agreement.

Overall, the changes stipulated in the Ta'if Agreement were intended to ensure a balance between the three centers of power in Lebanon (president, prime minister, and Speaker of the parliament), which have come to be collectively known as the "Troika." The new arrangement was also designed to ensure the broad representation of all political factions, and it effectively spelled the end of any Maronite aspirations toward hegemony in Lebanese politics. Therefore, it is possible to say that the Second Lebanese Republic has returned to and further codified a consociational system of government.[30] However, Syrian interference in Lebanese affairs and the presence of Syrian troops on Lebanese soil until 2005 suggest that postwar Lebanon was not a truly stable or democratic state. Rather, I will suggest that the recruitment of political elites and the direction of policy decisions in Lebanon were in practice driven by the political tutelage of the Syrian state.

The Syrian Variable

Syria's involvement in Lebanon between 1989 and 2005 should be regarded as a crucial variable in the development of the Second Lebanese Republic, just as French and American interventions were crucial during the First Republic. I argue that in postwar Lebanon, Syria acted as a reliable external party that was able to enforce the demobilization of the wartime militias (with the important exception of Hezbollah) and could oversee and guarantee the practices of power sharing among the various Lebanese factions. In many ways, Syria became the ultimate arbiter of Lebanese politics in the Second Republic.[31]

It is important to recognize that Lebanon was carved out of Syria by the French mandatory power in the early twentieth century. The loss of Lebanon, along with Palestine, Jordan, and Alexandretta (which became part of Turkey), reduced the size of Greater Syria. For this reason, many in Syria still see Lebanon as a rogue province and not as an independent state, which might explain Syria's attitudes vis-à-vis its neighbor. Syria has always had an important influence in Lebanon, and after the breakdown of the First Lebanese Republic in 1975 that influence grew exponentially. Naomi Weinberger has described Syria's involvement in wartime Lebanon in terms of three phases: an early attempt at mediation, an escalation to indirect intervention in the conflict, and then finally direct military intervention.[32] Weinberger also maintains that the goal of the Syrian intervention was not to support any one particular faction, but rather to restore stability and ensure the preservation and expansion of Syrian influence. Postwar negotiations in Lebanon showed that Syria had indeed succeeded in this goal of becoming a central power broker in Lebanese politics.

While many observers questioned the legality of the Syrian military intervention,[33] this initial action was followed by a series of moves on the part of Syrian president Hafez al-Assad to legitimize the Syrian presence in Lebanese territory. The first basis of legitimacy claimed by Syria was the 1978 decision of the Arab League to send an Arab Dissuasion Force (ADF) into Lebanon. Although this decision was initially made for the purpose of restraining Syrian action, it ended up having a legitimizing effect, as more than 80 percent of the proposed ADF force was composed of Syrian troops. When a relative calm returned to Lebanon following the first spate of violence, members of the Arab League began to call for the abolition of the ADF mandate and the withdrawal of Syrian troops. In the meantime, however, the effectiveness of al-Assad's policy in Lebanon had provided the intervention with a greater legitimacy. From the beginning of the 1980s, Syria had a measure of success in justifying its "special relation" with Lebanon on the basis of the important role of Lebanon in the Arab-Israeli conflict. Finally, in 1982, with Israelis laying siege to Beirut, the Arab League met in Morocco and signed a resolution officially ending the ADF mandate. This greatly reduced the legitimacy of Syria's presence in Lebanon—though al-Assad managed to include a clause in the resolution stipulating that the withdrawal of Syrian troops would be contingent on negotiations between the Lebanese and Syrian governments.

After having successfully abrogated the US-backed May 17, 1983, treaty between Israel and Lebanon, Syria contacted the leaders of the primary Lebanese militias in an attempt to create a national agreement that could end the civil war in Lebanon and establish the legitimacy of the Syrian presence. This came to be known as the Tripartite Agreement because it was founded on the cooperation of three important militias (the AMAL [Afwaj al-Muqawama al-Lubnaniyya] movement of Nabih Berri, representing the Shi'a; the Lebanese Forces of Elie Hobeiqa, representing the Maronites; and the Progressive Socialist Party of Walid Jumblat, representing the Druze). The Tripartite Agreement was never implemented, but in pushing for it, President al-Assad revealed his desire to broker a legal arrangement in Lebanon to justify the Syrian military presence and consolidate Syria's political influence.

The missed opportunity of the Tripartite Agreement was recaptured a few years later in the creation of the Ta'if Agreement. Syria helped to broker the agreement at Ta'if, and the Syrian regime insisted on the inclusion of two important clauses. First, Syria was given the right to deploy its forces in Lebanon for a period that could not be determined by external actors, but only by the Lebanese and Syrian governments. Second, Syria was given the right to react within Lebanon to threats to Syrian security. These two clauses of the Ta'if Agreement finally provided Syria with an internationally recognized legal basis for its continued presence in Lebanon. As the Ta'if Agreement came to be recognized by both the Arab League and the United Nations, Syria's mandate in Lebanon could no longer be questioned.

Postwar Treaties and the Consolidation of Syrian Influence

After the Ta'if Agreement, Syria and Lebanon signed a series of additional bilateral agreements. The more important ones are the Treaty of Brotherhood and Cooperation, signed in May 1991, and the Defense and Security Agreement, signed in September 1991. The Treaty of Brotherhood and Cooperation was without doubt the jewel in the crown of the Syrian claims in Lebanon. The six articles of the treaty confirmed Syrian influence in wide-ranging areas such as security, foreign policy, and economic affairs and established bodies and commissions to manage the cooperation between the two countries. Lebanese scholar Bou Melhab-Atallah has argued that this agreement "did not only regulate a usual bilateral relation . . . but went as far as to codify and legitimate unequal relations."[34] With the Ta'if Agreement, the Treaty of Brotherhood and Cooperation, and seventeen additional treaties linking Lebanese policy to Syrian interests, the Syrian hold on Lebanon was fully institutionalized.

The extent of Syria's influence on the configuration of the Lebanese elite in the postwar period can be seen at a glance by considering the presidential elections. Not only have the vast majority of Lebanese presidents since 1976 received Syrian backing,[35] but between 1990 and 2005 all Lebanese presidents were simply "Syrian candidates," loyal enthusiasts who were vetted by the Syrian regime and then parachuted into power. When a suitable candidate was unavailable, Syria did not hesitate to have its clients in Lebanon make adjustments to the Lebanese Constitution so that a Syrian enthusiast could fill the office. In 1995, for example, the constitution was amended under Syrian pressure in order to prolong the term of President Elias Hrawi, and in 1998 it was amended once again to allow the election of then general Émile Lahoud (under the original constitution, military commanders were not eligible for the office). This pattern was repeated in 2004, in spite of international protests, in order to prolong the mandate of President Lahoud.[36]

Syrian influence also appeared in the composition of the Lebanese Parliament. A seat in this institution is often the first step for entering the political elite in Lebanon. The discretionary nomination of forty parliamentarians in 1991 to fill seats vacated by deaths during the civil war, and to occupy twenty-nine newly created seats, led to a rapid introduction of new individuals into Lebanon's political elite. All of those chosen in 1991 had ties to Syria. Twenty-nine of these appointed parliamentarians were elected to the legislature of 1992, twenty-five to the legislature of 1996, and twenty-one reelected for the third time in 2000. Lebanese political scientist Bassel Salloukh affirms that "Syria ensured that her allies controlled a substantial percentage of parliamentary seats, and concomitantly held control over presidential elections, cabinet formation and legislation. This very visible Syrian hand was present in the 1992, 1996 and 2000 elections."[37] However, by 2005 this hand had all but disappeared. The Syrian clients in Lebanon's parliament had never been able to establish an independent basis of Lebanese support,[38] and after the Syrian military withdrawal almost all of these Syrian-backed parliamentarians lost their seats. In 2005 sixty-six MPs from the 2000 legislature (or about 51 percent) were reelected. Of these, only nine had first been appointed in 1991. Lebanese American journalist Michael Young distinguishes three phases of Syrian hegemony in Lebanon. The first was between 1990 and 1998, when "an amorphous structure of relations existed between Damascus and Beirut."[39] The second period began in 1998, as Syrian president Hafez al-Assad was instrumental in engineering the election of Émile Lahoud as president. The third period began in 2002 and ended with Syrian withdrawal from Lebanon.[40]

Syria manipulated Lebanese politics through its two principal representatives in Lebanon, Ghazi Kanaan and Rustom Ghazaleh. Kanaan, an Alawi and a close friend of the Assad family, was the head of Syrian intelligence in Lebanon for twenty years, from 1982 until 2002. In the postwar period, Kanaan was allegedly the most powerful figure in Lebanon, overseeing the country from the Beqaa town of Anjar, where the country's military and political leaders reported directly to him on all major issues. Kanaan in turn reported directly to the Syrian president.[41] He was often described as a "kingmaker," since Lebanese politicians were said to have required his approval before they could aspire to office.

The third and final period of Syrian hegemony began in 2002, when Rustom Ghazaleh took over from Kanaan as the head of Syrian intelligence (and de facto proconsul) in Lebanon.[42] Ghazaleh, a Sunni from a village in southern Syria, began as the Syrian intelligence chief in the town of Hammana in the Metn region before rising to replace Kanaan. Ghazaleh had obtained a doctorate in history from the Lebanese University. It was said that his adviser, Hassan Hallaq, actually wrote the dissertation and that half of Lebanon's political elite attended his defense. Likewise, numerous members of the Lebanese political elite traveled to Syria to attend the wedding of Ghazaleh's daughter.[43] Ghazaleh was considered the personal representative of new Syrian president Bashar al-Assad and was widely feared, or at least flattered, by the Lebanese political elite. Under Ghazaleh's oversight, Syrian abuses became more pronounced than was the case under Kanaan.

In addition to his involvement in geopolitical maneuvering, Ghazaleh (like many other Syrian officials) was entangled in a network of corruption and crime in Lebanon and often used political clout to protect these personal investments.[44] Ghazaleh was said to have been involved in the al-Madina Bank failure, Lebanon's largest financial scandal in recent memory. According to an investigative report conducted by journalist Mitchell Prothero, the collapse of al-Madina Bank in early 2003 was no ordinary loss—US$1.65 billion worth of depositors' assets simply disappeared. Further, Prothero indicates that the Lebanese government attempted to cover up the scandal and to intimidate journalists who investigated it, actions that many saw as signaling the involvement of Syrian heavyweights. Even before its collapse, al-Madina Bank was a locus of shadowy financial dealings between Lebanese and Syrian politicians, and it was alleged that the executive secretary of the bank, Rana Qoleilat, had made large payments to Lebanese and Syrian officials. Ghazaleh's family members, as well as Ghazaleh himself, were documented to have received large sums of money from Qoleilat.[45] According to a report by Fortress Global Investigations, a New York–based firm, "during a one-month period, ending in January 2003, Qoleilat used al-Madina funds to pay $941,000 to Ghazaleh's brothers. . . . The following March [Qoleilat] arranged for a $300,000 'donation' to Ghazaleh from the bank's funds."[46] Ghazaleh is said to have used his power to personally threaten the chairman of Lebanon's Central Bank, Riad Salameh, and to force him to freeze the investigation into the scandal.[47]

Democracy Aborted

The 1943 National Pact led to a brief time of prosperity, democracy, and social progress in Lebanon. However, in the years that followed the 1989 Ta'if Agreement, the democratic process was aborted and a similar golden era did not emerge. This point seems to indicate that power-sharing arrangements adopted after peace settlements do not necessarily lead to a flourishing of democracy.[48] Nancy Bermeo noted in 2003 that works on democratization have not given a systematic treatment of the effects of postwar settlements on the functionality of the resulting political systems. Bermeo concluded that while "pacts may make democracies more durable . . . they also make the deepening of democracy more difficult."[49] More recent studies have shown that elite pacts do tend to lead to formal democracy; indeed, formal democratic structures are more likely to emerge from negotiated settlements than from military victories. However, post–civil war democratization is primarily motivated by the need for political order and is empirically distinct from postauthoritarian democratization.[50]

Democratization after a war comes in two parts: military pacification and political reconstruction. The first of these involves mainly the demobilization of militias, whereas the second requires the structuring of a democratic system and the holding of multiparty elections.[51] In Lebanon the demobilization process was not the result of military victory by the state over the militias. It was a political act that started after the cabinet declaration of March 1991 that mandated the disbandment, disarmament, and rehabilitation of militias.[52] The militias were given one month to disarm and disband—with the important exception of Hezbollah, which was allowed to keep its weapons as a designated "resistance force" against Israeli occupation. In June 1991, Law 88 was promulgated, allowing the integration of six thousand militiamen into the Lebanese Armed Forces.[53] This perfect example of "cooperative disarmament" took place under the control of the Syrian Army, which acted as an outside monitor of the process, albeit not a disinterested one.[54]

Political reconstruction soon followed. Two years after the implementation of the Ta'if Agreement, the first postwar elections were held. Postsettlement elections serve a crucial purpose: they are the "foundation for a longer-term process of democratic consolidation through which new rules of the political game are institutionalized."[55] However, because of the nineteen one-sided agreements between Lebanon and Syria, and the latter's refusal to redeploy as outlined in the Ta'if Agreement, this secondary process of democratic consolidation was aborted in Lebanon. Syrian control over districting, the writing of the electoral law, and the election process created a system that cannot be termed free and fair, leading Christian elites to completely boycott the 1992 and 1996 elections. Hence, although the Lebanese political system after Ta'if had some of the trappings of a democracy (for example, regular elections), it cannot be described as a true democracy even in the narrowest definition of that term: a system based on free and fair elections with universal suffrage where basic civil liberties are guaranteed. Although postwar social and political reconstruction took place as an initial form of "peace-building,"[56] democracy never took hold in Lebanon. The system governing the country in the period of Syrian control was consociational in that it was based on power sharing, but it cannot be called a consociational democracy.

Conclusion

The Lebanese political system remained stable in the period between 1990 and 2005, in large part because of Syrian intervention in Lebanese political affairs. However, this initial overview has shown that although the postwar system was stable, it was not democratic. The Ta'if Agreement attempted to institute a new formula of power sharing among the various segments of Lebanese society, but this agreement was undermined by Syrian interference in the political process and by Syrian clientelism in the recruitment of new elites. Even after the 2005 Syrian withdrawal, the legacy of Pax Syriana remains. Influences established through three decades of control cannot be eliminated overnight, and Syria still has an extensive network of allies and agents in Lebanon who frequently act as spoilers in the political process. They have been accused of attempting to destabilize the Lebanese state through a series of assassinations and bombings that started with the assassination of Rafiq Hariri.

Postwar Lebanon is once again ruled by a stable, consociational system of government, but the establishment of stability may be only temporary if democratization remains superficial. To fully understand the operation of power in Lebanon and the prospects for democratization, it is necessary to look more closely at the interaction of political actors within the system.

2

Postwar Elite Interaction

The period following the Lebanese civil war saw not only a new formula of power sharing, as exemplified in the Ta'if Agreement, but also
the emergence of a new political elite composed of Syrian-supported
politicians. The Ta'if Agreement was first and foremost an arrangement
among elite groups. Although Arend Lijphart's theories of consociational
democracy can be used to explain this political system and the formal
structures of its government, it is of limited use in understanding the
complex interactions of the actors in the system. In this chapter I will
supplement Lijphart's perspective with an additional concept central to
modern elite theory: the notion of elite settlements. American sociologists Michael Burton and John Higley define settlements as "relatively
rare events in which warring national elite factions suddenly and deliberately reorganize their relations by negotiating compromises."[1]

The implementation of elite settlements can initially occur without
the inclusion of all players. Using this perspective, it is possible to describe
the interaction among the different actors in the Lebanese political system as progressing in three stages between 1989 and 2005. First, there
was the initial elite pact of the Ta'if Agreement, in which a central group
of elite factions negotiated their differences, while many other factions
remained excluded. The second stage involved the progressive incorpora-
tion of other groups into the political process and their acceptance of the
"rules of the game" under Syrian hegemony. Finally, in the third stage
Lebanon saw a realignment of members of previously excluded groups
and their co-option by other political forces, a process I call "factionalization." Overall, the political system in post-Ta'if Lebanon was characterized by the consolidation of power by elites who had emerged in the

1990s and the marginalization of dissidents who sought to change the structure of the political regime.[2]

The Ta'if Agreement: An Elite Settlement

Two sets of circumstances encourage the creation of elite settlements.[3] The first is the existence of a conflict wherein all factions incur substantial losses. The protracted Lebanese civil war corresponds to this condition. The second is the occurrence of crises that threaten to bring about a resurgence of violence. Such crises are typically centered on heads of state whose errors of judgment, abuses of power, or personal weaknesses become public after a particular event. Such incidents threaten to exacerbate the discontent of the elite and to push disagreements to a point of no return. In this section, I show how the Ta'if Agreement grew out of such circumstances and how the provisions of the agreement were constructed.

The 1988 Presidential Crisis and the War of Liberation

In 1988 the last president of the First Lebanese Republic, Amin Gemayel, attempted to prolong his presidential term for an additional two years. Assuming that the French would support his actions, he blocked the upcoming presidential elections.[4] On September 22, 1988, the night before the end of his term, Gemayel appointed the Lebanese Army commander General Michel Aoun as the head of an interim military government, and the position of president remained unfilled. This appointment marked the beginning of one of the most turbulent periods of contemporary Lebanese history.[5] The military government appointed by Gemayel was equally divided between Christian and Muslim officers. However, the Muslim officers immediately resigned in order to support the legitimacy of the cabinet, headed by Prime Minister Salim al-Hoss. This action led to a period when Lebanon was ruled by two separate governments: the government of Michel Aoun, which portrayed itself as "constitutional," and the government of Salim al-Hoss, which argued that it had the greater mandate under the National Pact. Al-Hoss's cabinet was in fact the last government confirmed by parliament, and with the resignation of the Muslim officers, Aoun's government did not include any form of Muslim representation.

Aoun's military government, which lasted from September 22, 1988, to March 14, 1989, was characterized by a monopoly on decision making. This monopolization was especially manifested in Aoun's decision to begin a "war of liberation"—a decision that was made unilaterally and without counsel from other military officers.[6] Aoun had been nominated to power at a crucial point in the history of the region. Iraq had just ended its long war with Iran and was getting ready to settle accounts with Syria, which had sided with Iran in the war. For that reason, Iraqi weapons began to flow toward anti-Syrian factions in Lebanon and most especially toward the Lebanese Army under the command of General Aoun.[7] These weapons, in addition to his assumption of Iraqi support, encouraged Aoun to oppose Syria.

In January 1989 Aoun attended the meeting of the Arab League in Tunis. He was led to believe that he was accepted by the Arab leaders as a peer, especially after Yassir Arafat of the PLO and Saddam Hussein of Iraq assured him of their support.[8] Upon his return to Lebanon, Aoun decided to end the practices of the militias that had taken over the institutions of the state during the civil war (see chapter 3). He first turned the army against the primary Christian militia, the Lebanese Forces, but that war ended after the intervention of Maronite patriarch Mar Nasrallah Boutros Sfeir.[9] Then, encouraged by the support of the French, who were hoping to extend their role in the region by exacerbating the tense situation in Lebanon,[10] Aoun turned toward Syria and that country's long-standing involvement in Lebanese affairs. On March 14, 1989, he declared his "war of liberation" against Syrian domination. The Christian enclave that had been spared the difficulties of the civil war started its descent into tumult, and Lebanon was once again overtaken by violence, and what Albert Mansour called the "obsession of the war of liberation" continued until the signing of the Ta'if Agreement.[11]

Arab and International Mediation

Aoun's bet initially played in his favor. Whereas the United States did not support Aoun's aspirations and did not add Lebanon to its list of priorities, France did side with him. A summit of the Arab League was called in Casablanca, Morocco, in May 1989, to find a solution to the Lebanese problem. During this summit, Syria was almost isolated, and all other Arab governments were in agreement that it was time to withdraw the Lebanese issue from Syria's control. However, King Fahd of Saudi Arabia intervened in support of Syrian president Hafez al-Assad. Because of this support, although Syria was excluded from the commission in charge of the Lebanon problem, the recommendations of the summit did not include a demand for Syrian withdrawal.[12] The summit resulted in a plan to invite Lebanese parliamentarians to meet—outside of Lebanon if necessary—to create a document of political reform that could become the foundation of a new national contract. It was suggested that afterward, the Lebanese Parliament would meet in Beirut to ratify this document, that new presidential elections would then be held in Lebanon, and that a new government convened by the elected president would take the appropriate steps to implement political reform.[13]

In the meantime, Patriarch Sfeir called for a meeting of Lebanese Christian parliamentarians. Twenty-three deputies attended the meeting, and they issued a communiqué asking for a return to dialogue. Aoun's bid for power was further undermined when the United States intimated that his radical anti-Syrian policies had ruined its plans for the region. US leaders were anticipating an increase in tensions with Saddam Hussein's Iraq (owing to Hussein's growing hostility toward US allies Kuwait and Saudi Arabia), and the US government was attempting to build an anti-Hussein coalition in the region. Syria was an important component in this effort. The US regime therefore felt an imperative to distance itself from Aoun's Iraq-supported anti-Syria campaign and to resolve the Lebanese problem by any means necessary. The European Union also asked France to decrease its support for Aoun and not to bring the issue before the United Nations Security Council. The European Union informed Syria that its cooperation to reduce the tensions would enable Washington to turn a blind eye to the Syrian military presence in Lebanon.[14] The adventurous policies of Michel Aoun might very well have succeeded had the national interests of the United States not intersected with a continued Syrian presence in Lebanon.

Signing and Implementing the Ta'if Agreement

On September 29, 1989, under the auspices of the Arab League, sixty-two surviving members of Lebanon's 1972 legislature arrived in the city of Ta'if in Saudi Arabia. When the parliamentarians arrived, their first impression was that the meeting would not last very long, as Saudi authorities had granted them visas for only four days. However, the deliberations and negotiations stretched out for more than three weeks. The final meeting of the parliamentarians in Ta'if was on October 22, 1989. The latest version of the document that they had created was read, and the Speaker of the parliament asked for a vote. The parliamentarians approved it unanimously with three abstentions.

Michel Aoun was informed about the agreement by the Arab emissary Lakhdar Brahimi. On the following day, he held a press conference to reject the agreement and to accuse the United States of plotting against Lebanese sovereignty. Afraid to come back to Lebanon, the parliamentarians from the areas under Aoun's control took refuge in Paris and after extensive negotiations went to northern Lebanon, to a military airport not controlled by Aoun, in order to elect a new president of the republic. On November 5, 1989, René Mouawad was elected to the presidency. In the meantime, Michel Aoun, who still considered himself the legitimate head of state, had formally dissolved the parliament.[15] On the day of the presidential election, Aoun met with the members of his military cabinet as well as other prominent Christian leaders, including the head of the Lebanese Forces, Samir Geagea, and the head of the Free National Party, Dany Chamoun. Geagea tried to convince the gathering to accept the election of Mouawad and to cooperate with the president-elect, but he was unable to win their support.[16]

On November 22, 1989, after celebrating Lebanon's Independence Day, President-Elect Mouawad was assassinated when a car bomb exploded near his motorcade, killing him and twenty-three others. Just two days later, the parliament met again, this time in the Beqaa valley, and elected Elias Hrawi as president. Hrawi announced that it was time to expel Michel Aoun from the presidential palace. On the evening of November 28, after Hrawi's threat was announced, a crowd of several thousand people arrived at the presidential palace to serve as human shields for Aoun. Samir Geagea was then forced to announce that the Lebanese Forces were going to side with Aoun. The tension increased over the following months, until Aoun himself decided to get rid of Geagea and the Lebanese Forces to consolidate his control of the Christian enclave. On February 1, 1990, the army under the command of Aoun attacked the position of the Lebanese Forces. This assault was called the "war of forceful unification" by Aoun, while Geagea dubbed it the "war of cancellation." As official history is written by winners, it is under that latter name that this conflict came to be known.[17]

Aoun's Defeat

In addition to Aoun's conflict with the Lebanese Forces, larger international events were afoot in the wake of the ratification of the Ta'if Agreement. In August 1990, Saddam Hussein of Iraq invaded Kuwait. This move prompted a strong reaction in the international community, especially in the United States, and on September 13, 1990, Syrian president Hafez al-Assad met with US secretary of state James Baker to formalize an alliance that would affect both the crisis in Kuwait and the situation in Lebanon. The United States agreed not to interfere if Syria deposed Michel Aoun. Several actors, including the Vatican and the new Lebanese government, had tried to reintegrate Michel Aoun into the political process, but Aoun was stubborn in his rejection. He thought that Syria would not dare to attack him. On October 13, 1990, however, Syrian military planes bombed Aoun's stronghold in the Baabda region. A simultaneous assault on the regions controlled by Aoun was then launched by Syrian and Lebanese forces under the command of the new Lebanese government. Aoun took refuge in the French embassy and asked for a cease-fire.

He would remain there until August 1991, when he finally departed into exile in France.

The crisis created by General Aoun and his refusal to accept the Ta'if Agreement led to a feeling of urgency among Lebanese political elites. This sense of crisis, combined with the broader international alignments in the region during the Gulf War period, allowed Syria to have a free hand in Lebanon and to enforce (some aspects of) the arrangement specified in the Ta'if negotiations. It is important to note that the Ta'if Agreement was not substantially different from the earlier Syrian-sponsored peace negotiations of 1983 and 1984; in fact, a number of very similar white papers and drafts of agreements had been sponsored and rejected during the years of active hostilities. More than the specific provisions of the agreement, it was the precarious circumstances and regional alignments in Lebanon in 1989 that convinced the nation's elites to accept a compromise that they may not have otherwise achieved.

The Characteristics of a Peace Settlement

Marie-Joëlle Zahar has pointed out that the Ta'if Agreement is unusual in the context of other accords that have ended civil wars. The parties directly involved in the conflict were not the primary negotiators, and the agreement was reached during the height of the conflict rather than as the result of a military victory or stalemate.[18] This difference can be understood when we regard the Ta'if Agreement as an elite settlement. Facing a serious political crisis and a potential for escalating violence, such a pact is grounded in the effort of diverse elites to find a way in which to reestablish stability. Time is of the essence in this context, and the fear of consequences leads diverse factions to moderate their rigid principles and fixed positions. Concessions are made that would not otherwise be considered.

An elite settlement is forged in secret and direct negotiations among the leaders of important factions. In the case of the Ta'if Agreement, the secrecy of the negotiations was preserved by keeping the press at bay. The Saudi hosts asked the press not to mention what was happening in the meetings and explained that the parliamentarians were to be in charge of informing the public of the results of their deliberations.[19] Contrary to other negotiations that attempted to solve the Lebanese problem, to which only warlords and the heads of militias had been invited, the Ta'if discussions brought together the members of the parliament as representatives of the Lebanese people. The main reason for this change was that previous attempts to reach a peace agreement had been scuttled by conflicts among radical political actors who were directly involved in the conflict. In contrast, Prime Minister Salim al-Hoss insisted that the Ta'if negotiations take place among parliamentarians. This insistence was based on his faith in the judgment of the parliamentarians and his desire to revive the role of the parliament.[20]

Another aspect of the creation of an elite settlement is the predominance of experienced political leaders in the negotiations. In Ta'if, newcomers to the political scene played a peripheral role at most. For example, and contrary to previous negotiations in the 1980s, warlords such as Nabih Berri and Walid Jumblat were excluded from these discussions.[21] At the Ta'if meetings, the negotiators were mainly sexagenarians and septuagenarians with lengthy experience in politics. These surviving parliamentarians were able to forge a written agreement and to convince their communities to support the concessions and guarantees that they made in private. In this very early stage of postwar interaction, an agreement was forged among a group of concerned elites, while many of the more aggressive actors in the conflict remained excluded from the negotiations.

Inclusion Process

In the initial years of the Ta'if Agreement, many important actors (most notably, Christian leaders) did not feel that they could see themselves as part of the new settlement. This situation was exacerbated by the legitimization of the Syrian presence in Lebanon and the incursion of Syria-sponsored clients into the political elite during the years 1991–92. Some Christian warlords who had been active in the hostilities, such as Michel Aoun and Samir Geagea, were formally excluded and banished to exile or imprisonment. This exclusion led to a widespread phenomenon that came to be known in the local press as "Christian disenchantment," as most Christians did not feel represented by the Syrian-sponsored elites. The electoral process under Syrian hegemony was far from equitable, and most Christian elites boycotted the legislative elections of 1992. During the following decade, however, these same Christian leaders gradually came to accept the postwar reality. The participation of the Lebanese Forces in the municipal elections of 1998 indicated that the new postwar political system had been accepted by most of the Christian elites. Indeed, a succession of electoral defeats at this time convinced dissidents that they would need to fully embrace the legitimacy of existing political institutions and learn how to beat the leading coalition at its own game in order to avoid a permanent exclusion from politics.

The dissident elites who slowly adapted to the new "rules of the game" came to recognize that participating in the settlement would be the most direct route to empowerment. Owing to the confessional allotment process, elections in Lebanon are primarily about the politics of sectarian representation and not about direct competition between factions. Thus, participating in elections was seen as a way to obtain a platform for one's outlook, rather than a process of confrontation or debate with opposing views. The European Union Election Observation Mission's 2005 report explained that "traditionally, elections in Lebanon are not meant to delineate a framework for competing political parties, governmental programs, or public policies. . . . Their primary function is to ensure the participation of the elites and the representation of the country's regions, confessions, and political families, through a specific system of seat allotment, which actually limits political competition and confines it within each confession."[22] In other words, dissidents found that they could participate in the settlement without actually having to negotiate their positions or make accommodations in their outlooks. This feature of the consociational system (along with the forceful presence of Syrian guardianship) was vital in creating an era of renewed stability in Lebanon. It did very little, however, to promote democratization or change in the underlying attitudes of Lebanese elites.

The 1992 Legislative Elections

The Ta'if Agreement included provisions that called for the eventual sovereignty of Lebanon and the redeployment of Syrian troops, but these aspects of the agreement were never implemented. Muslims were largely satisfied with the arrangements and in general accepted the nomination of new Lebanese elites who had strong ties to Syria. However, most Christians did not feel the same way. In 1992, with the blessing of Maronite patriarch Sfeir, the legislative elections were largely boycotted by the Christian candidates and by the Christian electorate. From Paris, exiled Christian leaders Michel Aoun, Amin Gemayel, and Raymond Eddé also called for a boycott of the elections. Samir Geagea, the leader of the Lebanese Forces, was against the elections as well, although for different reasons. Geagea had expected to achieve prominence in Lebanese Christian politics after the defeat of Aoun, but was instead confronted with a decline in his popularity and influence. In 1992 he hoped to improve his status by following the popular mood of the Christian community and by avoiding the embarrassment of running as a candidate in an election in which he would likely have been defeated.[23]

Like Geagea, Maronite patriarch Sfeir had also participated in the isolation of Aoun and supported the Ta'if Agreement. Despite this support, the Maronite community had lost its traditional privileges in the constitutional reforms that followed the peace settlement. These reforms had rebalanced the Lebanese political system, something that the patriarch and other moderate Maronite leaders had expected and been ready to accept since the 1980s. Under the influence of Syria, however, the implementation of the reforms went too far in shifting influence to Syria and its Muslim allies. The patriarch felt that the new regime had cast aside his community, and he therefore joined the opposition in 1992. The secession of a religious figure of his stature reinforced the opposition and greatly increased its legitimacy; in addition, however, his involvement also reinforced the confessional character of the boycott.[24] This led to a greater entrenchment of the Muslim-Christian divide and cast the resistance against Syrian interference in Lebanon as a purely sectarian matter. A number of Christian politicians who wanted to participate in the elections, such as the leaders of the Kata'eb Party, were forced to abandon their position and join the boycott. The elections nevertheless took place, and the resulting changes in parliament only reinforced the schism between the government and the Christian community.

The 1996 Elections

In 1996 a number of Christian leaders seemed prepared to change their position on electoral participation, as the boycott had only led to further marginalization. As one Lebanese analyst explained, they had the intent of "fighting with the state's weapons."[25] From Paris, however, the "National Union" led by Amin Gemayel, Michel Aoun, and Dory Chamoun called again for a boycott of the elections, and Raymond Eddé also voiced continued opposition. It seemed that the Christian opposition outside of the country was committed to marginalizing its community in advance by encouraging its members to step out of the democratic game.[26] Nonetheless, several Christian leaders in Lebanon who did not necessarily approve of the government and its policies decided to participate in the process. Christian deputy Albert Mukhaiber visited the seat of the Maronite patriarch on June 15 to discuss the negative consequences of the boycott of 1992 and to suggest that a continued boycott would be counterproductive. The patriarch adopted a more moderate position and encouraged voters to follow their own conscience.[27] Fifty-eight men who had boycotted the 1992 elections met at Mukhaiber's home on July 16 and published a communiqué calling for participation in the elections. The Christian camp, which had been unified in its opposition in 1992, thus began to split. Even though the majority of the Christians who ran for office in 1996 were not elected, their participation created a precedent for the return of the Christian community to the political process.

The 1998 Municipal Elections

The municipal elections of 1998 showed a further move of Christian elites toward the mainstream political process. For the first time in the Second Republic, members of the Lebanese Forces, the Kata'eb, and the

Aounists participated in the elections (the LF and the Kata'eb are discussed in more detail in chapter 3). Their candidates were well received in regions with large Christian populations, and a number of Christian candidates were elected to office in municipalities where their constituencies were preponderant. The importance of the Lebanese Forces was especially felt in the *qada'* (district) of Bsharri in northern Lebanon. Bsharri is the home district of Samir Geagea, the Lebanese Forces commander who was imprisoned in 1994 in connection with a variety of political assassinations. The region remained stalwart in its support of the Lebanese Forces despite Geagea's imprisonment, and in 1998 the party's candidates won seats in the majority of towns and villages in Bsharri. The Lebanese Forces also had some success in elections in Beirut, and in Mount Lebanon two candidates close to Geagea ran but were not elected.

The Christian Kata'eb Party also participated in the municipal elections, though the percentage of seats won by this party was relatively small. Even in the heavily Christian region of Mount Lebanon, the Kata'eb won only 1.58 percent of the municipal seats.[28] In contrast to the Lebanese Forces, who were able to control entire councils in the district of Bsharri, the Kata'eb sympathizers achieved only a few seats in the Batrun, Kura, Akkar, and Bsharri districts. In Beirut, traditionally one of the bastions of the Kata'eb, their electoral results were also disappointing. As for the Free Patriotic Movement (FPM) of General Aoun, it managed to get 4.36 percent of the votes in the Mount Lebanon district.[29] In Beirut the Aounist candidates joined the elections on the opposition list and received a small percentage of the vote of the Druze and Christian communities.

The 2000 Legislative Elections

By the year 2000, the vast majority of opposition leaders had been incorporated into the political process established by the pro-Syria regime. Only a handful of Christian elites continued to call for boycotts, and the Maronite patriarch kept a neutral position, suggesting only that all Christians should be unified, either for or against the elections. A number of prominent Christian elites won parliamentary seats in this election, and Lebanese analysts began to increasingly argue that the boycott had failed to achieve its purpose and was losing its grip among the opposition community.[30] Within the space of a single decade, the oppositional political elite who had initially refused to accept the settlement of Ta'if had largely come to affirm the legality of the agreement and agreed to play by the rules established therein.

The 2004 Municipal Elections and 2005 Legislative Elections

In May 2004 the Christian opposition parties lost ground in local elections in the Mount Lebanon district because of the control exerted by pro-Syria regime elements over that region. Unexpectedly and perhaps suspiciously, the candidate lists supported by Michel Murr, a client of Syria, won in forty of the forty-eight Christian municipalities in Mount Lebanon. In northern Lebanon, however, the Lebanese Forces won all twenty-one seats in the Bsharri municipal council.[31] In general, Christian opposition parties did not make many inroads in these elections, but participation remained high.

The 2005 legislative elections were held in the wake of the Cedar Revolution and the withdrawal of Syrian troops. The elections showed that without the Syrian presence, many of that country's political clients who did not have a real constituency in Lebanon would not be able to achieve reelection. The 2005 legislature saw a very high rate of turnover, with new parliamentarians representing 47.66 percent of the deputies.[32] However, despite this circulation, the consociational system ensured that the main parliamentary blocs remained identical to the factions of the previous legislatures.

The elections showed changes within the Christian representation, as Michel Aoun had returned from his exile in Paris to head a candidate list and run for election in the Mount Lebanon area. As a result, the main stake of the election in that region became a choice among Christian leaders. The elections were heavily contested, with an initial field of 170 candidates vying for 34 seats. The turnout in Mount Lebanon was higher than in any other region, with 54.46 percent of the electorate turning up for the vote, and it reached an all-time high of 62.55 percent in Kisrwan-Jbeil, where Aoun was running as a candidate. The most noticeable result of this election was the unexpected landslide of Aoun's electoral victory in Kisrwan-Jbeil and Metn; his victory pushed aside the scions of prominent political dynasties that had traditionally dominated the region's political scene. With his electoral victory, Aoun became the most important Christian leader in Lebanon, heading the country's largest Christian bloc. The majority of the 15 parliamentarians who were elected as part of Aoun's bloc in the 2005–9 legislature were unknown candidates, individuals close to Aoun who obtained office simply by being on his candidate list.[33]

The Lebanese Forces also ran candidates in the elections of 2005, with Setrida Geagea heading the list and calling for her husband's release from prison.[34] The party managed to win 6 seats in the new parliament: 2 in Mount Lebanon and 4 in the North, one of whom was Mrs. Geagea herself. The Kata'eb Party also won 3 seats in the election: 1 for the Arabist faction of Karim Pakradouni and 2 for the reform faction headed by Gemayel.

Elite Factionalization

The slow inclusion of dissenting elements in Lebanese politics in the 1990s was followed by an attempt on the part of the pro-Syria government to split the Christian leadership. After the death of Syrian president Hafez al-Assad and the legislative elections of 2000, Syria and its Lebanese allies began secret negotiations with the Maronite Church, the heads of important political dynasties, and the leadership of former militias. Syria wanted to forge a credible coalition of Christian leaders willing to abandon their demands for a Syrian withdrawal from Lebanon. In exchange, Syria was willing to offer cultural autonomy and a protection of Christian political privileges.[35] This led to significant internecine struggles within the ranks of the Kata'eb and the Lebanese Forces. Within each group, political elites supported by the pro-Syria political establishment started a campaign aimed at controlling and marginalizing the forces that were asking for Syrian withdrawal.

Michel Aoun's Free Patriotic Movement was the only major Christian group that the government did not try to divide or co-opt. This omission can be explained by two factors. First, Aoun and the majority of his cadre were outside of Lebanon between 1989 and 2005, and the second tier of his followers was not willing to make concessions to the demands of the government. Second, contrary to the Lebanese Forces or the Kata'eb, the rejection of the Syrian presence on Lebanese soil and of Syrian interference in Lebanese internal affairs was at the heart of the Free Patriotic Movement's raison d'être. This rejection is what gave the movement credibility and legitimacy in the eyes of its popular base. Thus, any perceived alliance with the Syrian "occupier" would have meant an immediate loss of legitimacy for the organization.

Conclusion

Through a process of inclusion and factionalization, the majority of the Christian elite who were alienated by the settlement at Ta'if were gradually brought into the pro-Syria governmental fold. While marginalized dissident factions splintered off from the primary opposition groups, the majority of postwar elite leaders came to share a consensus on two specific issues: a fear of violence and an embrace of the rules of the political game. This relative unity of purpose permitted Lebanon to overcome the chaos of the civil war and to reestablish a more or less stable consociational system. Although the co-option of dissident factions into the postwar elite settlement promoted stability, it also tended to ensure that the process of democratization would remain superficial. An important component of this democratization process was the weakness and instability of Lebanese political parties. Because of their rigid confessional alignments, Lebanese parties remained fundamentally paternalistic organizations, with no internal democratic procedures and no clear ideologies. In the following chapter, I will turn to a detailed discussion of these political parties and their failure to act as stable platforms for elite recruitment—while indicating one notable exception to the norm.

3

Political Parties

During the prewar period, Lebanese American scholar Michael Suleiman developed the thesis that although political parties existed in Lebanon, these organizations could not be thought of as the functional equivalents of parties in Western democracies.[1] Suleiman noted that Lebanese political parties did not emerge until the early twentieth century and that their primary purpose was to lend a modern aspect to older structures based on ties of kinship and religion. Despite the advent of the modern Lebanese state, religion continued to permeate all aspects of political life, and political representation in the First Republic was completely based on one's religious affiliation. Consequently, almost all political parties operating in Lebanon during the prewar period had a sectarian character.[2] In addition, the stability of these parties' ideological platforms was minimal in comparison with the influence of individual party leaders. The majority of Lebanese parties were the products of founding personalities who tried to combine traditional concepts of leadership (za'ama) with modern or Western ideas of political representation. The orientation of parties largely conformed to the outlook of their leader, rather than the other way around. Therefore, party-based ideologies have never played a strong role in shaping Lebanon's governmental policies, and the function of political parties has often been limited to their use as propaganda machines for individual political actors.

The limitations of Lebanese political parties that Suleiman noted in the prewar period were only exacerbated by the onset of the civil war. The sectarian prewar parties took an active role in aggravating the conflict, and most commentators agree that they were "predisposed politically and ideologically to transform themselves into militia forces."[3] This enthusiastic embrace of violence, sometimes involving brutal behavior even toward the parties' own sectarian communities, alienated the majority of the Lebanese public. During the war, Lebanese political parties lost any sense of democratic credibility that they may have had in the prewar period, and the Lebanese came to regard the concept of political parties with mistrust or even hostility. Therefore, after the end of the violence, new political organizations avoided registering as parties.[4] Although new organizations did emerge during the period of postwar Syrian hegemony, such as Rafiq Hariri's "Future Movement" and Michel Aoun's "Free Patriotic Movement," it is only since 2006 that some of these organizations have once again begun to formally describe themselves as political parties. For the purposes of my analysis here, such organizations will be referred to as parties regardless of their official designation.

Since Lebanese political parties are mostly organized around the charisma and patronage networks of individual leaders, the list of these parties is quite long.[5] In most cases, the examination of individual elites (see chapter 4) is of greater significance than is the examination of their party organizations. Nevertheless, some Lebanese elites remain more closely tied to party apparatuses than others, and there are a handful of parties that have played an important role in modern Lebanese history. These prominent parties consolidated their influence during the civil war, when the collapse of the Lebanese state and the absence of functioning state institutions led aspiring elites to turn to sectarian parties and their militias as the principal venue for political advancement. The party leaders who emerged during this period can be called "war elites" or, perhaps more to the point, "warlords."[6]

The most important parties that prospered during the civil war and survived to have an influence in postwar Lebanon include the Kata'eb and its offshoot the Lebanese Forces (composed of members of the Maronite community), the Progressive Socialist Party (composed of members of the Druze community), and Hezbollah (composed of members of the Shi'i community). The Kata'eb Party and the Progressive Socialist Party were formed during the prewar period, and prior to the outbreak of the conflict they maintained a balance between the roles of patronage organization and modern political party. During the war and in the postwar period, however, these parties—as well as the Lebanese Forces, which was formed during the conflict—developed into wholly personality-based organizations, without any consistent platform or ideology. In the influential typology of political organizations developed by Richard Gunther and Larry Diamond, they would be classified as "elite-based parties"—ones that have little formal organization and are centered on patron-client relationships.[7]

In contrast, Hezbollah has moved in the opposite direction, developing from a small militia in the 1980s into a coherent and widespread political organization in the postwar period. Today Hezbollah is the only political party in Lebanon that retains an explicit ideology and a clear organizational structure. Unlike the Kata'eb Party and the Progressive Socialist Party, leadership positions in Hezbollah are elected rather than inherited. In Gunther and Diamond's typology, Hezbollah would be considered a "mass-based party" of the "religious fundamentalist" variety.[8] Its coherence is based on a strict application of religious doctrine, and its role in providing social services within the Shi'i community increases the party's appeal among the more destitute segments of Lebanese society.

The Kata'eb

Hizb al-Kata'eb al-Lubnaniya is often referred to in English and in French as "the party of the Phalanges" (*Kata'eb* is the Arabic translation of *Phalanges*, a Greek word meaning "battalions"). The formation of the party was inspired by the era of the "shirts" in Europe, when paramilitary organizations proliferated in Nazi Germany, Fascist Italy, and elsewhere.[9] Indeed, the Kata'eb's first president, Pierre Gemayel, participated in the 1936 Olympic Games in Berlin, where he was inspired by the "discipline, order, purpose and nationalist zeal" of the German spectacle.[10] On November 21, 1936, Gemayel joined fellow Christians George Naccache, Shafiq Nassif, Émile Yared, and future Lebanese president Charles Helou in founding a paramilitary organization that would be directed toward the creation of an independent and Westernized Lebanon. The party's leaders were young, middle-class Christian professionals with ties to France. Beyond their nationalist zealotry and their desire to protect

Christian interests, the early objectives of the party leaders were some-what vague.[11]

The Kata'eb became a strong voice for nationalism in the struggle for Lebanese independence that took place between 1937 and 1943. A few days before the group's first anniversary, the French-controlled government formally dissolved the party—along with other paramilitary organizations such as the Sunni-oriented Najjadah Party—and the Kata'eb's headquarters was seized by French-controlled government troops. This persecution only strengthened the movement, however, and Gemayel's incarceration along with eighty other party members led to widespread demonstrations by Kata'eb supporters. The authorities' decision to arrest Gemayel along with other more notorious proponents of Lebanese statehood transformed the leader of the Kata'eb into a pillar of Lebanese politics, lending symbolic capital and revolutionary legitimacy to his organization. The Kata'eb persevered, and even prospered, as an outlawed party until the achievement of Lebanese independence in November 1943.

After the success of the revolutionary movement, the Kata'eb enjoyed both official recognition and widespread popularity among Lebanese Christians. The following decades were a period of uncertainty and transformation for the party, however, since its identity as a paramilitary and revolutionary organization did not straightforwardly translate into one of a peacetime political party. Important moments in this transformation occurred in 1945, when the Kata'eb first put forward candidates for election, and in 1951, when Pierre Gemayel himself ran (unsuccessfully) for parliament. In the early 1950s, the party developed a more formal bureaucratic apparatus and began to participate systematically in the electoral process. This move signaled a full embrace of the consociational Lebanese political system under the National Pact—although the Kata'eb also continued to maintain a paramilitary aspect and to organize combat training programs for its members.[12]

During the 1958 crisis in Lebanon, the Kata'eb's military organization assisted US troops in putting down antigovernment insurrection and in maintaining the stability of the Westward-leaning government. The party was rewarded with ministerial appointments in the new government that was organized following the crisis. The legitimacy thus obtained completed the party's transition into the Lebanese mainstream. The Kata'eb was victorious at the polls in the following decade, winning a significant number of parliamentary seats.[13] Pierre Gemayel became the parliamentary representative of Beirut in 1960, and he retained this position until the breakdown of the state during the civil war. By the early 1970s, the Kata'eb had become a political giant, with an estimated membership of between sixty and seventy thousand. The party members were men and women who mostly came from the lower middle classes. Eighty-five percent were Maronites, but other sectarian groups were also represented in the organization, including minority Christian communities, a number of Shi'a, a small representation of Druze, and also some members of the Jewish community.[14]

The party ideology as it coalesced during this time leaned toward a version of Lebanese nationalism called Phoenicianism (this ideology is discussed in more detail in chapter 7). The Kata'eb saw themselves as the protectors of the Lebanese nation and, in particular, of the ostensibly civilizing influence of Western, that is, non-Arabic, culture in the region. The Kata'eb understood Lebanon as a nation with a purpose, and they often invoked Christian imagery to explicate this idea. As described by the scholar Ghassan Hage, "The spirituality and the mission embodied in Lebanese civilization are essentially Christian . . . in a somewhat Hegelian sense, as being the objectification of a Christian spirit without which there would be no civilization."[15] Politically, this ideology translated into an extreme version of nationalist patriotism, in which the line between the actions of the party leader and the working of divine will was often blurred. The party maintained strict control over its parliamentary representatives, and it propagated the view that the individual success of party members derived purely from their adherence to the goals of the leadership.[16]

The Role of the Kata'eb in the Civil War

By the time of his death in 1984, Pierre Gemayel had created a new political dynasty in Lebanon, one that would figure prominently in the modern history of the nation. As Lebanon descended into civil war, the legacy of the Kata'eb was mainly carried forward by Pierre's two sons, Bashir and Amin Gemayel. The different leadership styles of these two individuals would have a significant effect on the trajectory of Lebanon's sectarian conflict.

Bashir Gemayel, the younger of the two brothers, was a charismatic and articulate leader who quickly rose to power within the ranks of the Kata'eb. His ambition was clear from the beginning: Bashir's colleague Joseph Abou Khalil describes the younger Gemayel as "being in a hurry to take over his father's place as the leader [of the Kata'eb] and as a Za'im [of the Maronites]."[17] Whereas his elder brother, Amin, seemed more cautious and more willing to take a backseat role in carrying on the family legacy, Bashir became a military and political firebrand. In Abou Khalil's description, he emerged as a wartime leader who saw force as the only effective way to establish power.[18] In addition, Bashir came to reject any possibility of cross-confessional collaboration; he was an advocate for a Christian state and was proud to claim that through the agency of his party, the consociational Lebanese National Pact of 1943 was "dead, buried, and we put a big stone on its tomb so that it does not resurrect."[19]

In 1970 Bashir was briefly kidnapped by Palestinian militants. He was released after only a few hours, but this event seems to have marked him profoundly and reinforced his already extensive prejudices against the Palestinian refugees in Lebanon. Bashir's anger came to the forefront in April 1975, when two members of his father's entourage were killed in an attack by unidentified gunmen, assumed to be Palestinian militants who were attempting to assassinate Pierre Gemayel. Kata'eb forces led by Bashir retaliated hours later by ambushing a bus carrying Palestinians, killing twenty-seven. This event is often regarded as the opening salvo of the Lebanese civil war.

Over the following years, Bashir became the principal military and political leader of the Lebanese Christian community. In 1976 he consolidated his power as the head of the Kata'eb militia, and then he simultaneously became the commander of the new Christian coalition called the Lebanese Forces (an organization that will be discussed in more detail below). Bashir's leadership resulted in an impressive string of wartime victories: he was able to force the Syrian Army to withdraw from the

Christian area north of Beirut, and then he likewise stopped the Lebanese Army from deploying in this area and forbade the presence of any armed forces besides his own militias. Part of Bashir's power in Lebanon came from his connections outside the country. He was backed by the United States, and President Ronald Reagan was said to be one of his staunchest supporters. Bashir visited the United States in 1981 with a vision: he wanted Lebanon to be a bastion of Western influence in the Middle East and to have the same "special" relationship with the United States that was enjoyed by Israel. The American administration was so enthralled with Bashir Gemayel that it created a secure, direct phone line to maintain contact with him.[20] Bashir also pursued amicable relations with Israel, and it is likely that his militias received funding and training from Israel.[21] It was rumored that Bashir met with Ariel Sharon, who was at that time Israel's defense minister, in order to discuss Israel's plans to invade Lebanon and root out Palestinian militants who were operating from within the country. That attack occurred in June 1982, and in the following month, with the country still under Israeli military control, Bashir was elected president of Lebanon.

On September 1, 1982, one week after his election, Bashir met with Israeli prime minister Menachem Begin. Begin demanded that Bashir acknowledge Israel's support of the Kata'eb's wartime efforts and that he sign a peace treaty between Israel and Lebanon. Bashir refused the immediate peace, arguing that he needed time to reach a consensus with Lebanese Muslims and with other Arab nations. As his country's president, Bashir wanted to create a strong, modern state in Lebanon, and he knew that such a project could not be undertaken without Muslim partners. Indeed, Bashir's concept of the Lebanese state was rife with contradictions. He wanted to be seen both as a savior of Lebanese autonomy and as an instrument of Christian civilization; he envisioned the country both as a multifaceted democracy and as a streamlined, militaristic defender of Western hegemony in the region. Bashir Gemayel was never given the opportunity to interrogate this contradictory vision as a peacetime president. Two weeks after his meeting with the Israeli prime minister, he was killed along with twenty-six others when a bomb exploded in the Beirut headquarters of the Kata'eb. Many of Bashir's supporters refused to believe that their leader had been killed. There had been several assassination attempts before, and Bashir had always miraculously survived, leading some to speculate that he was protected by supernatural powers. During his life and after his death, Bashir achieved a sense of religious presence beyond even his father's. He became popularly known among Maronites as "the Savior," and his speeches and opinions became enshrined as "teachings."[22] Indeed, Michael Young has argued that Gemayel "foreshadowed another figure, both similar and dissimilar: Hassan Nasrallah, Hezbollah's secretary-general. . . . Both men, in their disdain for Lebanon's past . . . demonstrated how illiberal too much yearning for revolution could be."[23]

The trajectory of Bashir's violent salvation mission continued after his death, as vengeful Lebanese Forces militiamen carried out the infamous Sabra and Shatila massacres (these events are discussed in detail below). However, Bashir's assassination also marked a new direction for the Kata'eb Party and for the Gemayel legacy. With US support, Bashir's older brother, Amin, emerged to become the new president of Lebanon. Amin Gemayel's leadership style was very different from Bashir's: he was less of a firebrand and more of a diplomat. Although Amin had been a member of parliament since 1970, he had mostly remained in the background and had spoken with a moderate voice. Amin's vision for Lebanon was different from the conception of his brother—he was opposed to a Christian alliance with Israel, and he did not burn any bridges with the Palestinians and the Syrians. The Christian community, which had become accustomed to Bashir's more radical politics, had some trouble adapting to this new style of leadership. Many came to see Amin as a traitor to the Maronite cause, and this belief led to a relative decline in the power of the Kata'eb as alliances shifted to the increasingly independent Lebanese Forces.

Despite Amin's relatively moderate views, Syria was not happy to have a Western-backed Gemayel heir in the presidency, and often-violent tensions between diverse sectarian groups continued to escalate. Political paralysis prevailed in Lebanon until the end of Amin's term in September 1988. When Amin's mandate expired, Lebanon was left with a political vacuum owing to the factions' inability to agree on a new president.

Amin appointed the Christian general Michel Aoun as the head of an interim military government, a decision that initiated a new, painful chapter in Lebanese history—Aoun's violent campaign against Syria and his subsequent defeat would help to usher in the postwar period of Syrian hegemony in Lebanon. Amin Gemayel himself went into semiexile after the end of his presidency, residing mainly in Paris for the next twelve years as Lebanon progressively fell under the sway of Syrian influence.

The Revitalization of the Kata'eb

The Kata'eb did not play a significant role in Lebanese politics during the immediate postwar period. In the year 2000, however, when the death of the influential Syrian leader Hafez al-Assad led to a renewed debate about the political future of the region, Amin Gemayel returned to Lebanon. A month later, his son, Pierre Gemayel II, the namesake of the Kata'eb founder, won a parliamentary seat as the representative of the Metn area. With this victory it began to appear that a new generation of Gemayels had emerged onto the Lebanese political scene.

Pierre II was only twenty-eight years old, and a political neophyte, when he obtained his seat in parliament. His election came as a surprise to many political observers. Pierre II predictably situated himself as a member of the opposition bloc (against the pro-Syria government). He argued that Lebanon enjoyed only "half-sovereignty," and he demanded an end to the military and political influence of Syria. Pierre II also spoke out against the military operations of Hezbollah in the contested Shebaa Farms region; in this opposition he argued against the official stance of President Émile Lahoud, who claimed that Hezbollah's actions were in agreement with Lebanon's strategic interests.[24] Pierre II quickly came to enjoy the support of a large segment of the Christian electorate. His role in the opposition led to his reelection to parliament in the 2005 elections that followed the Syrian withdrawal from Lebanon and to his subsequent appointment as the minister of industry in the cabinet of Fouad Siniora.

With the help of his father, Amin, Pierre Gemayel II attempted to revitalize the Kata'eb Party and to return it to its previous role as a major political force. He wanted to jolt the Christian community out of its long period of political "disenchantment" and to revive a more radical Christian voice in Lebanon. To block this effort, the pro-Syria government pursued the strategy of dividing the party and co-opting some of its cadre. Thus, in the early years of the twenty-first century, the Kata'eb fractured into a pro-Syria faction, headed by Karim Pakradouni, and an anti-Syria faction, which remained under the control of the Gemayel family. Indeed, after the municipal elections of 1998, the pro-Syria government initiated a policy of divide et impera in order to dilute the influence of the Kata'eb. After the principal Kata'eb leader, Georges Saadeh, was co-opted to the government position, the party began to consolidate into two factions: one group that supported the politics of the state—including the Syrian presence in Lebanon—and another group that remained in the opposition.

In March 1999, Mounir al-Hajj was elected as secretary-general of the party and started a campaign in favor of the Syrian presence in Lebanon. During the 2000 parliamentary elections, he was invited to join the electoral list headed by the minister of the interior, Michel Murr. However, al-Hajj did not win as expected, mainly because of the candidacy of Pierre Gemayel II. Gemayel entered the fray in the last days of the electoral campaign and managed to gather the support of the Kata'eb partisans. Al-Hajj was humiliated by this fiasco, and the majority of the party's political bureau members called on him to resign. The two factions of the party began to struggle for the control of the Kata'eb: the opposition faction was centered on former president Amin Gemayel, who had returned to Lebanon in July 2000 after twelve years of exile, while the progovernment faction was headed by al-Hajj's second in command, Karim Pakradouni.

Initially, Pakradouni had expressed his support for Gemayel's return to the helm of the party; however, he soon changed his mind and started to adopt a radically pro-Syria position. Fearing that Gemayel might win a majority of the votes within the electoral assembly of the Kata'eb, Pakradouni and al-Hajj reduced the number of interparty representatives from Metn, traditionally the fief of the Gemayel family, and appointed several of Gemayel's opponents to the empty seats. The interparty elections took place in October 2001, and Pakradouni easily won with 80 percent of the vote, becoming the new leader of the Kata'eb. A few hours after his election, he announced that the Kata'eb would from then on "be the party of the President, the army and the judiciary."[25] Pierre Gemayel II accused Pakradouni of having launched a "coup d'état" against the party's rightful leaders, adding, "All that is built on oppression and fraud will not last."[26]

From October 2001 to the 2005 elections, Pakradouni was one of the most eloquent advocates of the Syrian presence and hegemony in Lebanon. His loyalty was rewarded with a ministerial post in the April 2003 cabinet. Under Pakradouni (an Armenian and the first non-Maronite Kata'eb leader) the party's relations with Damascus attained their peak, and the Kata'eb officially participated in all pro-Syria demonstrations. Day after day, however, the party's sympathizers were gradually decreasing in number. With the co-optation of its leader and its division into two inimical factions, the Kata'eb lost its prominence as a major Christian party. The victory of Pakradouni in the party elections did not indicate a consensus within the Christian community, but was rather an indicator of the resignation and discord reigning within the community following the Ta'if Agreement. The Kata'eb ceased to serve as a political outlet for the Maronites, becoming instead a puppet organization loyal to the regime and to Syria.

In a 2002 interview with the *Washington Report*, Amin Gemayel said that his "duty" would be to restore his party to the status it had enjoyed under the leadership of his father. He added that the Kata'eb had been paralyzed because of intercommunal rivalries and Syrian intervention in Lebanon: "The Syrians fear the resurrection of the Phalange [Kata'eb] with someone like Amin Gemayel at its head," he said. Indeed, under his leadership the party would symbolize "the true representatives of the people assuming their leadership role."[27] In July 2005, a court verdict dethroned Pakradouni from the leadership of the Kata'eb and set the stage for Amin Gemayel to take back the helm of his father's party. Pakradouni declared he would appeal the new ruling and would not evacuate the party's headquarters pending the Court of Appeals' verdict.

In early September 2005, Lebanon's English newspaper, the *Daily Star*, mentioned the possibility that the two factions might be sorting out their differences.[28] This prediction came to pass later in the same month when the two factions came together in a widely publicized reconciliation. Amin Gemayel stated that the "breeze of a new era blows on the Phalange Party," and added, "There is no crack in the Phalange Party as people used to say, and there was no division in the literal meaning of the word."[29] He expressed his joy at the reunification of the party and his reform movement, saying that "there could be no better reunion."[30] After the unification of the party, Pakradouni kept his position at the helm, while Amin Gemayel was declared the party's "supreme leader" for life.

The reconciliation between the two factions of the Kata'eb after Syrian withdrawal signaled the end of Syria-backed factionalization in Lebanese politics—indeed, as Pakradouni's incentive for siding with the Syrians disappeared following their withdrawal, it was in his interest to return to the fold of the traditional Kata'eb. Pakradouni ultimately resigned from the party in early 2008.

Pierre Gemayel II paid for his political convictions with his life. He was gunned down by unknown assassins in November 2006. It has been speculated that Pierre II's assassination was an attempt by pro-Syria groups to force the dissolution of the Lebanese cabinet, as it is stipulated in Lebanese law that the cabinet must be adjourned if one-third of its members become unavailable. With the walkout of the five Shi'i ministers and one of their allies that month, followed quickly by Pierre II's high-profile assassination, the government came very close to collapse.[31] Ultimately, however, stability was maintained, and the death of Pierre II did not reverse the fortunes of the Kata'eb or intimidate other members of the Gemayel family into withdrawing from politics. In 2009 Sami Gemayel, Pierre II's brother, was elected as the new representative of the Metn region, and Nadim Gemayel, the son of Bashir Gemayel, also achieved a seat in the legislature, representing Beirut's first district.

The Lebanese Forces

The Lebanese Forces organized in August 1976 as an informal coalition of Christian militias. It was commanded by Bashir Gemayel and mainly controlled by members of the Kata'eb.[32] The goal of the LF was to bring together and coordinate the operations of diverse Christian factions, including the National Liberal Party, the al-Tanzim Party, and the Guardians of the Cedars, as well as the Kata'eb forces. The men and women who composed the rank and file of the LF were primarily young Maronites from the lower-middle-class and working-class areas of Beirut. Most were volunteers, but starting in 1982 the LF also began to conscript recruits from Christian communities. In the early 1980s, the LF militia was estimated to contain twelve thousand members.[33]

Whereas the organization was first and foremost combat oriented, the collapse of government services during the 1980s led the LF to increasingly adopt civic responsibilities in the areas of Beirut that were under the militia's control. Members of the LF maintained public order and provided police functions in their enclave; they also organized public transportation, managed traffic, created a consumer protection program, and instituted a system of price controls to prevent inflation. The LF created programs for social relief that aided citizens victimized by the war; it also promulgated an antidrug movement and sponsored cultural heritage tours for the children of Lebanese Christians who were living abroad. The militia collected revenues by enforcing duties on shipping and surcharges on luxury items such as cinema tickets and restaurant meals. The LF even created an office of foreign affairs that worked to mobilize expatriate communities and to communicate the militia's points of view to an international audience. It is reasonable to conclude that, for Lebanon's Maronite community, the LF became the functional equivalent of the state during the civil war.

After the death of Bashir Gemayel in 1982, there was a struggle over the command of the Lebanese Forces. Unhappy with the more moderate direction of the Kata'eb leadership under Amin Gemayel, two young LF commanders, Elie Hobeiqa and Samir Geagea, orchestrated an internal coup and took control of the militia in 1985.[34] In January of the following year, Geagea became the sole head of the LF after overthrowing Hobeiqa, who was widely accused of betraying the Lebanese Christian sector by cultivating ties with Syria.

As members of the generation that had come of age during the civil war, Hobeiqa and Geagea were more headstrong, and more entrenched in a combat mentality, than was the prewar Christian leadership under Pierre Gemayel I. The prewar establishment of the Kata'eb was made possible through charismatic leadership and diplomacy, but the institutionalization of the organization's power during the 1960s and 1970s meant that the subsequent generation of leaders did not need to rely on charismatic leadership to retain control of their followers. During the 1980s, as Amin Gemayel worked inconclusively to move the Kata'eb back toward the relatively deliberative and philosophical Christian nationalism of his father, the Lebanese Forces broke away and diverged ever more sharply into the realm of zealotry.

Elie Hobeiqa: Warlord, War Criminal

Born in 1956, Elie Hobeiqa was a loyal follower of the Kata'eb during his adolescence. After the outbreak of the civil war, he became known as a ruthless warrior in the Christian cause. Hobeiqa became the head of the security agency of the Lebanese Forces in 1978, a position that allowed him to cultivate high-profile contacts with the Israelis and with the CIA in the United States. During the Israeli invasion of 1982, he acted as one of the LF's main liaison officers with the Israeli army. In his memoirs of the Lebanese Forces, Joseph Abou Khalil describes Hobeiqa as a perfect product of the war and its sectarian barricades, a great strategist and a pragmatic thinker who remained aloof from emotionality and philosophical debate. According to Abou Khalil, he was a silent participant in the meetings of the LF commanders, one who spent his time doodling and answered questions only when he was directly addressed. The war was his raison d'être. Abou Khalil alleges that Hobeiqa learned the arts of war and military intelligence at the hands of Israeli trainers, excelling in both fields.[35]

Following the assassination of Bashir Gemayel, LF militiamen under Hobeiqa's command entered the Sabra and Shatila refugee camps and massacred the Palestinians who were residing there. No precise account of this atrocity is available, but estimates of the number of Palestinians killed range between seven hundred and thirty-five hundred individuals.[36] Although Hobeiqa denied any personal involvement in the massacres, his claim was refuted by Israel's own Kahan Commission, which was convened to investigate the role of Israeli forces under Ariel Sharon in allowing the militiamen to enter the camps.[37] Hobeiqa's reputation for atrocity was further compounded in March 1985, when at the request of the Saudis and the CIA he ordered the assassination of Shi'i ayatollah Muhammad Hussein Fadlallah, who was at the time perceived by the West as the spiritual leader of Hezbollah.[38] The LF bomb that was intended to kill Fadlallah both failed in its objective and resulted in the deaths of eighty uninvolved civilians, leading the CIA to break off its relations with Hobeiqa.

Just a few days after the attack on Fadlallah, Hobeiqa joined Samir Geagea in wresting the leadership of the Lebanese Forces. Hobeiqa's leadership style as the commander of the LF proved to be extremely authoritarian. It is reported that Hobeiqa was an admirer of Machiavelli's writings on the maintenance of political power and that he embraced the Machiavellian ideal of forceful autocracy in governance.[39] Hobeiqa made the LF into a refuge for the unemployed and for ordinary thugs. He used the LF militia to impose his personal rule on the Christian enclave and put prominent members of the Kata'eb under house arrest. All of this activity led to a growth of resentment in the Christian community. However, among the many mistakes that Hobeiqa made in consolidating his power, the most significant was his attempted rapprochement with Syria. Christian outrage at Hobeiqa's involvement with the Syrian leadership came to a head in December 1985, when Hobeiqa agreed to sign the Syrian-sponsored Tripartite Accord on behalf of the LF. Realizing that the accord would legitimize Syrian intervention in Lebanon, Christian factions led by Samir Geagea seized control of the LF in January 1986. Hobeiqa fled to France, and then to Damascus—where he was encouraged by the Syrian regime to return to Lebanon and establish a new militia in the areas under Syrian control. In the closing years of the civil war, Hobeiqa became fully a Syrian client. He was rewarded for this new allegiance with important positions in the first decade of the postwar, Syrian-influenced government.

In 1999 Hobeiqa's former bodyguard Robert Hatem (alias Cobra) published a book that changed Hobeiqa's life. Titled *From Israel to*

Damascus, the book described in detail the atrocities carried out by Hobeiqa during the civil war. Hatem attributed numerous assassinations and war crimes to his former boss, among which was an assassination attempt against Salim al-Hoss. Al-Hoss, then prime minister of Lebanon, opened an investigation into this event, which had cost the life of his driver as well as the lives of several innocent bystanders. Syria assured Hobeiqa that the investigation would be inconclusive; however, the polemic that ensued was the beginning of the end of Hobeiqa's political career. In 2000 a lawsuit was filed in Belgium against Ariel Sharon for his role in the massacres at Sabra and Shatila. This event renewed the public debate over Hobeiqa's role in the massacre. Hobeiqa proclaimed his innocence and promised to reveal proof to that effect during the trial. He was, however, to take his secrets to the tomb: on January 24, 2002, Hobeiqa was killed in a bombing attack. The actors behind this assassination are still unknown, but the Lebanese government has accused Israel of ordering Hobeiqa's death to protect Prime Minister Sharon from his embarrassing accusations.

Samir Geagea: The Prisoner

Samir Geagea was born in 1952 to a modest Maronite family, and like Hobeiqa, he was active in the Kata'eb Party during his youth. Geagea was studying medicine at the American University of Beirut in 1975 when the initial battles of the civil war began. Because of the division of the city into Christian and Muslim enclaves, he was forced to transfer to the University of St. Joseph, which was located in the Christian area. He soon interrupted his studies, and then abandoned them altogether, in order to participate in the fighting.[40] At the request of Bashir Gemayel, Geagea joined the newly formed Lebanese Forces, and in January 1983 he was appointed commander of the LF divisions in the Shuf-Aley sector of Mount Lebanon. Later that year, in what came to be known as the "Battle of the Mountain," Geagea's units were defeated and forced to abandon their territory. Geagea attributed this humiliating loss to the declining rigor of the LF leadership in the wake of Bashir's assassination.

In March 1985 Geagea joined Elie Hobeiqa and other disaffected LF commanders in wresting control of the militia from the Kata'eb. It is likely that a contributing factor in the split between the Kata'eb and the LF was a widespread resentment of the Gemayel family dynasty among rural and lower-class Christians. Geagea, who came from humble origins, was an ideal conduit for this resentment. He cultivated a populist voice, questioning why the primary Christian leadership should always remain in one family.[41] Indeed, his ambition was to become one day president of the Lebanese Republic.[42] However, despite the populist nature of his following, Geagea is often described as being similar to Hobeiqa in his monopolization of power in the LF and in his pursuit of "unlimited ambition."[43] After he became the sole leader of the LF in 1986, Geagea went from being a warrior to being an organizer in charge of the social, political, and military programs of the organization. His rejection of several proposed candidates for a presidential successor to Amin Gemayel was instrumental in ushering in the interim military government led by Michel Aoun. Geagea at first maintained a reluctant support for Aoun's government, a position that he came to regret after Aoun launched his "war of annihilation" against the Lebanese Forces.[44]

With the signing of the Ta'if Agreement and the ousting of Michel Aoun from the presidential palace, the LF reinvented itself as a pro-Western political party. It developed a platform that was oriented around the preservation of religious minority rights and maintaining Lebanon's independence from Syria. Geagea's marriage in January 1990 to Setrida Tawq, the daughter of a well-off family from the traditional Lebanese elite, sealed his rise from humble populist to established member of the ruling class. Geagea was introduced to his wife by her uncle Gebran Tawq, a parliamentarian, and the wedding was attended by more than 550 official guests, including representatives of the Lebanese president, the prime minister, and the Speaker of the parliament.[45] In December 1990, the first cabinet of the Second Republic was formed, and Samir Geagea was appointed as a state minister without a portfolio, in an attempt to include him in the Ta'if settlement. However, Geagea refused to take up his post, arguing that the new government was controlled by "Syrian-backed leftists."[46] This intractability led to difficulties for Geagea. In June 1992, he ran for the Kata'eb Party's presidential election but lost to Georges Saadeh. The new leader of the Kata'eb then dismissed Geagea from the party's politburo, along with a majority of Kata'eb district leaders who were Geagea sympathizers.

The Lebanese Forces' rocky fortunes under Syrian hegemony came to a head in 1994, when Geagea was arrested in association with a bombing attack on the Our Lady of Deliverance Church in the town of Zouk Mikael. The bomb exploded under the church's altar during Sunday services while worshipers were receiving communion, killing eleven people and wounding more than fifty others. Whereas the bombing shocked the Lebanese public, Geagea's arrest in April, his subsequent indictment, and the call for the death penalty enraged the Lebanese Christians. Geagea was subsequently sentenced to life imprisonment on several different counts. He was first tried for the assassination of Dany Chamoun and his family and was declared guilty.[47] For this conviction, Geagea received a death sentence that was eventually commuted to life imprisonment. He was also accused of being behind the 1987 assassination of former prime minister Rashid Karami. Ironically, Geagea was not declared guilty of the original crime that had initiated the government intervention, the bomb that exploded in Our Lady of Deliverance Church. Following his trial, the Lebanese Forces Party was officially disbanded, and many other party members were arrested and tortured. Geagea remained incarcerated in solitary confinement for the next eleven years, while his supporters argued that the Syrian-controlled Lebanese government had merely used the alleged crimes as a pretext for jailing Geagea and banning the anti-Syria party.[48]

The Lebanese Forces

After the period of conflict between the Lebanese Forces and the interim government of Michel Aoun, the Lebanese Forces leader Samir Geagea endorsed the Ta'if Agreement. Assured by the stipulations of the agreement that the Syrian presence was temporary, the Lebanese Forces demobilized and disarmed in 1991 as part of a deal with the new government. The militiamen were incorporated into the Lebanese Army, and the organization established itself as a purely political party. In the early 1990s, when Syria did not redeploy its troops and withdraw as promised, Geagea refused to participate in any of the postwar cabinets and vigorously opposed the Syrian hegemony in Lebanon.

Geagea was the only Lebanese warlord tried for war crimes. A general amnesty law had been passed in 1991 (Lebanese Law 84/91) stipulating that war crimes committed against the populace would be pardoned, whereas those crimes committed against political and religious leaders would not. This law was used by the Syria-backed regime to sideline Geagea and ensure that the Lebanese Forces would not intervene in the postwar political order.[49] Geagea's imprisonment also gave the government the means to negotiate with and intimidate his followers. Several of these partisans, including his wife, Setrida Geagea, moderated their opposition to the regime after his arrest. The outlawing of the LF did not destroy the organization, but greatly weakened it by undermining the institutional mechanisms that allowed for the election of a responsible leadership and the formal adoption of a political platform.

After boycotting the legislative elections in 1996, the Lebanese Forces participated in the municipal elections of 1998 and managed to gain control of several municipalities. At this point, however, the new leaders of the Lebanese Forces began to diverge. Fouad Malek, who had been Geagea's deputy before his arrest, did not want to participate in the boycott of the 2000 legislative elections. He argued that it was the refusal to participate in the post-Ta'if political process that had allowed the regime to arrest Geagea and outlaw the party in 1994. Malek's faction was of the opinion that the Lebanese Forces did not have a chance of winning seats in the parliament unless their candidates were part of progovernment electoral lists. They pointed to the increases in gerrymandering, the electoral law, and other mechanisms installed by the state to manage the election results. Setrida Geagea saw things differently. Suspecting that Malek and others were only looking after their own interests, she and her followers joined the groups that boycotted the 2000 elections.[50]

After the elections, Malek started to look for a compromise with the regime. Rumors abounded that the minister of the interior, Elias Murr, had promised that the ministry would give the Lebanese Forces back its license if the "moderates" were to consolidate their presence at the head of the party and to marginalize Setrida Geagea. Such a move would have allowed Malek to reclaim close to seventy million dollars in Lebanese Forces assets that were confiscated by the state in 1994.[51] From the perspective of the government, there was a growing concern about the umbrella organization of anti-Syria Christian leaders called the Qornet Shehwan coalition, which first convened in April and May 2001. Three highly ranked members of the Lebanese Forces, supported by Setrida Geagea, joined the coalition, and members of Aoun's Free Patriotic Movement also participated as observers. These actions led Syrian leaders to accelerate their efforts to create Christian support for the existing regime. During this period of time, which occurred simultaneously to the Syrian promotion of Karim Pakradouni as the pro-Syria leader of the Kata'eb, it seems reasonable to believe that similar overtures were presented to encourage a malleable and pro-Syrian leadership in the Lebanese Forces.[52]

In July 2001, Malek started to openly defy the authority of Setrida Geagea. His critiques of her ideas and actions were not well received by the Lebanese Forces partisans, and in November 2001, the organization's leaders announced the expulsion of Malek from the party. One of these leaders went so far as to accuse Malek of wanting to "liquidate the cause of the LF and their program."[53] By the end of 2001, however, Setrida Geagea had been marginalized, and other factions in the Lebanese Forces announced that Malek had been named secretary-general of the party. In January 2002, Malek's faction of the Lebanese Forces was allowed to hold a political conclave in a monastery north of Beirut. This gathering was perceived by the Lebanese press as a first step toward the reintegration of the Lebanese Forces into the political system. Desiring the approbation of the state, in 2002 Malek adopted expressions of solidarity with Damascus. However, the Syrian-backed Ministry of the Interior continued to refuse to give him the official recognition that he wanted. The lack of enthusiasm among the Lebanese Forces partisans led the pro-Syria regime to doubt Malek's ability to transform the organization into a vehicle of political solidarity. Malek had been incapable of mobilizing supporters, despite the fact that he was allowed to hold meetings and to ask for support in the name of the organization, privileges that were denied to Setrida Geagea's faction.

The Lebanese Forces were therefore divided during their years of political banishment, and the 2002 conclave was allowed only because the pro-Syria government was trying to promote Malek's faction. As with the Kata'eb, the government split the Lebanese Forces by co-opting one of its leaders and creating division.

The Revitalization of the Lebanese Forces

After the 2005 Cedar Revolution forced Syrian troops to withdraw from Lebanon, the parliament passed legislation that freed Samir Geagea and reinstituted the Lebanese Forces as a recognized political party. Geagea was released from prison in July 2005. Upon obtaining his freedom, he was reported to have said, "I have spent eleven horrific years in solitary confinement in a six-square-meter dungeon three floors underground without sunlight or fresh air. But I endured my hardships because I was merely living my convictions."[54] Several years later, Geagea made a public statement of contrition, apologizing in 2008 for his brutal past and his actions during the civil war.[55] After Geagea's release and apology, the newly sanctioned "Lebanese Forces Party" registered a significant following among Christians, and it also gained a measure of support from Sunni Muslims and Druze. These supporters include not only older members of the war generation, but also a significant number of Lebanese youth. The LF had five parliamentarians in the 2005 legislature and currently has eight representatives elected in the 2009 Lebanese Parliament; among them is Samir's wife, Setrida Geagea, who was first elected in 2005.

The Progressive Socialist Party

The Progressive Socialist Party was established in 1949 by the Druze leader Kamal Jumblat, in coordination with a number of his friends and supporters from diverse sectarian backgrounds.[56] Jumblat was the scion of a feudal family that for several hundred years has maintained a strong leadership role in the Druze community. He was educated in Paris at the Sorbonne, where he studied sociology and psychology, and then in Lebanon at St. Joseph University, where he studied law. His path to power in Lebanon was paved by his mother, Sitt Nazira, who had taken over the leadership of the clan after her husband was assassinated in 1921. Nazira was a key figure in the politics of the Druze community for more than a quarter of a century, and this fact allowed her son to almost effortlessly become an important political actor. Kamal Jumblat was elected to parliament at the young age of twenty-six, and three years later he received his first ministerial appointment.

Jumblat's elite education and exposure to European intellectual life made him into something of a radical within the political scene of the First Lebanese Republic. His progressive ideals were completely at odds with the culture of elitism that had prevailed in the region since the days of the Ottoman Empire.[57] Kamal Jumblat established the Progressive Socialist Party as a challenge to "politics as usual" and as a platform for utopian thinkers with a commitment to social justice. The charter of the PSP put forth a nonsectarian vision of Lebanese democracy that would transform the conditions of workers, promote human rights, and bring about interconfessional peace. The PSP's call for secular democracy was posited in opposition to the Maronite-Sunni alliance that constituted the National Pact of 1943. Jumblat was an outspoken opponent of the confessional system, largely because the structural division of power excluded members of the Druze community—as well as other minority confessions—from holding any of the major political posts in the Lebanese government. Jumblat believed that the mainstream understanding of the Lebanese nation distorted and downplayed the role of the Druze in Lebanese history. However, he also believed that a socialist transformation of Lebanese politics would make room not only for a greater representation of the Druze, but for a complete transcendence of confessional lines as well.[58] The confessionally diverse leadership of the PSP in the early days of the organization seemed to lend credence to this ideal.

Nonetheless, the early leadership of the PSP remained a loosely knit group, largely dependent upon Kamal Jumblat's patronage. In the decades leading up to the civil war, this group expanded, and the party underwent a gradual transformation that altered its demographic makeup as well as its ideological vision. The social composition of the party leaders shifted from one of educated and well-established professionals to become increasingly dominated by rural and lower-middle-class activists. This shift, which would continue during the war, helped to move the party toward a more militant, rather than utopian, version of leftism. In addition, the PSP became increasingly dominated by Druze recruits, lending a newly sectarian character to the party. The most likely explanation for this change is that with increased confessional tension, potential non-Druze PSP members were drawn off by other sectarian alliances, leaving the PSP to become a primarily Druze organization.[59]

When the violence of the civil war erupted, the PSP quickly militarized. It entered the conflict on the side of the Left and of the Palestine Liberation Organization. Since the PSP understood itself as the champion of the underprivileged, Kamal Jumblat's military alliance with the Palestinians was logical. However, it had a negative effect on the organization's credibility among Christian sympathizers, who largely abandoned the PSP after the start of the war. In addition, the militarization of the PSP created significant ripples in the party's internal politics. The onset of the war led to a hardening of the party line and exacerbated the transfer of leadership from utopian thinkers to proletarian pragmatists. These changes in the party were of great significance, but they gave way to an even greater transformation in March 1977, when Kamal Jumblat, the PSP's founder and patron, was assassinated.[60] Kamal Jumblat's death left the mantle of the party leadership in the hands of his relatively inexperienced son, Walid.

Walid Jumblat and the Confessionalization of the PSP

Walid Jumblat was not politically active prior to the assassination of his father, and his ascension to the head of the PSP occurred amid significant challenges. Walid had to confirm his own readiness to lead the party, as well as the viability and identity of the party within an increasingly bloody sectarian conflict. Despite his lack of experience, Walid was successful in taking the helm of the party leadership and in establishing the military power of the PSP. However, this victory came at the expense of the final transformation of the PSP from a secular party with socialist aspirations to a militant organization exclusively representing Druze interests. Walid's priority after taking the mantle of leadership was to mobilize the support of the entire Druze community behind the PSP. The Druze largely responded to Walid's call, as they felt threatened by the encroachment of Christian militias and viewed the PSP as the only organization that could provide a means of defending the Druze community.[61]

As part of his bid to affirm his leadership, Walid stepped up the role of the PSP militia in the territorial battles of the civil war. In 1983 the PSP took part in the infamous "Battle of the Mountain" and emerged as the victorious faction. In the course of this conflict, the PSP ousted the northern divisions of the Lebanese Forces (under the command of Samir Geagea) and effected an "ethnic" cleansing of the Shuf region by forcing the Maronite population to leave. This victory allowed Walid Jumblat to become the uncontested leader of the Druze and an important player on the Lebanese political scene. The forced displacement of Maronites and other sectarian groups from the Shuf region led to the collapse of many social institutions, since although the area is the historical heartland of the Druze community, only a very small percentage of institutional positions in the region were held by the Druze.[62] To rectify this situation, Walid stepped in and created his own civic apparatus: a local government under the control of the PSP that he named the Civil Administration of the Mountain (CAOM). The Lebanese government, under the control of Amin Gemayel, reacted swiftly and violently to what was perceived as an attempt to create a Druze canton; nonetheless, the CAOM remained in control of the Shuf region for the remainder of the civil war.

The boundaries between the CAOM and the PSP were blurry at best. Walid Jumblat endeavored to create a formal distinction between the two entities, but the vast majority of CAOM officials were party members, and many had personal ties to the Jumblat family. In addition, the CAOM executive committee remained under the authority of PSP regional directors, and the administration of CAOM projects was largely overseen by the party.[63] Thus, as with the Lebanese Forces in the Christian enclave, the PSP through the CAOM largely took over the functions of the state in the area under its control. An office of financial affairs was created, and revenue was collected through formal taxes and road tolls. The CAOM even had its own retail chain of household goods and clothing, known as Farah Shops.

One of the projects of the CAOM was the formalized socialization of Druze youths, the effects of which have been studied by Judith Harik.[64] Students in the PSP-controlled area were required to study party ideology and to take part in paramilitary training. Druze youth brigades, called the "Scouts of the Martyr Kamal Jumblat," were created and held up as a role model for younger children. This investment in "educational" programs created a fierce allegiance to the PSP and to the person of Walid Jumblat among the younger generation of Druze, a legacy that extended into the postwar period. As Harik explains, by the end of the war, the PSP militia "counted only some 4000 fighters . . . [but] it was well known that unlike any of the other Lebanese groups, the Druze could mobilize thousands more at short notice."[65] The effectiveness of Walid Jumblat in organizing his community's resources allowed the PSP to successfully compete against the much larger Christian factions. Druze victories during the conflict were not limited to the Shuf region, but extended into other parts of Lebanon, including Beirut. The PSP's partial control of the western areas of the capital provided the organization with significant negotiating power at the end of the war.

The Role of the PSP after the Civil War

The PSP participated in the abortive peace conferences that took place in Geneva and Lausanne during the conflict, and Walid Jumblat was appointed as minister of public works in the 1984 national reconciliation government of Rashid Karami. When the Ta'if Agreement finally put an end to the fighting in 1989, the Druze leader emerged onto the national scene as an influential political actor. In the postwar government, the Druze were allocated eight parliamentary seats and two ministers in every cabinet. Most of these Druze parliamentarians and ministers have been Walid's allies or clients. Walid himself was elected to parliament in 1992 and has retained his seat ever since.

A political chameleon, Walid adapted and survived through many changes in the postwar political scene. He "was willing to ally himself with anyone and any group if he believed that it was in his interest to do so."[66] In the 1990s, he was Syria's ally and remained very cautious in his criticism of Lebanon's powerful neighbor. At the same time, however, he was able to reconcile with his previous sectarian enemies, the Maronites, and to partially project the image of a cross-confessional leader. By the mid-1990s, the PSP under Walid's leadership had regained at least a portion of its prewar diversity, with a political bureau composed of six Druze, four Christians, four Shi'a, and three Sunnis. The political representation of the Druze in the post-Ta'if system is significantly overproportional in comparison with the community's demographic numbers, and in creating a more diverse PSP Walid appears to be laying the groundwork for a cross-confessional base of support that will help him to retain his influence in case the representational playing field is leveled.

After the death of Syrian president Hafez al-Assad, Walid gradually adjusted his position along with the general direction of Lebanese public discourse. He became more critical of Syrian influence in Lebanon and allied himself first with businessman Rafiq Hariri, then with the pro-Western coalition known as the "March 14 Alliance" that was established after Hariri was killed. Walid was one of the political powerhouses who publicly accused Syria of masterminding Hariri's assassination. In late 2009, however, Walid seemed to be changing sides yet again. After the 2009 legislative elections, he withdrew from the March 14 Alliance, saying that his participation had been driven by a temporary necessity after the Cedar Revolution. He once more praised Syria and resolved his problems with its leadership. He called his visits to the United States after Hariri's assassination and his meeting with President George W. Bush a "black spot" on his personal history. Jumblat appears to have concluded that the pro-Western alliance has no future in Lebanon and that it is safer to chart a more neutral course. He has allied himself with the Hezbollah-led opposition that allowed it to form a government in June 2011 after a four-month stalemate.

This transformation in the behavior of the PSP's leader might signal a change in the political winds of the region. Indeed, Walid Jumblat is seen by many as Lebanon's "political weathervane"—he is regarded as one of the smartest politicians in the country, and throughout his career he has been successful in choosing the winning side at the early stages of the contest.[67] By the end of 2011, Walid Jumblat seemed to have read the situation in Syria as spelling the end for the Assad regime. He had broken ranks with the Syrian regime once again, calling on Iran and Russia to reconsider their policies toward Syria. However, he refrained from publicly calling for regime change in Lebanon's powerful neighbor.

Perceiving himself as a link in a long familial chain, Walid Jumblat is said to be currently preparing his eldest son, Teymour, to succeed him in perpetuating the Jumblat family dynasty. He has already given Teymour a leading position in the party, and Teymour is today one step away from becoming the leader of the PSP. However, Walid has sent mixed signals in this regard. In November 2011, Walid Jumblat declared his preference to see power transferred to someone else, and not necessarily someone from his own family. In an interview with journalist Ghassan Charbel, Jumblat said that "it is better if he [Teymour] does not work in politics" and that "he should remain far from the political world."[68] He acknowledges having taught Teymour about their enemies and questioned the wisdom of bequeathing enemies to one's children. He also added that his son "deserves to know that at the end of the day politics are not worth it."[69]

Hezbollah

Among Lebanese political parties, Hezbollah has emerged as the only organization with a coherent and stable platform, one that has remained relatively unaffected by the changing tides of the political scene.[70] One member of the Christian opposition whom I interviewed in 2001 explained that "the postwar elite is one that is only interested in money and that is willing to make concessions to Syria based on different degrees of servitude. The only exception is Hezbollah, which has its own logic, a main goal, and, most important, a model for society. This simply does not exist among other groups." This statement is a testament to Hezbollah's reputation for efficiency and honesty and to the respect that it has gained even among its political opponents.

The Origins of Hezbollah

Hezbollah is a relative newcomer on the Lebanese political scene. The leaders of the party emerged from Harakat al-Mahrumin (the Movement of the Deprived), an organization established in March 1974 by the Iranian cleric Musa al-Sadr along with sympathetic Christian leaders. Al-Sadr had come to Lebanon in the late 1950s, at the invitation of local religious leaders in Tyre, in order to assume a prominent role in the Shi'i community of that city. During the 1960s and 1970s, he mobilized the Shi'a both socially and politically. Harakat al-Mahrumin was at first a cross-confessional movement, but as Lebanon began sliding toward civil war al-Sadr firmly positioned the organization as the defender of the Shi'i community. In 1975, believing that the safety of his flock was threatened by the growing confrontation, al-Sadr added a military wing to his movement. It was called Afwaj al-Muqawama al-Lubnaniyya (Brigades of the Lebanese Resistance) and was known by its acronym, AMAL, or "hope."

The formation of Hezbollah took place in response to the 1982 Israeli invasion of Lebanon. Feeling that the leadership of AMAL was too moderate, a group of clerics and laymen broke away from AMAL and established a separate militia to more actively resist the Israeli occupation. After drawing in an increasing number of Shi'i militants, Hezbollah formally announced itself in February 1985 with a manifesto titled "An Open Letter: The Hezbollah Program." This document, addressed "to the downtrodden in Lebanon and the world," elaborated a perspective in which humanity is sharply divided between the ranks of the oppressors and the oppressed and in which the perceived imperialist ambitions of the United States are identified as the "primary root" of the suffering that was inflicted on Lebanese Muslims during the Israeli occupation. The stance taken by Hezbollah during these formative years was profoundly informed by the context of the 1982 invasion and the siege mentality that it prompted among Lebanese Muslims.

Ideology: Fighting the Oppressors

The oppressor-oppressed dichotomy embraced by Hezbollah militants has its roots in the writings of Iranian leader Ruhollah Khomeini. These views, which served as a catalyst for the 1979 Iranian revolution that brought Khomeini to power, posit an ongoing conflict not only between the oppressed (*mostazafin*) and the oppressors (*mostakberin*) of the world, but also between the *nations* of the oppressed (*mellat-e mostazaf*) and the "governments of Satan" (*hokumat-e shaytan*).[71] Khomeini's writings became a central part of a widespread Shi'i view that anthropologist Michael Fisher has labeled the "Karbala paradigm."[72] This phrase refers to a legendary battle that took place in the area of Karbala in 680 CE, in which Hussein bin Ali (revered by Shi'i Muslims as the third imam and the grandson of the Prophet Muhammad) led an uprising against the dominant reign of the Umayyad caliph. The story of Karbala is one of the founding myths of Shi'ism, evoking ideas of martyrdom, sacrifice, commitment, and passion. In Khomeini's politicized interpretation of this story, the oppressed Iranian masses came to represent Hussein and those individuals who died with him during the battle of Karbala, while the Iranian shah and his regime were associated with the tyrannical Umayyad rulers. After Khomeini seized power in Iran, the allegorical role of the oppressor was also meted out to various "foreign imperialist powers."[73]

In Lebanon Hezbollah adopted a slightly modified version of this doctrine, in which "the fight against the oppressor state" became "the fight against the invading or occupying state." The Hezbollah manifesto described the threat of Western invasion as a more or less permanent condition of Lebanese life, and it attributed this condition to the desire of Western leaders to destroy the Muslim people. The "Open Letter" states that "America, its Atlantic Pact allies, and the Zionist entity in the holy land of Palestine, attacked us and continue to do so without respite. . . . This is why we are, more and more, in a state of permanent alert in order to repel aggression and defend our religion, our existence, our dignity." Revealing the grounding of the organization's ideology in the anticolonial movement, Hezbollah notably associated the actions of Israel with the imperialist history of other Western powers, and especially with the United States. The "Open Letter" declared that the goal of Hezbollah was to "expel the Americans . . . and their allies definitely from Lebanon, putting an end to any colonialist entity on our land." The last paragraph of the manifesto stated, "We see in Israel the vanguard of the United States in our Islamic world."[74]

In addition to the militaristic goal of resisting Israeli and Western occupation, Hezbollah also quickly co-opted Musa al-Sadr's original mission of providing social services to Lebanon's Shi'i community. While the military wing of the party carried out operations against Israel and its allies in Lebanon, the sociopolitical wing of Hezbollah developed an extensive network of charitable organizations. Some of these charities were oriented toward providing services related to the armed resistance (for example, the charities al-Shahid [the Martyr] and al-Juraha [the Wounded]), but others delivered services to a wide group of needy users (for example, al-Mu'assassa al-Tarbawiyya [Educational Institution] and al-Qard al-Hassan [the Good Loan]). Hezbollah also provided support to more autonomous charitable organizations, three of which are branches of Iranian institutions: al-Imdad (Assistance), al-Hay'a al-Suhiyya (Health Organization), and Jihad al-Bina' (Struggle for Construction).[75]

During the first years of its existence, Hezbollah launched operations that were directed primarily against Israel and its local Lebanese allies in the Southern Lebanon Army. The SLA controlled Israel's "security zone" in southern Lebanon and handled civilian governmental operations in the area. It was estimated to consist of around three thousand men, mostly Christians, led first by the renegade army major Saad Haddad and then after January 1984 by Antoine Lahad.[76] The SLA became notorious for operating the Khiam Detention Center in southern Lebanon, where detainees, especially Hezbollah members or sympathizers, were held without trial and systematically tortured and ill-treated.[77] In the course of its conflict with the SLA, Hezbollah came to be seen as a primary opponent of Israeli power in Lebanon. Hezbollah was also said to have been behind several sensational actions in the mid- to late 1980s, such as the hijacking of TWA flight 847; the kidnappings of David Dodge, Terry Waite, and Terry Anderson;[78] the killing of former

CIA bureau chief William Buckley; and the killing of French sociologist Michel Seurat. However, Hezbollah has strongly denied any involvement in these operations.

"Lebanonization"

After the Ta'if Agreement, Hezbollah's leaders made a concerted effort to transform the militia from a revolutionary faction aimed at creating an Islamic state into a Lebanese political party representing the interests of the Shi'a within the confessional framework. Emblematic of this change was the participation of Hezbollah representatives in the first postwar legislative elections in 1992. According to Na'im Qassem, the deputy secretary-general of Hezbollah, the period leading up to the elections was one of significant disagreement and realignment within the organization: "Parliamentary representation of Hizbullah was not a clear choice. . . . [A]t the time, [it was] a decision that called for deep internal debate."[79] Among the issues under debate was the legitimacy of Hezbollah's participation in a pluralistic government, "a parliament based on a confessional political system that does not represent Hizbullah's view of an ideal system."[80] Ultimately, however, after Hezbollah's political participation was endorsed by Ali Khamenei, the new supreme leader of Iran, the organization decided to embrace the postwar Lebanese government. Since that time, Hezbollah has participated as a political party in all of Lebanon's legislative and municipal elections.

As part of the realignment of the party, Hezbollah's secretary-general, Abbas Musawi, issued a four-point political program. In addition to a continued resistance against Israeli occupation, this new program called for a process of discussion and reconciliation with Hezbollah's former enemies within Lebanon, a policy of *infitah* (opening) to other groups and especially to Christians, and a project of using the Hezbollah organization to alleviate social problems at the grassroots level.[81] The term *Lebanonization* has been used to describe the official shelving of Hezbollah's demand for an Islamic state in Lebanon and its acceptance of a more domestic role within the multisectarian Lebanese polity. There are a variety of reasons for this initial Lebanonization of Hezbollah, including the

1989 death of Supreme Leader Ruhollah Khomeini of Iran, who was an inspiration and mentor to the early Hezbollah militants; the favorable terms of the Ta'if Agreement, which helped convince Hezbollah leaders that they could achieve most of their goals within the system; and the end of the Cold War, which led to a decrease in the regional power of Iran and Syria owing to the loss of Soviet support. Finally, the assassination of Hezbollah's leader, Abbas Musawi, by the Israelis in 1992 led to the election of Hassan Nasrallah as the new secretary-general and incited an internal reevaluation of Hezbollah's political strategy.

The Effects of the Israeli Withdrawal

Between 1992 and 2000, Hezbollah maintained a war of attrition in southern Lebanon, eventually driving Israel out of the country by ensuring that the human and financial costs of the occupation remained high. During this time, a broad consensus developed in Lebanon in support of Hezbollah's doctrine of resistance. Israeli actions during "Operation Grapes of Wrath" in 1996, which included a massacre of refugees at the UN compound in Qana,[82] had the effect of firmly uniting both Christians and Muslims in a nationalist stance against the Israeli occupation. By 1998 the election of the staunch Hezbollah ally Émile Lahoud as president of Lebanon indicated the ascendancy of the organization's political power.

After the Israeli withdrawal from southern Lebanon in May 2000, a dispute arose over a fifteen-square-mile border region called the Shebaa Farms. Lebanon and Syria asserted that the area was Lebanese, while Israel declared it part of the Golan Heights and, therefore, Syrian territory—though still occupied by Israel.[83] The continuation of the dispute was exacerbated by Israel's refusal to supply maps showing the location of land mines that were left behind in Lebanon, as well as its refusal to liberate Lebanese prisoners of war. Hezbollah seized upon these issues to argue that the Israeli withdrawal was incomplete and that there was still a need for resistance. At this point, however, many Christians and Sunnis in Lebanon began to see Hezbollah's rejection of the new boundary line and the bid to "liberate" the Shebaa Farms as a somewhat trivial excuse to maintain the posture of resistance.[84] Indeed, since Hezbollah's self-defined role and highest priority was to resist the Israeli occupation, the withdrawal of Israel prompted a crisis within the organization. There was a wide-ranging internal debate as to whether Hezbollah would shift its focus exclusively to the Lebanese political and social arenas or maintain a broad posture of resistance in reference to perceived imperialism in the Middle East as a whole.[85] Perhaps unfortunately for the stability of the Middle East, Hezbollah's internal party discussions settled on the latter course in 2000, and the mission to continue resistance with a particular focus on the Israeli-Palestinian theater was blessed by Ayatollah Ali Khamenei of Iran. It is important to note, however, that the option of continuing a broad posture of resistance was a source of debate within Hezbollah and was ultimately a *strategic choice*, not an immutable feature of the organization.

Refocusing on Lebanon

After Rafiq Hariri's assassination in February 2005, Hezbollah was forced to turn its attention back to the internal political scene in Lebanon. In a bid to express support for Syrian involvement in the country, Hezbollah organized a massive demonstration on March 8, which was attended by an estimated four hundred thousand people—mainly Shi'a. In response, Hariri's followers and their allies organized a counterdemonstration on March 14, the one-month anniversary of the assassination. According to most estimates, this demonstration was attended by about one million people, or a quarter of the total Lebanese population.[86] A month later, owing to both Lebanese and international pressure, Syria was forced out of Lebanon. When the 2005 legislative elections took place later in the year, the group that came to be known as the March 14 Coalition took seventy-two seats, short of the two-thirds needed to unseat pro-Syria president Émile Lahoud. Hezbollah and its allies captured thirty-two seats, and the newly returned Michel Aoun and his allies won twenty-one seats. Hezbollah, which also held two cabinet positions, attempted in December 2005 to stop the formation of the Hariri tribunal that was to look into the assassination of the former prime minister. When the

Lebanese Parliament passed a motion to authorize the tribunal, the Shi'i ministers walked out of the cabinet, which led to a gridlock that lasted for two months. Prime Minister Fouad Siniora eventually reached a compromise with Hezbollah that allowed the government to go forward; Siniora's concessions involved the acceptance of Hezbollah as "a national resistance organization," a position that sheltered the group from international calls for its disarmament.

The Summer 2006 War and Afterward

The dispute over the Shebaa Farms region simmered on through the early years of the twenty-first century, and hostilities between Hezbollah and Israeli forces continued in that theater as a smaller-scale version of the limited engagement that had marked the occupation. This state of affairs broke down in the summer of 2006, when Hezbollah kidnapped two Israeli soldiers for use in a prisoner exchange. Although this action had a precedent in previous Hezbollah-Israeli prisoner exchanges, and was arguably within the "rules of the game" that until then had defined the scope of the conflict, this time Israeli forces responded with a massive attack against Lebanon.[87] Israel's retaliation led to more than a thousand deaths—mostly civilians—with several thousand injured, roughly one million displaced, and economic losses estimated at twelve billion US dollars.[88]

During this renewed conflict, the majority of Lebanese rallied around Hezbollah, despite the fact that the country was at the time divided between the "March 8" (pro-Syria) and "March 14" (anti-Syria) camps. When the 2006 war with Israel broke out, internal calls for the disarmament of Hezbollah and criticisms of its stance of resistance, which had been steadily building in Lebanon since 2000, momentarily stopped. While the war raged, 87 percent of Lebanese supported Hezbollah's military response to the Israeli attacks—notably including 89 percent of Sunnis and 80 percent of Christians.[89] In spite of the destruction in Lebanon, Hezbollah's stance of resistance gained an enormous amount of symbolic capital during the war. The organization emerged victoriously intact in the wake of the Israeli onslaught, a survival that was touted as a "divine victory" in the eyes of Islamists both in and beyond Lebanon.[90] While expressing remorse about the extent of the violence, Hezbollah's leader, Hassan Nasrallah, took the opportunity in a televised address to characterize his organization as the "spearhead of the *umma* [the entire Islamic community]," and to describe the conflict with Israel as "surpassing Lebanon. . . . [I]t is the conflict of the umma."[91] This broad statement of resistance struck a chord most notably with Palestinians, and pro-Hezbollah sentiment exploded in the West Bank and Gaza. The perception of Hezbollah's victory was further reinforced by the preliminary report of Israel's Winograd Commission, which harshly criticized the conduct of the war and the performance of Israeli leaders.[92]

Hezbollah's Weapons Turn Inward

The momentum that Hezbollah gained during the 2006 invasion did not prove to be lasting, and renewed opposition against Hezbollah's militaristic stance was quick to emerge after the end of the Israeli attack. In November 2006, in an attempt to increase their power within the government and to forestall calls for Hezbollah's disarmament, the Shi'i ministers again staged a walkout. For the next year and a half, the government remained deadlocked as members of Hezbollah and AMAL, as well as supporters of the Christian leader Michel Aoun, camped outside Prime Minister Siniora's office in Beirut in an open-ended sit-in aimed at forcing the government to resign. The stalemate lasted until May 2008, when the government announced a decision to investigate Hezbollah's private telecommunication network, accusing the party of violating the nation's sovereignty.[93] Hezbollah's reaction was swift, and fighting started almost immediately. Hezbollah gunmen, unchallenged by the army, quickly seized control of West Beirut in a telling demonstration of the organization's military prowess.

By the time the government reversed its controversial decision, the conflict had led to the deaths of at least 65 people, and more than 250 others had been wounded. The consequences for the country were dire. The fighting terrified much of the population of Beirut, especially its Sunni and Christian communities, and Hezbollah's use of its military might against the very nation that it claimed to protect was seen by many as a dangerous precedent.[94] Such armed disobedience reopened the gate to violent sectarian conflict, and it is a move that is not likely to be forgotten. The events of May 2008, while anchoring Hezbollah more firmly in its Shi'i constituency, led to a significant loss of support among other communities.[95]

After the battle, Lebanon's political process was no longer deadlocked, and Hezbollah's use of violence against domestic targets proved to be a tactical success in the short term. When a new cabinet was announced in July 2008, Hezbollah and its allies gained a number of additional positions and took control of a full one-third of the ministerial body. It seemed as though the organization had successfully used its weapons to increase its political clout. The results of the 2009 parliamentary elections, however, told a very different story, as Sunnis and Christians, fearful of a Hezbollah-dominated Lebanon, gave the majority to the Western-leaning "March 14" Coalition.

Hezbollah's New Charter

In November 2009, Hezbollah issued a new manifesto that seemed to consecrate the party's "Lebanonization." In comparison with previous Hezbollah dispatches, this policy statement displayed a significant reduction in Islamist rhetoric. It made no mention of a potential Islamic republic in Lebanon, and it affirmed that "consensual democracy constitutes an appropriate political formula to guarantee true partnership."[96] However, the organization has not changed its reductive views regarding the actions of the United States and Israel.

In a section titled "Hegemony and Mobilization," the new manifesto describes the dangers of US influence, stating that Americans believe "the world is owned by the superpower, and that such power has the right to rule out of sheer superiority at more than one level. . . . Western expansionary strategies—particularly those of the US—took on an international dimension characterized by unbounded greed." The manifesto adds that after the September 11 attacks in the United States, "'Terrorism' was transformed into an American alibi for hegemony. Persecution, seizures and arbitrary detention, absence of the most basic elements of fair trial . . . , direct intervention in state sovereignty, and the transformation of sovereignty into a registered US trademark have all been used in the quest to legalize arbitrary criminalization of countries and the collective punishment of their people." According to Hezbollah's interpretation, "It is doubtless that US terrorism is the mother of all terrorism." The 2009 manifesto also maintains that the "central and most prominent goal of American hauteur is represented by dominance over the people in all forms through political, economic, or cultural dominion or through the looting of public wealth. At the forefront is the pillaging of oil wealth." To achieve this goal, Washington has resorted to general policies and working strategies that include "ensuring all means of stability for the Zionist entity," "undermining the . . . potentials of our people," "supporting satellite states and tyrannical regimes in the region," "taking control of the strategic geographical zones in the region," "hindering the rise of any form of renaissance in the region," and "implanting feuds and divisions in various forms." This list of grievances allows Hezbollah to conclude that "American oppression has left our nation and its people with no choice but to resist for a better life."[97]

Hezbollah has emerged as a force to be reckoned with in Lebanon after the summer 2006 war. It is now able to force its will on the government by acting as a spoiler or by using military means. Indeed, it appears that Hezbollah and its allies will be able to impose their will on Lebanon at least for the foreseeable future. However, were the Alawi regime in Syria to fall, Hezbollah's supremacy in Lebanese politics would probably be diminished.[98]

The Charismatic Leader: Sayyed Hassan Nasrallah

Perhaps the most notable characteristic of Hezbollah's leaders is that, unlike other prominent political figures in Lebanon, they have not been the heirs of family legacies, destined a priori to become players on the political scene. The current secretary-general of Hezbollah, Hassan Nasrallah, was born into a modest Shi'i family in 1960. He joined the AMAL movement when he was fifteen and followed Abbas Musawi, his mentor and predecessor, into the ranks of Hezbollah. Nasrallah was not part of the inner circle of the party's founders, and he did not play a prominent role in the organization during the civil war. He gradually became recognized for his leadership qualities, however, and when Musawi was assassinated in 1992, Nasrallah was elected as Hezbollah's new secretary-general.

When Nasrallah took the helm of the party, the modus operandi of Hezbollah changed drastically. Nasrallah is a charismatic leader in the Weberian sense of the term; the loyalty and admiration that motivate his followers seem to be based on personal magnetism and the inspiration of conviction, rather than on rational self-interest or traditional political alliances.[99] His populism and his speeches are seen as "free of the evasive embroidery of most other politicians,"[100] and the perception that he is speaking truth to power helps gather admirers among members of his community and beyond.

After Nasrallah was elected and began to explicate the party's platform, the popularity of Hezbollah in Lebanon seemed to multiply. The efficiency of the organization also increased, and its attacks on Israel became more deadly. Nasrallah's growing importance in the Lebanese political sphere was recognized by the international community in June 2000, when Kofi Annan, secretary-general of the United Nations, made an official visit to the Hezbollah offices in Beirut. Although Nasrallah is not a part of the Lebanese government, his influence exceeds the power of many other elected or appointed members of the political elite.

British journalist and longtime observer of Lebanon David Hirst referred to Nasrallah as a "warrior-priest."[101] Indeed, Nasrallah's persona seems to hark back to the warriors of old who combined in their person the divine and the secular in order to smite the enemy of the faith. Although he is both a warrior and a priest, his martial characteristics are the ones that prevail. In an interview with Hirst, Timur Goksel, another longtime observer of Lebanon and former head of the United Nations Interim Force in Lebanon says, "Some people think . . . that Nasrallah was really meant to be a general not an Ayatollah."[102]

After having climbed through the echelons of a structured party by means of intelligence and charisma, Nasrallah is probably one of the only members of the Lebanese political elite who is not attempting to build a political dynasty. Indeed, the democratic nature of Hezbollah's internal politics seems to preclude such a happening. Nasrallah's eldest son, Hadi, was killed in 1997 in a battle against Israeli soldiers, a personal loss that added to the leader's political mystique. Nasrallah refused to accept the return of his son's body until Israel acquiesced to giving equal treatment to the bodies of the other Hezbollah dead. This single-minded devotion to the cause has made Nasrallah a hero among many disaffected Lebanese Shi'a, and it has helped to maintain his credibility beyond his community even in the wake of declining support for Hezbollah's tactics.

A number of Nasrallah's admirers in Lebanon and the Arab world have even written hagiographies comparing the charismatic traits of their leader to the features of Imam Hussein, the hero of the battle of Karbala.[103] Nonetheless, in recent years Nasrallah seems to have fallen out of favor with the Iranian leadership, a circumstance that may prove to have a significant effect on his position within Hezbollah. Nasrallah's position may be threatened by other party members who have remained more loyal to Iran, such as Na'im Qassem, Hezbollah's deputy secretary-general, or Sheikh Nabil Qawuq, a rising star and Nasrallah opponent who has been described by members of Hezbollah as the de facto governor and security chief of southern Lebanon.[104]

The Disappearance of Sunni Parties

An intriguing feature of postwar Lebanese politics is that the Sunni community is the only major sectarian group that did not end up with a representative party composed of former militia leaders. Indeed, most of the Sunni militias that existed on the eve of the civil war or that emerged during its first five years (for example, al-Mourabitoun)[105] had effectively disappeared by the mid-1980s. The absence of a militia leader who would act as a protector of the Sunni community can be in part explained by the role taken by Palestinian forces in Sunni protection during the civil war. Most Lebanese Sunnis were ambivalent in their support of a distinct, multiconfessional Lebanese state and were sympathetic to the

Palestinian exiles, who shared their religious affiliation. Instead of developing independent Lebanese leaders, they rallied behind Yassir Arafat and the PLO.[106] A second factor contributing to the nonemergence of a Sunni party based on a wartime militia is Syrian opposition. Fearing that a powerful Sunni militia in Lebanon might have a spillover effect and encourage Syrian Sunnis to rise up against the Alawi regime, Syria's leaders actively—and violently—discouraged the development of any such organization during the civil war.

In the years following the civil war, two notable Islamist movements gained in popularity among Lebanon's Sunni community. The first was the Jama'a Islamiyyah, the Islamic Group, an organization strongly influenced by Egypt's Muslim Brotherhood, and the second was the Jami'yat al-Mashari' al-Khairiyah, or the Association of Islamic Charitable Projects (known as al-Ahbash, or the Ethiopians). Although these organizations did not have as great of an impact on the Lebanese political scene as did the central parties discussed earlier in this chapter, they became a recognizable part of the national discourse and thus merit a brief examination here. The postwar period also saw the emergence of the vigorous, Sunni-dominated "Future Movement," created initially by businessman Rafiq Hariri and then cultivated by his son Saad after the elder Hariri's assassination in 2005.[107]

The Jama'a Islamiyyah

The Jama'a Islamiyyah grew out of an earlier organization called 'Ibad al-Rahman (the Worshipers of the Merciful), which was established by Muhammad Omar Daouq in Beirut in the aftermath of the creation of the state of Israel. The membership of 'Ibad al-Rahman quickly reached several thousand, and its influence spread to other cities with large Sunni populations, including Tripoli and Sidon. In 1952 it received an official permit and established its headquarters in one of the Sunni centers of Beirut, the Basta neighborhood. Although there is no clear indication that there was a formal relationship between 'Ibad al-Rahman and the Muslim Brotherhood in Egypt, the two associations collaborated, harmonized, and synchronized their activities.

By the late 1950s, the influence of 'Ibad al-Rahman began to diminish owing to the influence of secular Pan-Arabism and the rise of Gamal Abdel Nasser as the new Arab hero. This decline led to a crisis within 'Ibad al-Rahman; Omar Daouq wanted his association to remain an educational, moral, and proselytizing institution, but many of his followers did not believe that such a path could resist the secular call of Pan-Arabism. These followers soon created a new association that corresponded more to their aims and aspirations. The new association began to work in 1957 under the name Jama'a Islamiyyah and eventually received a formal permit from the Ministry of the Interior in June 1964. According to the permit, the founders were Fathi Yakan, Sheikh Faisal Mawlawi, Zuhair al-Obeidi, and Ibrahim Masri.[108]

The choice of the name Jama'a Islamiyyah instead of using the Muslim Brotherhood brand was important and quite clever—it gave the impression that the association was purely of Lebanese origin. It effaced the Jama'a connection with the Muslim Brotherhood and thereby made the organization more palatable in the era of Pan-Arabism (to which the brotherhood stood in opposition). During the mid-1960s, the Jama'a Islamiyyah published a pamphlet titled *Hatha huwa al-tariq* (This Is the Way). This document was a direct adaptation of the influential *Ma'alim fi al-tariq* (Milestones), written by Muslim Brotherhood ideologue Sayyed Qutb. Although not naming its source explicitly, the booklet clearly demonstrated the ideological affiliation of the Jama'a with the Muslim Brotherhood.[109]

During the 1970s, the writings of Fathi Yakan, one of the founders of the Jama'a and its primary ideologue, went further in the direction of radicalism by adopting the language of the *takfiri* movement then prevalent in the Egyptian Muslim Brotherhood.[110] This radicalization is likely an expression of the Sunni community's retrenchment during the civil war and their feeling of being under siege (especially in Yakan's hometown of Tripoli). At the beginning of the civil war, the Jama'a created a militia, al-Mujahidun. In the early years of the war, al-Mujahidun fought at the side of the leftist forces against the Christians. However, the Jama'a "decided to dismantle its militia and move away from military activism. . . . [T]he entrance of Syrian troops in summer 1976 into Lebanon had changed the dynamics of the civil war," as the Syrians came in to support the embattled Christians.[111] The Jama'a did not have a militia during most of the civil war and emerged as a significant political faction only in the first years of the postwar period.

Yakan had a change of heart in the years following the Ta'if Agreement. His writings became critical of radical Islamism, and he tried to offer a more pragmatic approach (though not condemning or revising his previous works).[112] According to Robert Rabil, this change was probably linked to Yakan's two operational concepts in Islamic activism, *al-Mabda'iyah* (principium) and *al-Marhaliya* (periodicization or gradualism).[113] As a part of this new direction, a number of Jama'a leaders decided to participate in the postwar elections. While still professing a belief in the apostasy (*kufr*) of secular regimes, Yakan issued a manifesto offering Islamic justifications for the Jama'a's willingness to participate in the Lebanese elections. According to German scholar Sebastian Elsasser, Yakan led this development by arguing that political participation "must be regarded not as something tolerated by Islamic law, but a religious duty."[114] Yakan gave four arguments: "parliamentary work can be counted as one of the methods of the Islamic practice of Hisba, which means 'enjoining good and forbidding evil'"; "participation in parliament does not mean having to accept un-Islamic policies, but allows the Islamic activists in parliament to resist such policies and to point out Islamic alternatives"; "parliament is an excellent stage for dawa (proselytizing)"; and "working in parliament gives the chance to promote the interests of the people."[115] Quickly adapting to the inclusiveness of the Ta'if settlement, Jama'a leaders openly advocated parliamentary participation with the goal of changing secular regimes into Islamic regimes. As for secular laws contradicting sharia that might be issued by the parliament, according to Yakan, "all a Muslim parliamentarian has to do from an Islamic legal perspective is to openly oppose the law and clear his conscience before God and the people."[116]

Based on these arguments, eight Jama'a candidates participated in the first postwar elections of 1992. The results were surprising in relation to the Jama'a's previous marginality in Lebanese discourse: three of the candidates were able to win seats in Beirut and Tripoli, and those candidates who did not win received a very high number of votes. These elections showed the emerging strength of the Jama'a's social network. By the time of the 1996 elections, the Jama'a had become a significant political player and a component of strong electoral alliances. The surprising event in 1996 was Fathi Yakan's declaration of an unwillingness to run for office, while at the same time his wife, Mona Haddad, announced her candidacy. Yakan's withdrawal from the electoral battle was accompanied by talk of "treason" and personal embarrassment. These tensions within the Jama'a weakened the group and undermined its credibility. The Jama'a came out of the 1996 elections with only one parliamentary seat, a defeat that came as a shock to the organization's supporters. This situation was only worsened in the legislative elections of 2000, when the Jama'a was thoroughly trounced. One of the reasons for this failure was electoral redistricting. In addition, Rafiq Hariri had at this time become a primary voice for the Sunni community, drawing supporters away from other groups such as the Jama'a.

Over the following decade, the Jama'a withdrew from electoral politics and focused on institutional rebuilding. While operating somewhat under the shadow of Rafiq Hariri and the events surrounding the 2005 Cedar Revolution, the Jama'a continued to slowly attract new adherents and develop its power base. Recently, in June 2010, the Jama'a reemerged on the political scene with a new manifesto titled "The Political Vision of the Jama'a Islamiyyah in Lebanon."[117] In this manifesto, the organization asserted that "political action is an indelible part of the Jama'a path" and that "political work is a reflection of Jama'a thinking and of the program that the organization is trying to accomplish." The manifesto listed seven general goals, which seemed to indicate a retreat from a hard-line Islamist position:

1. creating a Muslim individual who can coexist with others and respect human rights and freedoms
2. promoting Islam to all citizens while rejecting sectarian and racial entrenchment

3. contributing to the opening of the Muslim society to all segments of society in Lebanon and considering dialogue and cooperation as the basis for the relation between the different Lebanese factions
4. participating in a constructive manner in all of the institutions of civic society with the goal of reforming and strengthening it
5. participating in politics in a manner that corresponds with sharia
6. calling for Arab unity and the creation of an international Arab organization modeled after the European Union
7. refusing to accept the "Zionist entity"

The impact that the reemergent Jama'a will have in Lebanese politics remains to be seen. The organization seems to be focusing on a call for Muslim unity and has expressed an interest in forming a strong relationship with its counterparts in the Shi'i community who believe that resistance against Israel is a "strategic issue," that is, Hezbollah. This interest is in part a response to Shi'i-Sunni divides that emerged in the May 2008 conflict between Hezbollah and the Lebanese government. The Jama'a strongly affirmed the role of the resistance in Lebanon and decried the internecine conflict. The Jama'a also acknowledged the impact of the Palestinian presence on Lebanese territory. While calling for a regulation of the refugee camps, the Jama'a affirmed that the Palestinian people have "a right to self-defense" and recognized that Lebanese laws have unfairly deprived Palestinians of their civil and human rights.

Al-Ahbash

The founder of al-Ahbash[118] was Sheikh Abdallah ben Muhammad ben Yousef, also known as al-Habashi ("the Ethiopian").[119] Al-Habashi and his students and followers first became important in Lebanon in the 1970s, taking advantage of the lawlessness and the breakdown of the state institutions brought about by the civil war. During this early period, the movement had no interest whatsoever in state politics and was focused instead on proselytizing and internal organization. In these early years, al-Habashi put the majority of his efforts into the education and development of his students. His teachings have been described as a blend of elements drawn from both Sunni and Shi'i theology, with additional trappings of Sufi spiritualism.[120]

Al-Habashi rarely came up with new legal opinions (*ijtihad*) about important or critical issues. However, he issued many edicts (fatwas) on small questions of conduct. His critics complained that he broke with traditional practice by issuing fatwas on detailed and sensitive issues that most contemporary Muslim scholars have avoided debating. For example, he issued rulings on the permissibility of handshakes between the sexes, on the tolerability of women leaving the house against the desires of their husbands in order to seek knowledge, and on the acceptability of anal sex with one's wife.[121] These fatwas led opponents to accuse al-Habashi of exaggeration and radicalism in the use of "legal tricks." Others accused him of having "Jewish origins" and referred to him as "Sheikh al-Fitna" (the Sheikh of Discord).[122] However, while these rulings stirred up distaste for al-Habashi among his contemporaries, they also brought attention to his movement. Traditionalist scholars of the Salafi school began to issue counterstatements against al-Habashi's fatwas, and the al-Ahbash movement became increasingly important in interpretive tensions among Sunni clerics.Al-Habashi continued to stay away from any discussion of politics until the Israeli invasion of 1982. In later years, some of his students insisted that al-Habashi counseled them to wage jihad against Israel; however, it is clear that he did not create a military organization for that purpose, nor did he call for jihad publicly or in writing.[123] In 1983 the followers of al-Habashi co-opted the leader of a preexisting community organization, the Association of Islamic Charitable Projects, and convinced him to cede the leadership to Nizar al-Halabi, one of al-Habashi's most promising students.[124] Under this new management, the Association of Islamic Charitable Projects was completely transformed: a new executive committee was instituted; specialized offices were created to deal with issues such as finances, law, education, health, media, and foreign relations; and, most important, the goals of the organization were significantly altered to conform to the al-Ahbash platform. However, there was no military or explicitly political aspect of this platform. Since there was no mention of political aspirations, the organization was allowed to retain its original charter as a community association, and it soon became the legitimized public face of the al-Ahbash movement.

The new Association of Islamic Charitable Projects grew rapidly during the war years. It created a network of fifteen modern schools—as well as additional vocational and technical centers—in Sunni majority areas such as Beirut, Tripoli, and the Akkar region. It established a radio station named Nida' al-Iman (Call of Faith), a magazine titled *Manar al-Huda* (Beacon of Salvation), a publishing house, a youth program, sports clubs, and health clinics. The movement even took on an international character, founding branches in more than forty countries on five continents.[125] This quick growth made critics wonder about the sources of funding for the organization. The most likely explanation is simply that al-Ahbash appealed to a relatively affluent segment of Islamic society. The constituency of al-Ahbash was the Sunni middle-class, especially the "intellectuals, professionals, and businessmen, [and] particularly the traditional Sunni commercial families of the urban centers." According to Hamzeh and Dekmejian, there was "a convergence between the values, aspirations, and socioeconomic interests of the Sunni middle-classes and the contents of Shaykh Habashi's message—that is, intersectarian accord and political stability; an enlightened Islamic spiritualism; within a modern secularist framework; a Lebanese identity wedded to Arab nationalism; and an accommodating attitude toward Arab regimes, particularly the Syrian government."[126]

In a time in which disenchantment and bitterness were widespread among Sunni professionals, al-Ahbash filled a social void. Some commentators have suggested that with the persecution of the Muslim Brotherhood in Syria in the 1980s, the Palestinian-Syrian struggle in Lebanon, and the rising star of Hezbollah, the professional Sunni community simply could not accept a void. The nontraditional interpretations of al-Habashi appealed to the sensibilities of the professional class, while leaving room for affiliations with the left-leaning Syrian leadership. Al-Ahbash became known for having a "special relationship" with Syria, and Daniel Nassif went so far as to describe the organization as "a propaganda tool used by Syria's secular, Alawi-dominated regime to combat Islamic fundamentalism, manipulate the Lebanese Sunni Muslim community, and gain acceptance for the Alawi sect within Islamic religious circles."[127] In both its political affiliations and its religious interpretations, al-Ahbash thus stood in opposition to traditionalist factions such as the Jama'a.

The political dimension of the al-Ahbash movement first became apparent in the 1990s, when Nizar al-Halabi vied for the position of mufti of Lebanon, the primary office of Sunni religious authority. The idea that he might win the office did not appear farfetched, especially since al-Ahbash had Syrian support and had developed a strong alliance with other Lebanese factions. During the 1992 legislative elections, al-Ahbash put forward two candidates: Taha Naji in Tripoli, who did not win but provided a strong showing, and Adnan al-Trabulsi in Beirut, who was elected. Al-Halabi was assassinated in 1995 by members of the Salafi group Osbat al-Ansar. It is likely that this killing was carried out to prevent the al-Ahbash movement from taking control of the mufti of Lebanon office. The new parliamentarian al-Trabulsi described it as "a clear message against the moderate path . . . against all honorable citizens and a clear blow to the Syria of Assad's Syria."[128] The subsequent capture, trial, and death sentences for the murderers of al-Halabi in 1997 did not go unnoticed. Traditionalist Sunni factions were appalled. Fathi Yakan of the Jama'a wrote a letter to President Elias Hrawi, asking him to stay the execution sentences and suggesting that the trial was a cover-up for Israeli assassins who were seeking to create strife among Lebanese Sunnis.[129]

The death of Nizar al-Halabi was a real crisis for al-Ahbash, and it was compounded by the group's resounding failure in the 1996 elections when al-Trabulsi failed to keep his seat in parliament. This trend continued in 2000, when al-Trabulsi, the leading al-Ahbash candidate, received only 15.5 percent of Sunni votes. Like other Sunni movements, al-Ahbash was beginning to fall into the shadow of Rafiq Hariri's network. Hariri received 84 percent of the *total* votes in Beirut in the 2000 legislative elections, and none of the other candidates in his network received less than 70 percent of the total votes in their districts. In addition to the overall weakening of Sunni Islamist groups in relation to Hariri's secular network, al-Ahbash had to contend with the legacy of its Syrian affiliations, which greatly weakened the group in the years after the Cedar Revolution. In the 2005 elections, al-Ahbash candidates again failed to win any parliamentary seats, and the movement appeared to be falling into decline.

Conclusion

Political parties in Lebanon lost the trust of the majority of the country's population during the civil war, when the main political associations transformed themselves into militias and descended ever further into sectarian zealotry. The inflexibility of these organizations helped to prolong the war, and their quest for international support led a variety of other nations to become more deeply embroiled in Lebanon's internal politics. The bloody clashes between militias were disastrous not only for the parties' adherents, but also for countless innocent bystanders, and they destroyed a significant portion of Lebanon's civic infrastructure. War elites who cultivated profit and prestige from the violence often saw no reason to seek a settlement, and indeed, it was only the decision of the prewar parliamentarians to conduct negotiations without inviting the military leaders that finally led to an armistice in Ta'if.

The three main parties in postwar Lebanon—the Lebanese Forces, the PSP, and Hezbollah—transitioned practically overnight from being militias to being peacetime political organizations. They have proved to be slow to move beyond the entrenched sectarian positions of the war years, and the arrangements for confessional power sharing that were established at Ta'if have left little room for the growth of new cross-confessional, platform-based parties after the Western model. Thus, political parties have not yet been able to play an "integrative" role in stabilizing and secularizing the Lebanese political scene.[130] In 2003 Lebanese scholar and politician Farid el-Khazen noted that the "parties have maintained a political discourse that is little different from that of the war . . . [which] has not helped to improve their credibility beyond a small circle of partisans."[131] As of this writing, the situation described by el-Khazen has not greatly improved, and we must look into the future for the development of parties that will act as a stabilizing rather than a dividing factor in Lebanese politics.

4

State Elites and the Legacy of Corruption

The consociational nature of the Lebanese political system is associated with relatively weak national institutions, overseen by individually strong sectarian elites who are the political representatives of the country's various religious communities. An understanding of the composition of the political elite can therefore be had by examining the elites who hold the high offices of the state, including the presidency, the Council of Ministers, and the parliament. Whereas the standard Western understanding of such positions is based on assumptions of institutional stability and bureaucratic functionality,[1] the Lebanese have a greater tendency to interpret the power of state offices as being the result of individual status. The significance of an institutional position in Lebanon is defined more by the personality and the networks of power created by the individual who holds the position and less by institutionalized duties and powers inherent in the office itself. This situation is a long-standing feature of Lebanese politics, and the collapse of the state during the civil war helped to further ensure that the institutional offices of the Second Republic are today perceived to be only as politically stable as are the individuals who hold them. Since the functioning of Lebanese political institutions is so strongly shaped by individuals, a study of the state elites is important, not only in its own right but also as the most direct route to understanding the workings of the state's institutional framework.

A study of the individuals who lead Lebanon's state institutions allows us to map the postwar political elite, and it can provide information about the modes of elite recruitment and socialization. To analyze the composition of the elite, it is also useful to identify the different resources and power bases that establish the political capital of these individuals.[2] Distinguishing among the various economic, symbolic, professional, and personal resources that allow one to enter political life in postwar Lebanon allows us to develop a taxonomy of these elites. As a heuristic device, I will mention the categories of new businessmen, notables, technocrats, former warlords, and clients of Syria. These categories are of course not exclusive, and more than one kind of resource base might overlap in a single political figure. After introducing a wide cross-section of these elite actors, I continue in the second part of this chapter to discuss the issue of corruption and how the misappropriation of state funds became a central feature of elite power networks during the postwar government. The financialization of Lebanese political power and an associated increase in corruption have contributed to the country's economic woes and to the widespread emigration of talented young Lebanese.

The Presidency

The Lebanese president has traditionally been a Maronite Christian, and this arrangement was codified in the Ta'if Agreement. Many see him as the main representative of the Christian community in the state institutions. The diminished role of the president in the Second Republic, as specified in the Ta'if Agreement, was therefore a source of anguish for many Christians. In addition, the presidents of the Second Republic have consistently cultivated personal ties with the leaders of Syria, which has frequently led to frustration and disenchantment within the Christian community.

In the period of Syrian hegemony between 1990 and 2005, Lebanon saw the election of only three presidents. The first, René Mouawad, was assassinated before he took the oath of office. The second, Elias Hrawi, was effectively the first president of the postwar republic, holding the office from 1989 until 1998. He was then succeeded by Émile Lahoud, who remained the country's president until 2007. From the perspective of the Christian community, none of these men was an obvious choice for the position of the presidency. All three were close to Syria, and both Hrawi and Lahoud had their terms of office extended for three years at the behest of the Syrian regime. Indeed, a constitutional amendment was needed for this extension, and in Lahoud's case a similar amendment was needed for his election, since his status as an active military commander at the time of the election would have otherwise made him ineligible. Brief biographies of these three men will illustrate the social and economic resources that they brought to bear in their bids for the presidency.

René Mouawad: The President-Martyr

Born in 1925, René Mouawad was the son of a notable Maronite family from Zgharta in northern Lebanon. He studied law at the University of St. Joseph and officially entered politics in 1957, when he was elected to the National Assembly. He was reelected in 1960, 1964, 1968, and 1972 and was appointed to three terms as cabinet minister. Like his successors, Mouawad maintained unusually close ties with Syria. Indeed, it was later revealed that immediately after the Ta'if negotiations, Mouawad borrowed one of Sunni businessman Rafiq Hariri's planes and flew to Damascus in order to discuss the Lebanese political situation with Syrian president Hafez al-Assad.[3]

René Mouawad's presidency lasted only seventeen days. He was assassinated on Lebanese Independence Day, November 22, 1989. It has never been established who was responsible for the crime, though the Syrian leadership was suspected of being behind it.[4] After the assassination, Mouawad's position in the parliament was inherited by his widow, Nayla Mouawad, who was then reelected to that position in 1992, 1996, 2000, and 2005. In 2004 Nayla Mouawad announced her own candidacy for the office of president, but these elections were never held because of the extension of President Lahoud's term. Many considered Nayla Mouawad to be only a "placeholder" for the family name, and in the 2009 legislative elections she stepped down for her son, Michel

Mouawad, who was by then old enough to be elected to parliament in his father's seat.

Elias Hrawi: A Secondary Notable

Elias Hrawi was the scion of a Maronite family of large landowners from the city of Zahle in the Beqaa valley; his family members had been represented in the Chamber of Deputies since the beginning of the country's independence in 1943. Hrawi was elected as a deputy of Zahle in 1972 and served in the Lebanese cabinet from 1980 to 1982. Hrawi participated in the unsuccessful peace conferences of Geneva and Lausanne in 1983 and 1984 and was also involved in brokering the abortive Tripartite Agreement in December 1985. He was a crucial participant in the Ta'if Agreement because of his closeness to the Syrian leadership in Damascus.[5]

Hrawi was elected as president two days after the assassination of René Mouawad. The unusual circumstances of his election made him a weaker president than any of his predecessors since the independence of Lebanon in 1943. The Ta'if Agreement had already reduced the powers of the presidency, and the assassination of Hrawi's predecessor lent an air of vulnerability to the office. In addition, Hrawi had to confront a strongly entrenched interim prime minister, General Michel Aoun, who refused to accept the Ta'if Agreement and continued to operate from the presidential residence in Baabda. During the early years of the Hrawi presidency, Syria took advantage of this vulnerability to consolidate its hegemonic role in Lebanon.[6] The Ta'if Agreement, which had no explicit provisions for the withdrawal of Syrian troops, was fully endorsed by the Chamber of Deputies on August 21, 1990. President Hrawi then also endorsed the Treaty of Brotherhood and Cooperation between Syria and Lebanon on May 22, 1991, and later in that same year he signed the Pact of Defense and Security to establish coordination with Syria in matters of military strategy, internal security, and the exchange of intelligence information. After such extensive support of Syrian involvement, it is unsurprising that in 1995 Syria encouraged an amendment in the Lebanese

Constitution that would allow the continuation of Hrawi's term for an additional three years.

During Hrawi's presidency, there emerged a division of power that became known as the "Troika." It was formed by Hrawi along with the Speaker of the parliament, Nabih Berri, and the prime minister, Rafiq Hariri. These men played a three-way game of "tug-of-war," with two of them often banding together against the third in a pattern of shifting alliances based on the particular issue under consideration. There was no systematic ideological foundation for these agreements and disagreements; they were purely based on sectarian and personal interests. The ultimate arbiter of the Troika was Syria, and the three politicians often took the road to Anjar to see Syria's viceroy, Ghazi Kanaan, or to Damascus to see Syrian president Hafez al-Assad in order to resolve their internal disputes. This reliance on Syrian arbitration to mediate between the three primary Lebanese political actors became an important factor in increasing Syria's hand in Lebanon and its interference in internal affairs.

The Lebanese are divided in their opinions of Hrawi. Supporters point to the fact that he tried to end the actions of militias and bring closure to the civil war, and they attribute to Hrawi a belief in the coexistence of the various religious factions in Lebanon. His critics, on the other hand, often mention that he disarmed all of the Christian militias but only most of the Muslim ones, making an exception of Hezbollah. They also emphasize that he defended the interests of Syria and accuse him of furthering the Syrian colonization of Lebanon. In another policy area, Hrawi was admired by some as an unlikely reformer: he attempted to change the law to allow civil marriages, thereby reducing the influence of the clergy in this important aspect of Lebanese life. This effort resulted in faint voices of support from an eclectic mix of liberals and left-wingers, although they were quickly drowned in the sea of threats emanating from various Christian and Muslim religious figures. Ultimately, however, Hrawi's most fateful decision in the eyes of many was his acceptance of an extended term of office. Former president Amin Gemayel argued at the time that such a decision would set a precedent and undermine the fragile postwar constitution, and indeed the precedent was followed nine years later when Émile Lahoud decided to extend his own presidential term, leading to frustration and anger among many segments of the Lebanese population.

Émile Lahoud: The General-President

Émile Lahoud was born into a militarily and politically active family in the northern part of the Metn region of Lebanon. His father, Jamil Lahoud, was an army general who was elected to parliament in 1960 and 1964 and was appointed as the minister of public works and social affairs in 1966. Émile Lahoud entered the military academy in 1956 as a cadet officer in the navy and was quickly promoted to the rank of commander. During his military career, he went on long professional training missions to Europe and the United States, studying naval engineering in Great Britain and receiving military training in the United States in the 1970s.

When his maternal cousin General Jean Njeim was named commander in chief of the Lebanese Army, Émile Lahoud was moved into the military administration and was again rapidly promoted. After the Ta'if Agreement, Lahoud himself became the commander in chief of the army. During his term as commander in chief, Lahoud rebuilt the army, which had been weakened and thrown into conflict under the leadership of Michel Aoun. Lahoud more than tripled the number of standing troops through a reintroduction of mandatory military service, and he modernized the equipment of the army with weapons provided at a reduced price by the United States. Lahoud is also credited with unifying the army across sectarian lines, in part by creating multiconfessional brigades that were rotated among different regions of the country. Michel Aoun and other exiled opposition leaders, however, saw Lahoud's attempt to eliminate sectarianism as a mask that hid his willingness to "Syrianize" the army. Whereas Lebanese officers were previously sent to the United States, Britain, or France for training, under Lahoud's leadership they were increasingly sent to a military academy in Homs, Syria. This arrangement was one of the signs of the rapprochement between Lahoud and Syria that paved the way to Lahoud's presidency.

Lahoud was elected president in 1998, after Syria pressured the Lebanese Parliament into removing the constitutionally mandated waiting period between public service (that is, military leadership) and political candidacy. Lahoud's first year in office was a period of high hopes among the Lebanese, and especially among Christians, who were hoping to find in him a strong political representative of their community. The speech that Lahoud delivered upon taking his presidential oath promised a "clean" administration, where there would be no place for bribes and corruption. Many believed that he would usher in a new era of reform similar to the one created by President Shehab in the late 1950s.[7] Instead, Lahoud's presidency led to an increased militarization of politics and to an even more apparent Syrian interference in Lebanese political life.[8]

Like other politicians, Lahoud tried to use his presidency to root himself more deeply in Lebanese political life and to establish a political dynasty. He appointed his brother Nasri Lahoud as a judge at the military court and encouraged his twenty-five-year-old son, Émile Lahoud Jr., to run for office in the legislative elections of 2000. Lahoud Jr. ran on the electoral list of Michel Murr, his sister's father-in-law, and managed to get elected to parliament because of Murr's political importance and manipulations. Lahoud Jr. presented himself as "the candidate of the youth," promising to address youth-oriented issues such as the abolition of the military service requirements that his father had implemented and the lowering of the voting age from twenty-one to eighteen. Lahoud Jr. failed to accomplish these goals in his time in parliament, however, and he did not run for reelection in 2005. The extension of Émile Lahoud's presidential mandate in 2004 had turned Lebanese public opinion firmly against the family, and the Syrian withdrawal from Lebanon after the Cedar Revolution led Lahoud Jr. to realize that he stood no chance of being reelected. Like other politicians close to Syria, he withdrew from the race, spelling the end of the projected Lahoud dynasty. However, Lahoud's presidency did herald a new era of military presidencies in Lebanon. His successor in the presidency, General Michel Suleiman, was also formerly at the head of the Lebanese Army. Suleiman, yet another Maronite politician with close ties to the Syrian regime, was elected to the presidency in May 2008.

The Prime Minister's Office

After the reforms of the Ta'if Agreement, the role of the prime minister became crucial. The personal strength and international connections of Prime Minister Rafiq Hariri, in particular, came to play an important role in lending protection and a sense of pride to Lebanon's Sunni community and in projecting its importance within and outside of the country. Between 1992 and 2005, eight ministerial cabinets were formed in Lebanon. Rafiq Hariri headed five of them, while the other three prime ministers, Salim al-Hoss, Omar Karami, and Najib Mikati, each headed only one.[9] The membership of these cabinets varied, with each including allies of specific prime ministers as well as a mixture of traditional politicians and technocrats. The ministers of the postwar period fall under three categories based on their economic, symbolic, and social resources: the new businessmen, the notables, and the technocrats. An examination of the three most significant prime ministers during the period of Syrian hegemony gives substance to this schema, allowing us to understand each individual's trajectory to the premiership. Najib Mikati, a businessman from Tripoli, will not be discussed at length. He was prime minister for only about six weeks during the period under study, and the main task of his government was to supervise the 2005 legislative elections.

The New Businessmen

Since the end of the civil war, businessmen have played an increasingly prominent role in the Lebanese political scene. Money is always an important part of political life, and Lebanese politicians have always tended to be affluent; however, money acquired an even greater importance in recent years. Finances have become instrumentalized since the end of the war, and financial leverage has become one of the main trajectories by which new elites enter Lebanese politics. These businessmen have extensive international experience, and they often adopt political attitudes and behaviors that are far removed from traditional Lebanese tropes. Their experience in the business world is frequently interjected into their political dealings—they tend to moderate their embrace of traditional patronage networks with meritocratic values, extending their favor not necessarily to the sycophant or to members of a traditional community, but rather to the person who they believe is best suited for the job.[10] The electoral campaigns of these businessmen also have a different character than the campaigns of other Lebanese politicians; in the absence of an established political constituency, these men put great efforts into creating new charitable organizations and otherwise working to build a base of popular support.

Rafiq Hariri: The Merchant Prince

Rafiq Hariri, dubbed the "merchant prince,"[11] was until his assassination in 2005 an unavoidable actor on the Lebanese political scene. He was the precursor of a new trend in Lebanese politics, in which financial wealth could be translated directly into political capital. Hariri issued from a modest Sunni family from the southern Lebanese city of Saida. He worked in Saudi Arabia as a schoolteacher, and then as an accountant, before creating his first company in 1969. This venture failed a few years later, but Hariri was more successful with his second company. By 1978 he had accumulated enough wealth to buy the French construction giant Oger, and he began to develop close ties with the French establishment, including French prime minister Jacques Chirac. He also became a business partner with Fahd bin Abdul Aziz al-Saud, then crown prince and later king of Saudi Arabia. He was granted Saudi citizenship in 1980 and went on to become one of the richest men in the world.

Hariri initiated his trajectory to the peak of Lebanese political power in 1982. After the Israeli invasion, he put the resources of his company, then called Saudi Oger, at the disposal of the Lebanese government to repair the streets of the capital and to dispose of the rubble left in the wake of the wartime destruction. Critics accused him of having financed the civil war by providing money used to purchase weapons to the various militias and of encouraging the destruction of Beirut in order to rebuild it in his image. Elie Salem, who was the Lebanese minister of foreign affairs at the time, writes in his memoirs that "one day [Hariri] drove up to the presidential palace followed by a truck. He surprised us all when his workers emptied the truck and constructed . . . a mock-up of a new downtown Beirut as Hariri perceived it. The downtown area depicted in the model had been reconstructed along modern and efficient lines. Hariri was a dreamer, but with a difference: he often realized his dreams."[12] Hariri denied the allegations that he had ulterior motives in helping to rebuild the city.

In 1983 and 1984, Hariri participated in the peace conferences of Geneva and Lausanne as a special envoy of the Saudi king.[13] This attempt to bring peace to Lebanon was not fruitful; however, it marked an important step in Hariri's political ascension. The final culmination of his attempts to enter politics took place in 1989, when as a member of the Saudi delegation he helped to organize and then participated in the Ta'if conference. Hariri cultivated relationships with the various protagonists of the civil war and showered them with generosity.[14] He also created the Hariri Foundation, a nonprofit organization that gave scholarships to young Lebanese without regard to religious or political affiliations. By his own estimate, the amount of money Hariri spent on these efforts was on the order of a billion US dollars. This generosity led to a widespread network of support for Hariri throughout Lebanese society, though Hariri has objected to suggestions that his philanthropy was intended to improve his political standing.[15]

In the 1980s, Hariri also established good relations with al-Assad's regime in Syria, and he personally met with al-Assad more than fifty times in the following years.[16] He was especially close to former Syrian vice president Abdul Halim Khaddam, and he maintained relations with various other members of the old guard in the Syrian political elite, including Hikmat Shehabi and Ghazi Kanaan. These connections allowed Hariri to act as a mediator between Syrian and Lebanese political actors. After the war, his efforts were acknowledged, and he was appointed as the prime minister of Lebanon in 1992 with Syria's benediction. He formed two other cabinets during the presidency of Elias Hrawi, one in April 1995 and the other in October 1996. The third cabinet ended in 1998 with the election of Émile Lahoud to the presidency. Hariri turned down an offer to form the first cabinet under Lahoud, and Salim al-Hoss (who will be discussed in detail below) was appointed as the new prime minister.

Hariri, however, made a grand comeback to the political scene in the elections of 2000, when he and all of the candidates on his list won landslide parliamentary victories despite the attempts of the Lahoud regime to curtail his influence. After the elections, Hariri returned to his post as prime minister, though his relations with Lahoud remained tense.

In the meantime, Hafez al-Assad had been grooming his son Bashar to inherit power in Syria. Beginning in the late 1990s, a shift of power in that country from the old guard to a new, younger generation of politicians associated with Bashar al-Assad began to erode Hariri's influence in Damascus. Hariri became further alienated from Syria in September 2004, when the United Nations Security Council adopted Resolution 1559, coauthored by France and the United States.[17] The resolution called for the withdrawal of Syrian forces from Lebanon and the disarmament of Hezbollah. It is likely that the Syrian leadership held Hariri accountable for this turn of events, especially given his close ties to the French establishment that coauthored the resolution. However, in a May 2009 interview, the leader of the Progressive Socialist Party, Walid Jumblat, denied that Hariri ever supported the resolution, insisting that both he and Hariri were committed to the Ta'if Agreement's open-ended acceptance of a Syrian presence. Jumblat went as far as to assert that "1559 is the resolution that killed Hariri."[18]

Rafiq Hariri had asserted that he was not likely to be assassinated, because such an event would have regional repercussions that "no sane person would contemplate."[19] Nonetheless, Hariri was killed with a car bomb on February 14, 2005. As he had predicted, this assassination resulted in significant realignments of forces throughout the Middle East, including the rapid withdrawal of Syria from Lebanon in April 2005. In Lebanon Hariri's political mantle was taken over by his son Saad. Whether he had wished it or not, Hariri had with his "martyrdom" created a new political dynasty.

The Notables

Political life in the region once defined by the Ottoman Empire has traditionally centered on a set of elite individuals that Albert Hourani has labeled the "urban notables." These powerful individuals established family dynasties that continue to exert influence in Lebanon through their control of local resources and their popular acceptance as leaders in the community.[20] Among the Christian Lebanese community, the symbolic capital of the notables acquired a renewed importance following the military and political defeat of Christian warlords during the civil war. Many of the notable Christian families that had diverted their political influence into the creation of militias at the beginning of the civil war found themselves temporarily sidelined by the younger, more militarily oriented leaders who emerged during the hostilities. However, following the 1989–90 intra-Christian conflict between the Lebanese Forces under Samir Geagea and the Lebanese Army under Michel Aoun, and the subsequent concessions of the Ta'if Agreement, the traditional leadership of the notable Christian families reemerged with great vigor.

Muslim notables in the Beirut area seem to have lost much of their power to newcomers such as Rafiq Hariri, but they have managed to retain their hold on political representation in the northern parts of Lebanon. Indeed, the presence of notables in the political elite has a regional character. In both Christian and Muslim communities, notables play a more predominant role in northern Lebanon than they do in Beirut or in the South. This point may be explained by the fact that the North was less affected by the civil war than were other regions of the country, and thus retained more political continuity. The central locus of power for the northern notables is the city of Tripoli, where the Sunni leadership has long been monopolized by the Karami family.[21]

Omar Karami: The Last of His Dynasty?

Since the time of Lebanon's independence, the predominance of the Karami family has translated into the continual presence of a Karami representative in the Lebanese Parliament (with the single exception of the 1947 legislature). Abdel-Hamid Karami, Omar's father and the founder of the political dynasty, was one of the leaders of the independence movement. He was for a time incarcerated in the Rashaya fortress by the French government, a sign of revolutionary legitimacy that helped him to obtain the appointment of prime minister in 1945. Abdel-Hamid died in 1950, and his eldest son, Rashid, inherited the *za'ama* (leadership) of the family. Rashid Karami is perhaps the most well known of the politicians who issued from this family. He was elected to parliament in 1951 at the age of thirty-one and retained his seat until his assassination in 1987.[22] He was appointed prime minister for the first time in 1955 and headed several governments in the 1950s, 1960s, 1970s, and 1980s. Rashid Karami had no children to inherit the mantle of the family leadership, so after his assassination that role fell to his brother Omar.

Omar Karami received a law degree from Cairo University in 1956. He lived in the shadow of his successful brother for most of his life, and it was only with the latter's death that he had his first break in politics. Omar Karami was appointed as the Lebanese minister of education in 1989 and as the prime minister in 1990, in the first government formed under President Hrawi. This cabinet was forced to step down in December 1992 because of public demonstrations brought on by difficult economic conditions. Although he lost his prime minister appointment, Omar Karami retained his seat in the new parliament, which he had received during the post-Ta'if parliamentary nominations and to which he was popularly reelected in 1992, 1996, and 2000.[23] He was again appointed as prime minister in the period from October 26, 2004, to April 19, 2005, and it was under his watch that Rafiq Hariri was assassinated.[24] Omar Karami was not reelected to parliament in 2005 or 2009.

Omar Karami's electoral alliances varied from one legislature to the next, depending on the local situation in Tripoli and the state of his relations with Syria. In general, Karami owes a lot to Syria, especially after that country blocked attempts by Rafiq Hariri to dominate the Sunni influence in northern Lebanon in the 1990s. Syria used Karami as a counterweight to Hariri's influence and manifested a public interest in Karami every time that it wished to send a cautionary message to Hariri. For example, the presence of Syrian vice president Abdul Halim Khaddam at the June 2000 ceremony commemorating the assassination of Omar's brother Rashid Karami underlined the tension between Hariri and Syria in preparation for the forthcoming legislative elections.

Omar Karami inherited the *za'ama* from his brother in an unexpected fashion, and he did not seem to possess the diplomatic qualities that were carefully cultivated by the more prominent members of his family. He was often perceived as rash and inarticulate, and his frequent use of popular proverbs in his strong Tripoli accent made him the butt of jokes in the Sunni circles of Beirut. This lack of political aptitude caused Karami to rely increasingly on Syria's support for the maintenance of his position. With Syria's influence reduced after 2005, it is not surprising that Omar Karami was unable to retain his seat in parliament. It is unlikely that he will be able to transmit the political capital of the family to his son Faisal Karami. However, because of AMAL's and Hezbollah's pressure and Syria's interference, Faisal was appointed as minister of sports and youth in the June 2011 cabinet of Prime Minister Najib Mikati, despite the latter's reluctance and his rivalry with the Karami family for the leadership of Tripoli.

The Technocrats

In his work on technically skilled elites in Latin America, Roderic Camp has argued that it is not always possible to make a clear distinction between politicians and technocrats. Camp uses the term *political technocrat* to describe politicians who maintain, through education or experience, "specialized knowledge that gives them expertise in the positions held."[25] In Lebanon such political technocrats have been brought into the cabinet under tough circumstances, when there is popular dissatisfaction with the work of the government or when a quick fix is needed in resolving issues of economics or corruption. However, cabinets with a technocratic majority have usually failed in this mission, leading to a return to power of traditional politicians in subsequent cabinets.

Salim al-Hoss: The Incorruptible

Salim al-Hoss was educated at the American University of Beirut, where he received his master's degree in business administration in 1957, and at Indiana University in the United States, where he received his doctorate in economics and business administration in 1961. In the following decade, he was employed as a financial adviser for the Kuwait Development Fund, as the chairman of the Lebanese Banking Control Commission, and as the chairman of the Industrial Development Bank. Al-Hoss attained these positions based on his expertise, rather than as political appointments.

Al-Hoss served as the prime minister of Lebanon three times and was known for his honesty and incorruptibility.[26] His first appointment was made in 1976 by the newly elected president, Elias Sarkis, a former colleague of al-Hoss's at the Central Bank of Lebanon. Al-Hoss convened a cabinet of eight technocrats drawn mainly from the private sector, who were given the right to rule by decree because of the difficult situation in Lebanon following the start of the civil war. His second, and most controversial, term was from 1987 to 1990. When Rashid Karami was assassinated in May 1987, al-Hoss was appointed as the acting prime minister. Starting in January 1988, he boycotted the meetings of his own cabinet in order to protest the policies of President Amin Gemayel. Then, in September 1988, the outgoing president, Gemayel, appointed General Michel Aoun as the head of a temporary military government. Al-Hoss refused to accept this new regime, leading to the period of time in which the government of Lebanon was split into two rival administrations, one under Aoun and one under al-Hoss. After the negotiations at Ta'if, the new president, Elias Hrawi, asked al-Hoss to continue as prime minister. He formed a new government composed of fourteen cabinet members, including seven Muslims and seven Christians. In December 1990, with the defeat of Aoun and the end of the civil war, al-Hoss resigned from the position of prime minister. He was succeeded by Omar Karami and then by Rafiq Hariri.

In 1992 and 1996, al-Hoss was elected as a member of parliament representing Beirut, and in 1998, with Syrian approval, the new president, Émile Lahoud, appointed him again as prime minister. It is likely that Bashar al-Assad, the heir apparent in Syria who had taken over the management of Lebanese relations as part of his training for the presidency, encouraged al-Hoss's appointment as a way to curtail Hariri's influence.[27] Al-Hoss formed a streamlined cabinet of sixteen ministers, eleven of whom were first-time appointees. Half of the cabinet was composed of technocrats. Al-Hoss's priorities for the new cabinet included reducing the budget deficit, implementing administrative reforms, liberating southern Lebanon from the Israeli occupation, and repatriating Lebanese who had been displaced by the war. Two years later, however, his policies had not resulted in economic growth in Lebanon, and Syria began to transfer its support back to Hariri. After losing his parliamentary seat in 2000 to a previously unknown candidate who was on Hariri's electoral list, al-Hoss resigned as prime minister and declared an end to his political career. After Hariri's assassination in 2005, al-Hoss was considered as a candidate to return to the position of prime minister, but citing health reasons, he refused to accept the appointment.

Al-Hoss's relationship with Syria was not as close as the ties of other politicians. In his memoirs, al-Hoss says that he "believes in a special relation between Syria and Lebanon," but insists that he was "an ally of Syria not a client."[28] He points out that his appointment as prime minister in 1987, after the assassination of Rashid Karami, took place without Syrian approval and that it was remarked upon with displeasure by Syrian vice president Abdul Halim Khaddam. Al-Hoss also maintains that he did not consult with Syria when choosing his cabinets and that any Syrian interference in the affairs of the Lebanese state went not through him but through other channels.[29] He concludes his chapter on relations with Syria by asserting that the "Syrian military presence in Lebanon . . . should remain a decision taken by the executive in Lebanon, i.e., by the Council of Ministers, in agreement with Syrian officials,"[30] seemingly arguing for consultation between the Lebanese and Syrian governments on this issue and for a Lebanese obedience of Syrian decisions. This position can be seen as a post ex facto justification of his behavior in office when he toed the Syrian line.

The Parliament and Its Speaker

A seat in the Chamber of Deputies is the first step toward admission into the political elite in Lebanon, and ever since the time of Lebanon's independence this institution has been the place where aspiring politicians are schooled in the art.[31] Indeed, the vast majority of executive leaders are recruited after having served time as parliamentary deputies. During the immediate postwar period, the Lebanese Parliament saw an extremely high rate of elite circulation. Such a turnover can be seen as a measure of the rate of political change. Between 1942 and 1960, the average rate of turnover was 42 percent.[32] After the 1992 elections, however, 82 percent of the parliament was composed of new entrants to the elite. In the following years, this trend reversed itself; in 1996 35 percent of the parliamentarians were first-time deputies, and in the 2000 election the turnover rate was 29 percent.[33] It looked as though the composition of the elite was consolidating, until the "earthquake" of Hariri's assassination changed all calculations.[34] In the 2005 elections, the renewal rate of the elite surged back to 48 percent, with sixty-one new parliamentarians entering the legislature. The high rate of circulation in 2005 indicated a new era of change and the emergence of a new political elite that was less dependent on Syria.

The majority of parliamentarians hold a university degree (87 percent in 1996 and 90 percent in 2000). The influence of traditional notable families in this body has remained remarkably steady: notables made up 44 percent of the prewar legislature of 1972, and they made up 43 percent of the legislature in 1992, 41 percent in 1996, and 42 percent in 2000.[35] The percentage of rich businessmen in parliament, however, steadily increased in the postwar era. Such individuals made up 12 percent of the 1992 legislature, 19 percent of the 1996 legislature, and 24 percent of the 2000 legislature.[36] This trend is indicative of an increasing financialization of Lebanese politics, with electoral campaigns becoming more organized and expensive.[37] The postwar parliament is mainly composed of members of political dynasties who have not only the sociopolitical but also the financial capital to run for office, along with rich political entrepreneurs who use their fortunes as a stepping-stone to political power.

The official title of the Speaker of the Lebanese Parliament is the president of the Chamber of Deputies. The Ta'if Agreement lengthened the term of this position to four years or the duration of the legislature, making it into a powerful governmental office. In addition, no limit was set on the number of terms that an individual can hold the office. Since

1992 the office of president of the chamber has been monopolized by one man, Nabih Berri. Many consider Berri to be a warlord, as he is also the leader of the Shi'i organization AMAL, which operated as a militia during the civil war. Berri's trajectory to the summit of Lebanese politics is exemplary of this category of Lebanese elites.

Former Warlords

Anthony Vinci defines the term *warlord* as referring to autonomous individual actors who maintain their political independence by employing military and economic force.[38] This simple definition encapsulates the activities of the militia leaders who controlled various areas of Lebanon during the civil war. Vinci also argues, however, that the continuing authority of warlords stems not only from their capacity to wield force but also from their charismatic and patrimonial command over their community of supporters. Most warlords derive their power from multiple sources, including political and family networks within their clan, the manipulation of ethnic identity, and a willingness to use their power to enrich their supporters. They often function across national boundaries and maintain relationships with established politicians in multiple countries.[39] Such are the warlords that existed in Lebanon at the dawn of the Second Republic: the leaders of sectarian militias such as the Shi'i AMAL or the Maronite Lebanese Forces. The Ta'if Agreement was followed by a general amnesty that allowed some of these warlords to "recycle" themselves as politicians.[40] With Syria's support, they became eligible for election to parliament as representatives of their communities.

In the 1992 legislature, many of the members of parliament had been directly involved in the wartime violence. In the decade that followed, however, the majority of these warlords, especially the Christian ones, were progressively excluded from the political scene. By 2005 the main Christian military leaders had been marginalized: Samir Geagea was in prison, Elie Hobeiqa had been assassinated, and Michel Aoun was in exile. Before the Cedar Revolution, only two former warlords played an important role in Lebanese politics: Nabih Berri and Walid Jumblat. These two men represent two types of warlord-politicians: Berri came to power during the violence and then moved into politics, whereas Jumblat is the heir of an old and prestigious dynasty who turned to warlordism during the conflict and then revived his status as a patrician when peace returned.[41]

Nabih Berri: The Monopolizing Speaker

Nabih Berri emerged from a modest family that had emigrated from southern Lebanon to Sierra Leone. Berri was sent back to Lebanon for his education, and after spending a brief time in France, he returned to Lebanon with the intent of entering political life. He tried to run for the legislative elections of 1968 and 1972 on the electoral list of Kamel al-As'ad, a traditional Shi'i leader and a Speaker of the Lebanese Parliament during the First Republic. However, al-As'ad turned Berri down and refused to add him to the electoral list, a decision that was the start of a long-standing animosity between the two men. Berri then joined Imam Musa al-Sadr's Harakat al-Mahrumin and worked as a lawyer for that organization. When the movement created a political-military wing in 1975, Berri was one of its founding members. In 1980 Berri became the secretary-general of AMAL, which had grown out of al-Sadr's movement. Under Berri's leadership, AMAL became the principal client of Syria in Lebanon and began to receive weaponry from its patron.[42] Although the breakaway organization Hezbollah eventually overtook AMAL in the role of most prominent Shi'i militia, Berri's organization continued to function as an important player throughout the civil war and as a political force in the new millennium

When the war ended, the Syrian regime rewarded Berri for his loyalty by providing strong political support. He received an appointment to the new parliament after the Ta'if negotiations and was able to retain this position in the following popular elections. Berri was elected by his peers to the position of Speaker of the parliament, and this mandate was renewed in 1996, 2000, 2005, and 2009. Although a number of other AMAL leaders have also maintained parliamentary seats—even after the Syrian withdrawal—the personality of Nabih Berri seems to eclipse all others within the organization. He has used his position to place his sympathizers into various state offices, and this network of clients helps him to ensure the loyalty of his electorate and consolidate his place within the Shi'i community.[43] Hence, state organs such as the national television channel Télé Liban and the Lebanese University are bloated with Shi'i personnel loyal to Nabih Berri. Indeed, Berri saw the civil service as a means "to perform 'positive discrimination' in favor of the Shi'ites" and as a way "to gain influence against the other members of the Lebanese Troika; strengthen his position with the Lebanese working class; and . . . his position in Shi'ite areas by controlling local unions."[44] In interviews several Lebanese civil servants have explained to me that no Shi'a in Lebanon can get a position as a civil servant without Berri's approval.[45] It is also rumored that Shi'i students cannot register at the Lebanese University without the express permission of an AMAL cadre. In an unsigned article that appeared in Beirut's *Daily Star* on January 31, 2001, a university professor went so far as to say that members of AMAL "consider the university their property" and control its academic and administrative appointments.[46]

In addition to his policy of creating networks of clients, Berri depends on Syria to help maintain his power. He is seen by some as Syria's man in Lebanon. His position as Speaker of parliament for the past two decades has made him a powerful political player and a central actor on the Lebanese political scene. Although he has been described as favoring short-term gains and being petty[47] and corrupt,[48] he is the only member of the original Troika who is still in public office and has often acted in the past twenty years as a tiebreaker between the president and the prime minister. Israeli scholar Omri Nir has argued that Berri's rise in the past two decades was parallel to the rise of Hezbollah: "As Hizballah gained more power within the Shi'ite community and the general Lebanese political arena, Berri's importance grew," since he acted as a mediator between Western governments and Hezbollah.[49] According to one of Berri's Shi'i opponents whom I interviewed in 2002, "The South [of Lebanon] is 'Berriland,' where Nabih Berri behaves like an oriental despot. He is hated by the population because of his constant interference in their affairs, his corruption, and his land grabs. Berri would not physically survive one day without Syria's protection." Since Berri has not only survived but also remained in power after the Syrian withdrawal, such a statement has to be taken with a grain of salt. Nevertheless, it illustrates the depth of the antipathy that some people feel toward Berri, as well as the common perception of his relations with Syria. Currently, Berri is rumored in Lebanon to be grooming his youngest son, Basil, to continue the family legacy. However, according to a leaked cable from the US Embassy in Beirut, Berri is grooming Abdallah, a son from a previous marriage, to assume the successor role. The cable also indicates that Abdallah is disliked by members of the party and more interested in making money than running AMAL and notes that "Abdallah is like his father in one way: a widespread reputation for corruption."[50]

Syria's Clients

Although most of the officeholders in Lebanon between 1989 and 2005 were beholden to Syria in one way or another, some politicians based their power almost completely on their relation with the country's powerful neighbor. I use the category of "Syria's clients" in a restricted sense to describe members of the political elite who not only are sympathetic to Syria but also relied solely on Syria in establishing their presence and influence in the Lebanese political scene. These political actors did not begin with a strong electoral base, and in most cases they lacked the social, political, symbolic, or economic capital needed to create a popular constituency. In order to develop this capital, they employed clientelism, corruption, and in some cases fear, translating their Syrian backing into other forms of economic and political resources.

Michel Murr: The "Superminister"

Michel Murr comes from an entrepreneurial family in the Metn region. He is the strongman of the Second Republic, a "superminister," as he has dubbed himself. Murr has a long political history: he was first elected to the legislature in 1968 on the list of Pierre Gemayel, the founder of the Kata'eb, and he was appointed as a cabinet minister in 1969, 1977, and 1980. However, during the presidencies of Suleiman Frangieh (1970–76) and Amin Gemayel (1982–88), Murr was not appointed to any cabinet and for an unknown reason disappeared from the political scene. In 1985 he reemerged to endorse the Tripartite Agreement proposed by the Syrian regime to end the civil war in Lebanon. When the agreement was broken by the Christian militias, he fled the country and lived in exile from 1986 to 1989. There is some disagreement about where he spent these last years of the war; however, most commentators believe that he was living in Paris.[51]

Murr's early loyalty to Syria was rewarded after the Ta'if Agreement, when he returned to Lebanon to become one of the pillars of the Second Republic. He was appointed to the new parliament in 1991 and retained this position in the popular elections of 1992, 1996, 2000, and 2005. He was also appointed in the first postwar government as Lebanon's deputy prime minister and as the minister of defense. He kept his position as deputy prime minister for almost ten years and was also appointed as the minister of the interior and municipalities between 1994 and 2000. In 1992 Murr sealed his relationship with Syria through the marriage of his son Elias to Karine Lahoud, the daughter of Émile Lahoud, another strong Syrian ally. When Émile Lahoud was elected to the presidency, Michel Murr's access to power became almost unlimited, especially between 1998 and 2000, when he shadowed the weak prime minister, Salim al-Hoss. Murr also contributed to a vicious campaign against Rafiq Hariri's rising power in Lebanon, but his efforts in this regard were unsuccessful.[52] With the appointment of Hariri as prime minister in 2000, Murr was sidelined, and his son Elias was appointed in his stead as the minister of the interior.

During the height of his power as minister of the interior, Murr controlled the majority of the state security apparatuses, and he used this position to help secure his political constituency. According to Walid Jumblat, Murr imposed his security agents in key offices in the administration and the judiciary.[53] He also used the power of his office to control civil servants who became crucial for his electoral campaigns; these clients helped Murr to pressure voters by making public services conditional on the return of votes for Murr and for other candidates that he supported.

In the 1998 municipal elections, Jumblat alleged that "nobody dared to run as a candidate in the municipal elections against his [Murr's] daughter, Myrna. Some people even received death threats."[54] During the period of Syrian hegemony, Murr's control of the Metn region was nearly absolute. His hold was such that only his brother, Gabriel, dared to oppose him in the 2000 legislative elections.

Although he is not the scion of a political family, Murr is proud to say that he has founded a new dynasty in Lebanon.[55] His son Elias Murr was the minister of the interior from 2000 to 2005, bringing the length of the Murr family's control over this position to a total of eleven years. Elias Murr was wounded in a bombing on July 12, 2005, that killed one person and injured a dozen others. He was then appointed as the minister of defense and as the deputy prime minister during the first Siniora cabinet (2005–8), which was formed on July 19, and he kept his position as the minister of defense during the second Siniora cabinet (2008–9). Whether Elias Murr returns to the political scene remains to be seen. A damning cable released by WikiLeaks shows that in a March 2008 meeting with the American chargé d'affaires, Murr offered advice on how Israel could defeat Hezbollah and suggested Israel should take care not to alienate the Lebanese Christians in its next war with Hezbollah.[56]

The Council of Ministers

The changes of the power-sharing formula in the Ta'if Agreement increased the importance of the Council of Ministers, especially relative to the president. A large majority of these postwar cabinets have been composed of thirty ministers. They have lasted on average eighteen months, with a few notable exceptions, such as the government formed by Omar Karami in 2004 (which lasted six months) and the one formed by Najib Mikati in 2005 (which existed for only six weeks). The following sections explain the composition of four sample postwar cabinets that were convened between 1998 and 2005. In these sections I introduce a wide variety of politicians who were influential in the postwar political scene, thereby describing a larger cross-section of the postwar elite culture.

Salim al-Hoss's Cabinet

Salim al-Hoss's 1998–2000 cabinet was composed of sixteen ministers. In his memoirs, al-Hoss maintains that four of these ministers were his personal choice (Muhammad Beydoun, Issam Na'man, Hassan Chalaq, and Naser Sa'idi) and that he welcomed the addition of Joseph Sha-oul's name, as he "knew of his abilities, his intellect and his honesty."[57] Al-Hoss also suggested the names of two ministers, Michel Musa and Ghazi Ze'aiter. Al-Hoss claims that the suggestion to include two other individuals, Najib Mikati and Karam Karam, came from Syria.[58] The other members of the cabinet, not mentioned by al-Hoss in his account, include Michel Murr, Suleiman Frangieh, Anwar Khalil, Suleiman Trabulsi, George Corm, and Arthur Nazarian.

Ministers such as Joseph Shaoul, Naser Sa'idi, and George Corm were chosen primarily for their expertise and were put at the head of the ministries corresponding to their qualifications. They are perfect examples of the "political technocrat." Shaoul, a judge and dean of law at the University of the Holy Spirit in Kaslik who is considered one of the most important constitutional scholars in Lebanon, was appointed as the minister of justice. Sa'idi, who gained experience in positions as the vice governor of the Central Bank of Lebanon, the chief economist of the Dubai International Financial Centre, and a board member of the Hawkamah Institute for Corporate Governance, was appointed both as the minister of economy and trade and as the minister of industry. Corm, who had previously been an adviser to the minister of finance of Algeria and an adviser to the governor of the Central Bank of Lebanon, was appointed as the minister of finance.

Michel Murr, Suleiman Frangieh, Anwar Khalil, Najib Mikati, Karam Karam, and Ghazi Ze'aiter formed the bulk of the Syrian contingent in the cabinet. These individuals provide examples of the diversity of political resources that state elites bring to bear in their bids for office. Frangieh, for instance, is a notable and the heir of a political dynasty. His grandfather and namesake was the president of Lebanon in the early 1970s. At the same time, however, Frangieh is also very close to the Assad family in Syria and draws much of his political capital from that relationship. In contrast to Frangieh, Karam is an unexpected newcomer to the political scene. A physician with substantial academic credentials, Karam chaired the Department of Obstetrics and Gynecology at the American University of Beirut Hospital from 1987 until 1999. Rumors circulating in Beirut at the time were that he was rewarded with the ministry of public health in 1998 because he was able to help Bushra al-Assad, the only daughter and favorite child of Syrian president Hafez al-Assad, to conceive. Karam later served as the minister of tourism and as a minister of state. Thus, while Karam's initial appointment could be seen as based on his technical expertise, he ended up solely as Syria's man in government, serving in areas that were far removed from his medical background.

Rafiq Hariri's Last Cabinet

Rafiq Hariri's last cabinet provides a good example of the kind of governments that this prime minister convened. Operating from April 17, 2003, to October 26, 2004, the cabinet was composed of thirty ministers.[59] Several factions were represented in the cabinet, each linked to a major political figure. Fouad Siniora, Bahij Tabbara, and Samir Jisr, for example, were included in the cabinet because they were long-standing associates of Hariri. Marwan Hamadeh and Ghazi Aridi were included because of their association with Hariri's ally Walid Jumblat. Jean-Louis Qordahi and Elias Murr were Émile Lahoud's representatives in the cabinet, while Berri's men included Ali Hassan Khalil, Ayyub Humayyed, and Mahmoud Hammoud. Syrian allies included Suleiman Frangieh, Najib Mikati, Karim Pakradouni, Assem Qanso, and As'ad Hardan. Qanso and Hardan, in particular, were purely Syria's men in Lebanon and had little popular support. Qanso is the regional head of the Baath political party (the ruling party of Syria), and Hardan is the president of the Lebanese Syrian Social Nationalist Party, which advocates the dissolution of Lebanon into Syria.

Omar Karami's Cabinet

Omar Karami's cabinet operated from October 26, 2004, to April 19, 2005, and was also composed of thirty ministers.[60] This cabinet, for the first time in Lebanese history, included women ministers: Leila al-Solh and Wafa' Hamza. Al-Solh's appointment as the minister of industry was largely a symbolic gesture recognizing the economic and political importance of her powerful family. She is the daughter of Riad al-Solh, one of the founding fathers of the country and an important Sunni icon. She is also the aunt of the billionaire prince Walid bin Talal of Saudi Arabia, who was granted Lebanese citizenship by President Lahoud and was said to have political ambitions in Lebanon. Hamza, who was appointed as minister of state, was said to be a client of the Speaker of the house, Nabih Berri.[61]

Two of the cabinet members, Adnan Addoum and Wi'am Wahhab, merit particular consideration owing to their alleged closeness to Syria. Addoum is a legal expert and judge who was appointed as the Lebanese prosecutor general (state prosecutor) after the personal intervention of Ghazi Kanaan, the head of Syrian military intelligence in Lebanon. Addoum was removed from his post as prosecutor general in 2005, after the assassination of Rafiq Hariri. He was accused by Hariri's camp of muddying the investigation and for pushing suspicions away from Syria and toward Islamist groups. Wahhab was a member of the Progressive Socialist Party and worked in its media organ, *Sawt al-Jabal* (Voice of the Mountain), from 1983 until 1987. He was catapulted into national politics with his appointment to the Karami government. Often referred to as "the pit bull," he became a popular and loquacious media star, defending an extreme pro-Syria position. In November 2007, Wahhab was designated by the US Treasury as being "affiliated with the Syrian regime's efforts to reassert Syrian control over the Lebanese political system."[62]

Najib Mikati's Cabinet

Najib Mikati's first cabinet[63] operated from April 19, 2005, to July 19, 2005. It consisted of fourteen ministers and was formed to supervise the 2005 elections following the Cedar Revolution.[64] Mikati declared that "this government certainly groups all the Lebanese factions," meaning that he sought to include representatives of all political orientations.[65] This cabinet differed from the ones that came before in that it lacked the usual complement of Syrian clients. Instead, the cabinet included many relatively young and previously unknown technocrats who agreed to be a part of the caretaker government and not to run for the immediately upcoming elections. Among these individuals was Demianos Qattar, a lecturer in finance and a founding dean of the Antonine Business School, whose name was later on floated as a possible presidential candidate owing to his perceived neutrality and his popularity as minister.[66] Bassam Yammine, likewise, was a name that had never been heard in Lebanese political circles prior to his appointment in the Mikati cabinet. He was educated at the University of Chicago and Loyola Marymount University in the United States and had previously been an adviser to Suleiman Frangieh and a ministry liaison officer with the World Bank. The appointment of such individuals indicated a turn away from the past and a reduction in Syrian influence after 2005.

The Legacy of Corruption

Harvard political scientist Joseph Nye describes the two main categories of corruption as nepotism ("bestowal of patronage by reason of ascriptive relationship rather than merit") and misappropriation ("illegal appropriation of private resources for private-regarding sources").[67] Although nepotism is prevalent in Lebanon, it is hard to prove. Misappropriations are another matter, and there is ample evidence of Lebanese politicians viewing the resources of the state as their own private fiefdom. This theft of public resources, sometimes called "grand corruption,"[68] has occurred at the highest levels of the Lebanese state, by individuals who have the power to make economic policies and distribute state funding. Various elite actors often share the benefits of such behavior among themselves, thereby building networks of power that can resist public opposition and political change, even in nominally democratic governments.[69] It is therefore unsurprising to see widespread political corruption in a country like Lebanon, where social inequality is pronounced; where state, and especially judicial, institutions are weak; and where state bureaucracies largely function as extensions of entrenched political networks.

The postwar period in Lebanon, in particular, was characterized by a massive and institutionalized recourse to corruption,[70] which became the primary means for elite factions to consolidate and negotiate their hold on power. According to some estimates, corruption's share in government contracts varies between 203 and 704 percent.[71] This corruption has been denounced in numerous works of political criticism, published mainly in Arabic in Beirut.[72] These books most commonly address evidence of corruption in the cabinets headed by Rafiq Hariri, whom they accuse of masterminding systemic patterns of misappropriation. Other members of the political elite, including the president and the Speaker of the house, are not innocent of similar behavior. In Lebanese political criticism, however, the corruption of these other state leaders is usually mentioned only in relation to the alleged contraventions by Hariri. This oblique and selective mode of critique is not accidental; it has to do with Hariri's nontraditional use of economic wealth as his primary stepping-stone to political power. Hariri's reliance on economic power opens the door to charges of financial corruption, and it also changes the rules of political critique. As it was explained by one of Hariri's advisers whom I interviewed in 2002, "Rafiq Hariri is a businessman. The worse he can do to an author who defames him is to drag him to court and sue him. In contrast, [Nabih] Berri and [Walid] Jumblat are warlords. They would order the assassination of such an author." Perhaps the best way to characterize Hariri's premiership is with the phrase "effective corrupt leadership," coined by Mark W. Neal and Richard Tansey. Hariri's endeavors were perhaps different from more conventional forms of corruption in that he proclaimed "the intention to promote public good; and the ability to do it."[73]

The Troika: An Institutionalization of Corruption

As the Pax Syriana progressed, the "Troika" system composed of Nabih Berri, Rafiq Hariri, and Elias Hrawi became increasingly entrenched in Lebanese politics (Hrawi's role was later taken over by Émile Lahoud). This entrenchment of the Troika led one scholar of Lebanon to maintain that "under Syrian guardianship, Lebanon was acquiring the traits of a closed system and that its power-sharing distinctiveness was dissolving into a disfigured consociational oligarchy."[74] The shifting arrangements among these individual power brokers functioned in a collegial and informal manner based on compromises and mutual concessions. In the configuration that prevailed under Syrian tutelage, each member of the Troika maintained an individual fief within the state apparatus that was used to promote his individual power and to extract personal revenues. Smaller sections of the public pie were left to other important actors, such as Walid Jumblat and Michel Murr.

One of Hariri's most important areas of control was the Council of Development and Reconstruction (CDR), whose mission was to rebuild the country after the war. The CDR was led by men who were appointed by Hariri and maintained a personal loyalty to him. Both of the council's leaders, al-Fadl Chalaq and Nabil Jisr, had previously been private employees of Hariri. Indeed, most of the 270 staff members of the CDR were in one way or another personally accountable to Hariri.[75] In addition, during the 1990s, control of the three semiprivate institutions that were in charge of the reconstruction of Beirut and its suburbs was divided among important political actors. Solidere,[76] the company in charge of the reconstruction of the Beirut central district, was viewed as Rafiq Hariri's turf. Indeed, Hariri personally owned 10 percent of the shares in the company. Elyssar, the company that was charged with the restructuring of the mainly Shi'i suburbs of southern Beirut, was controlled by Nabih Berri in conjunction with Hezbollah.[77] Linord, the company charged with restructuring the mainly Christian area in North Beirut, was controlled by Michel Murr.[78]

Further examples of personalized control over state resources abound. The Council of the South, which was created after the Israeli invasion of 1982 to help victims of the aggression, is controlled by AMAL under the leadership of Nabih Berri. The Ministry of the Displaced, created in 1992 and charged with giving indemnities to internally displaced Lebanese, is ironically under the authority of Walid Jumblat, whose militia was responsible for the massive, forced removal of Christians from the Shuf Mountains during the 1980s. Although this ministry spent eight hundred million US dollars between 1991 and 1999, only 20 percent of the displaced were able to return to their villages. Only 9 percent of those people who returned were fully reimbursed for housing reconstruction. The overt mismanagement and embezzlement of these funds led to tension among Rafiq Hariri, Nabih Berri, and Walid Jumblat.[79]

The propensity toward personalized control of state institutions in Lebanon is often mediated through family networks. For example, Hrawi's son-in-law, Fares Boueiz, was appointed as Lebanon's minister of foreign affairs for almost the entire duration of Hrawi's presidential term. After Hrawi left office, the political fortunes of Boueiz vanished, at least temporarily. Hrawi's biological sons, who had an interest in the oil and gas sectors, were likewise the beneficiaries of the resources from the state's Ministry of Energy and Water during their father's presidency. President Lahoud continued this tradition, using his influence to place his son Émile Jr. in a parliamentary seat and to promote his son-in-law, Elias Murr, to minister of the interior. Although it is difficult to argue that Boueiz's or Murr's appointment is an example of nepotism and had no basis in the merit of their appointment, what is clear is that these politicians willfully used the power of their positions to promote their own private, clientelistic network and their own economic fortunes. In addition, it is highly probable that Lahoud received personal benefits from the various recovery and development plans that were orchestrated by the Murr family, in exchange for Lahoud's support of Murr family members' political careers.

"Horizon 2000" and the Fate of the Lebanese Economy

According to Lebanese economist and former finance minister Samir Makdisi, four phases can be distinguished in the Lebanese economy during the postwar period.[80] The first, from 1990 to 1994, was one of accelerated growth based on reconstruction spending. The second, from 1995 to 2000, saw a decline in growth, which became negative in 2000. The probable cause of this decline was extensive state borrowing at relatively high interest rates. The third phase followed the World Trade Center attacks in 2001 when the Lebanese economy underwent a partial recovery, owing to a renewed influx of capital from the Arab world, as Arabs felt unwanted in the United States and Europe. The economy continued to remain stable until the advent of the fourth phase brought about by the destruction of the country during the Israeli war in July 2006. It might be said that Lebanon's postwar economy has entered a fifth stage, in which it is struggling to contend with the legacy of corruption and wartime destruction. Because of the conservative policies of Lebanon's Central Bank, the country has not been strongly affected by the world economic crisis that began in 2008. Nonetheless, Lebanon's debt-to-GDP ratio was 153 percent in June 2009, raising questions about the ability of the country to manage the results of postwar spending.[81]

The centerpiece of Lebanon's immediate postwar economic policy was the reconstruction of downtown Beirut. Upon his ascendancy to the office of prime minister in 1992, Hariri launched the program called "Horizon 2000,"[82] an expenditure plan centered on the reconstruction of Beirut's downtown as well as the infrastructure of the entire country—including roads, electrical infrastructure, and telecommunications. The cost of the reconstruction was anticipated to come to US$14.3 billion. Banking on an anticipated era of peace with Israel, the goal of this program was to resuscitate the role of Lebanon as a commercial and financial hub and as an intermediary between the Western and Arab worlds. Hariri and his allies introduced a variety of new governmental policies to accelerate the modernization of the country's infrastructure. These policies were similar to the ones that followed Lebanon's independence in 1943. They privileged large companies and the wealthy elite, to the detriment of middle- and working-class Lebanese. The plan was based on extensive borrowing, and economist Toufic Gaspard has described it as "more of a wish list than a reasoned economic program."[83] The most extensive provisions of Horizon 2000 were soon shelved, reducing its scope to the reconstruction of downtown Beirut alone. Nonetheless, the project made a major contribution to Lebanon's increasing fiscal deficits and mounting public debt in the latter half of the 1990s.

In 1991 the company Solidere was created and charged with rebuilding the heart of Beirut, including the infrastructure and the public

utilities.[84] After judicial valuation, assets held by 120,000 original claim-
ants to property rights in the area were transferred to the newly created
entity, as were the rights to own and exploit important parcels of real
estate that would be reclaimed from a landfill. The company came to
monopolize many government-subsidized functions in the area, including the roles of city planning and construction regulation.[85] This transfer
of public funds and responsibilities to private monopolies was extended
to a variety of development projects and to newly privatized sectors such
as the postal service and garbage collection.[86]

Further debacles occurred in the newly developing area of telecommunications. In her book *Al-Khalawi: Ashhar fada'ih al 'asr* (The Cell
Phone: The Biggest Scandal of the Century), Lebanese journalist Aline
Hallaq links numerous members of the Lebanese elite to LibanCell and
Cellis, companies created in the early 1990s that, as Hallaq documents,
have been charged with roughly four hundred distinct violations of Lebanese laws. Hallaq explains that LibanCell was owned by Nizar Dalloul,
the husband of Hariri's stepdaughter, and that a majority of the shares in
Cellis belonged to Najib Mikati and his brother, Taha. Syrian elites also
demonstrated their interest in these lucrative activities. Khaled Shehabi,
the son of former Syrian chief of staff Hikmat Shehabi, tried to develop
a stake in LibanCell but was bought out by Dalloul. Likewise, Jamil
Khaddam, the son of former Syrian vice president Abdul Halim Khaddam, was at one time an important shareholder in Cellis.[87] In her book
Al-Khalawi: Akbar al-safaqat (The Cell Phone: The Biggest Deal), Lebanese journalist and presenter Ghada Eid has developed Hallaq's investigation, maintaining that Rafiq Hariri's connections in the world of finance
and business gave him an inside line on the importance of the developing
industry.[88] This fact likely explains Hariri's insistence, in the first three
cabinets that he formed, in reserving the telecommunications portfolio
for himself and his closest collaborators.[89] Eid alleges that Hariri wanted
to create a productive and profitable telecommunication sector in Lebanon, but not one that functioned at its full potential. She maintains that
Hariri's ultimate aim was to create a perceived need for privatization and
then to personally buy out the nation's public telecommunications infrastructure at a low price.[90]

In a separate book, Eid also alleges that the waste collection and treatment company Sukleen is only nominally owned by businessman Maysara Sukkar and that the actual financial impetus behind the company was Rafiq Hariri. Eid maintains that since 1995, Sukleen has received between US$110 and US$120 million per year, while estimates from other companies show that the job could be done for around US$50 to US$60 million per year.[91] She also explains that the exceptionally lucrative terms of Sukleen's 1994 contract with the government were achieved owing to patronage from Hariri, with the support of Ghazi Kanaan, the head of Syrian intelligence in Lebanon.[92]

The Lebanese economy was important for Syrian elites because many were personally invested or had familial investment in the success of Lebanese businesses, as evidenced by the interest of Khaddam and Shehabi in new Lebanese ventures in the early 1990s.[93] In the early years of the twenty-first century, as political change began to foment in Lebanon, Syria encouraged a separation of the economic and political arenas by allocating the economic portfolio to Hariri and the political dossier to Lahoud. The result was a gridlock in which Hariri's attempts at privatization were balanced against resistance from the president and his allies, leading to a freeze on economic policy changes and the further entrenchment of corruption. In some views, this stasis could be interpreted as a way to guarantee a peaceful balance of power. Scholar Michael Johnston has argued that certain types of corruption—what he calls "market" and "patronage" corruption—tend to act as forces for political integration and stability in divided societies.[94] In Lebanon widespread corruption combined with the deep-seated patronage system led to a relatively stable system in the postwar period, one that was based on the "division of spoils" and on the adage "You scratch my back, and I'll scratch yours." However, it also led to an inability to resolve systemic financial problems and abuses in the government, and it had a dampening effect on the pace of political reform. Lebanese patronage networks proved to be volatile and unpredictable. They added to the cost of doing business in Lebanon and discouraged foreign and local investors.[95] In addition, the power gridlock and the slow pace of reform in Lebanon had an unintended consequence: it contributed to the widespread and continuing emigration of the country's most promising youths.

Youth Emigration and "Brain Drain"

The stagnation of the Lebanese economy in the postwar era has been accompanied by increasing public debt as well as by the continuation of policies that favor the rich, leading to the consolidation of a governing coalition composed of wealthy businessmen, warlords, notables, and clients of the Syrian regime. The internal struggles among these ruling elites have more often than not culminated in gridlock. The educated youth that could potentially counterbalance the monopoly of the established elite are largely disenchanted by the lack of opportunities, corruption, and structural constraints that limit their ability to participate in the political process. For many, leaving the country seems a better option than does remaining behind to struggle against these obstacles. They therefore depart Lebanon en masse, taking up residence in Australia, Canada, the United States, and various European countries. Those youths who cannot find a way to emigrate permanently often leave the country for repeated work stints in the Gulf States or Africa, returning to Lebanon full-time only after their retirement.

Although Lebanon is an emigrant country par excellence, and has been so since the mid-nineteenth century—the Lebanese taking pride in their emigrants who have gone on to succeed in other countries—the situation has changed in recent years. We can divide emigrants into three categories: permanent emigrants who remain detached from their home country, emigrants who maintain a strong relationship with their homeland without residing there, and emigrants who work abroad but return often and maintain their primary residence in their home country.[96] In Lebanon it is this last category of emigrants whose ranks have swollen in recent years. Their pattern of travel tends to be a "circular migration," in which they repeatedly leave the country for contractually determined amounts of time to work on specific projects abroad.[97] Many of these emigrants are employed in the Gulf States, which generally do not offer the possibility of naturalization to foreign workers or to the children of foreign workers. Between 1997 and 2007, nearly half of Lebanese emigrants were on their way to such countries.[98]

The exodus of Lebanese of all ages began, unsurprisingly, during the civil war, but this depletion of the nation's human assets has not stopped after the Ta'if Agreement. In the period from 1992 to 2007, the number of emigrants was estimated to be at least 446,000 people.[99] These individuals have a much higher record of educational achievement than do people who remain in country; one study found that between 1975 and 2001, 25.4 percent of emigrants had a university degree, whereas only 8.1 percent of the nonemigrant population were university graduates.[100] This trend shows no signs of reversing. A 2009 study by Lebanese economist Jad Chaaban indicated that although the country was suffering from a national shortage of skilled professionals, nearly half of recent university graduates aspired to leave the country. As the title of the report on this study suggests, we are witnessing a significant "brain drain" in Lebanon.[101] This report concludes that whereas the ability of Lebanese universities to produce highly skilled professionals is not in question, the ability of the country to retain these individuals is suffering because of political instability and the high cost of living.

The phenomena of "brain drain" and youth emigration did not seem to bother the political elites whom I interviewed in Lebanon. When questioned on this issue, many of the interviewees pointed to the value of the monthly remittances that are frequently sent by emigrants to their families at home. In addition, interviewees also remarked that returning emigrants are a primary channel for the transfer of technological skills into the country. Some even commented approvingly on the fact that widespread emigration helped to reduce the amount of competition faced by themselves and their progeny. One interviewee ironically said, "Are we losing the brains needed to develop the nuclear sector in Lebanon?"— implying that the brain drain is no big loss for the country, as Lebanon will never have that kind of advanced technology. Therefore, in his view, the remittances these emigrants send more than compensate for the loss of human capital.

Conclusion

Whereas the prewar Lebanese elite was mainly composed of professionals, lawyers, and notables,[102] the postwar elite is largely made up of warlords, rich entrepreneurs from the Lebanese diaspora, Syria's clients, and notables who have retained or regained political influence. These groups have consolidated their hold on power through a mix of patronage and corruption. The gridlock of these established elites and the exclusion of the youth from political participation in the postwar era contributed to a significant increase in emigration, which is beginning to have a noticeable effect among the educated and professional segments of Lebanese society. The consolidation of power by elite cartels in the postwar era is to the detriment of Lebanon's future. In addition, trends such as the increasing value of brute wealth in political campaigns increasingly make politics the purview of a small circle of millionaires and boost the oligarchic aspect of Lebanese politics.

5

Strategic Elites

Whereas state elites act directly within the political arena, other groups that exist beyond state institutions can also have an effect on political decisions. They are the second half of what Italian scholar Vilfredo Pareto has called "governing elites," those people who either directly or indirectly affect decision making. Suzanne Keller has referred to them as the "strategic elite."[1] These unelected elites can be in the shadows, éminences grises who influence better-known politicians, or they can be outspoken opinion makers. In Lebanon these unelected strategic elites include military commanders, religious leaders, and important journalists.

The Military and Security Apparatus

In his seminal book *The Soldier and the State,* American political scientist Samuel Huntington describes the qualities needed to make a professional soldier, namely, expertise, responsibility, and "corporateness." In describing the ideal expertise of military officers, he invokes Harold Lasswell's notion of "the management of violence" and suggests that an officer should be "peculiarly expert at directing the application of violence under certain prescribed conditions."[2] The scope of these "prescribed conditions," however, is limited by Huntington's further expectations of social responsibility and sublimation of individual ambition. He argues that a necessary part of military professionalism is that soldiers must be detached from partisanship and remain under civilian authority, thereby ensuring that their actions will serve the interests of society as a whole. In Huntington's unambiguous formulation, "civilian control is essential to military professionalism."[3]

In comparison to other "developing" nations worldwide, the civilian control of the military in Lebanon has remained relatively strong. Under the First Republic, the army was intentionally kept small so that it could not have a disruptive effect on the consociational balance.[4] And although the role of the military has steadily increased, only three of Lebanon's twelve elected presidents have been military leaders: during the First Republic, Fouad Shehab (1959–64), and during the Second Republic, Émile Lahoud (1998–2004) and Michel Suleiman (2008–present). The commander in chief of the Lebanese Armed Forces has traditionally been a Maronite, so the move from this office to the traditionally Maronite presidency is not particularly surprising. What is surprising is that in contrast to other Middle Eastern states, Lebanon has had so few military leaders. It is notable that although the presidency has been offered to army commanders at various crucial times during Lebanese history, the position was more often than not refused.[5] In the following section, I will discuss some of the reasons for the notable lack of military rule in Lebanese history, as well as some of the recent trends that threaten to undermine this precedent.

A Brief History of the Lebanese Armed Forces (1945–90)

The Lebanese Armed Forces originate from the Troupes Spéciales du Levant established by the French colonial power in Lebanon and Syria after World War I. After Lebanon obtained its independence, control of these forces was transferred to the new Lebanese Republic. The new institution was small and uncoordinated, numbering only about three thousand men, and the officer corps was disproportionately Christian. The main mission of the French-led forces had been internal security, and this task continued to be the main concern of the LAF after 1945.[6]

The first commander in chief of the LAF was Fouad Shehab, who remained at the helm of Lebanon's military forces until he became president in 1958. Shehab emphasized professionalism and education in the army, and he tried to discourage client-patron relations between officers and politicians.[7] Today, Shehab's presidency is widely regarded as the golden age of Lebanon. He is perceived as a great statesman who stood up to traditional political leaders and established a number of forward-looking state institutions that still exist. Nonetheless, from 1958 to 1970, that is, under the Shehab and Helou presidencies, the Lebanese were convinced that the LAF was being used as a political instrument by the presidency, and the two institutions came to be seen as intertwined with one another. Shehab appointed army officers to important government posts, and the Deuxième Bureau, the army's intelligence branch, became an important force in the government. Because of its intimate relation with the presidency, the army was soon perceived by Lebanese Muslims as an instrument perpetuating Maronite control over the state. By 1968, when Israeli commandos attacked the Beirut airport in retaliation against an operation by the Beirut-based Popular Front for the Liberation of Palestine, the army had lost its legitimacy and was in the process of losing physical control of the situation in the country. It was increasingly unable to counter the activities of Palestinian fedayeen (guerrillas) who were using Lebanon as a platform to infiltrate and strike against Israel.

In 1970 the election of Suleiman Frangieh to the presidency curtailed the intrusion of the military into Lebanese politics. In addition to restricting the army's political influence, Frangieh dismissed many Shehabist officers outright, leading to the emergence of a new officer corps and greatly decreasing the effectiveness of the Deuxième Bureau.[8] When the civil war started in 1975, the army ceased to behave as a single entity. It was reorganized starting in 1977, with deserters encouraged to come back into the ranks and many career officers given an opportunity to resign in exchange for a generous financial package. The hope was to mend sectarian rifts and to balance the religious composition of the officer corps. An institutional reform program was put in place in March 1979 with the passage of the National Defense Law, which purported to update the military chain of command and to entrench civilian control over the military. The powers of the president over the army were curtailed, and the government's defense policies became the purview of the cabinet in addition to a newly created institution, the Supreme Defense Council.[9]

During the presidency of Amin Gemayel (1982–88), the LAF underwent further reorganization and training in cooperation with the United States and other members of the multinational forces in Beirut. Under the Lebanese Army Modernization Program (LAMP), the United States committed to helping the LAF both with the development of military leadership and with the acquisition and use of sophisticated weapons capable of facing the fire of the Lebanese militias. The Americans were surprised at the quality of the soldiers they were training. Colonel Tom Fintel, a US officer heading the LAMP program, noted that he would give them "high grades in every area" and that he would be "very happy to have Lebanese soldiers working under [his] command anywhere in the world."[10] Although the modernization aspect of the LAMP program was successful, in 1984 the army once again disintegrated for political reasons. At that time, the LAF was pitted against two powerful militias, the Druze forces of Walid Jumblat and the Shi'i AMAL militia of Nabih Berri. By the winter of 1984, 40 percent of the army had deserted, and Muslim officers and soldiers refused to obey orders and fight their coreligionists. Professionalism and the commitment to the civil authorities had taken a backseat to religious affiliation. From 1984 to 1988, the LAF was divided into two—one group of soldiers, which included the core of the units trained by the United States, obeyed the orders of the military command, while a second group was unwilling or unable to do so.

In June 1984, Michel Aoun was appointed commander in chief of the army, a choice that would greatly contribute to the polarization and politicization of the LAF. Ronald McLaurin has argued that as early as 1986, Aoun was already planning for his elevation to the presidency at the end of Amin Gemayel's term and that he did not keep this ambition a secret from his fellow army officers.[11] Aoun began by screening officer assignments and promoting junior officers who would be personally loyal to him, often at the expense of more experienced and better-qualified candidates. He also developed his own Praetorian guard, composed of the highly trained Ranger units and the military police, with the latter being groomed as Aoun's personal strike force. Aoun was indeed appointed by Gemayel as the leader of an interim government in 1988, but as was discussed in chapter 2, his legitimacy was challenged by the cabinet headed by Salim al-Hoss. In March 1989, Aoun commenced his "war of liberation" from Syrian domination. LAF forces started shelling Syrian Army positions in the western section of Beirut. Aoun was hoping that his call for an intifada (uprising) against Syrian occupation would be heard. However, the civilians in West Beirut did not rise up, and Aoun expanded his assault into an indiscriminate shelling of Muslim areas. As a result of this attack, the erosion of loyalty among LAF soldiers accelerated. By the early autumn of 1990, Aoun had only about four thousand army regulars under his command, while untrained volunteers made up the bulk of his forces. Most of the LAF soldiers had either deserted or shifted their allegiance to al-Hoss. The army was not only destroyed but also exhausted and demoralized. It had lost its national character and turned into another sectarian militia.

Aoun's control of the eastern area of Beirut can be described only as a military dictatorship. After the signing of the Ta'if Agreement, he had the houses of opposing politicians attacked, incarcerated foreign journalists critical of his policies, and informally censored the local press. He threatened to close any media outlet that mentioned the new president, government, or Speaker. Aoun's actions are a strong reminder that the greatest threats to the military professionalism described by Huntington are partisanship and political aspirations on the part of senior officers. In the following sections, I describe in greater detail the composition of Lebanon's military officer corps and the way that individual military men have interacted with the political process. The biographies of Shehab and Aoun both indicate how an inclusion of the military in the political process has been used in Lebanon during times of crisis, arguably with the goal of creating national stability.

Composition of the Officer Corps

The officer corps is mainly composed of Lebanese males who have trained at the military academy in Fayadieh.[12] In the preindependence period and the early days of the First Lebanese Republic, the officer corps was mainly constituted of upper-middle-class and middle-class men, about half of whom were from Mount Lebanon and more than half of whom were Maronites. President Shehab's military experience dates from this era, and the military officers that Shehab drew into the government mostly come from this tradition. Through the latter part of the First Republic and up to the 1977 reorganization, however, the percentage of Druze, Sunni, and Shi'i officers steadily increased, as did the geographical and economic diversity of the officers. Many of these officers became politically active during the civil war. A number of them developed ties with the militias of their sect, especially with the Maronite Lebanese Forces (not to be confused with the LAF itself) and with the Druze Progressive Socialist Party. Several officers ended up as senior militiamen. General Aoun's military experience was formed during this later, diversifying, phase of the LAF.

During 1977–78, at the time of the restructuring of the army that culminated with the National Defense Law in 1979, more than 100 officers were encouraged to retire. Fifty-three were of the rank of colonel or above. The majority of the retired officers were Christians, mainly Maronites, and the purpose of the forced retirements was to diversify the composition of the military elite. In 1983, during the second restructuring of the army, an additional 91 officers were asked to retire, and again the majority was Maronite. These changes were resented, leading some military Christians to become politically reactionary. In 1991, after the defeat of General Aoun, there was an additional wave of mainly Christian retirements: 253 officers, including more than 100 at or above the rank of colonel, left the LAF.[13]

Fouad Shehab and the Deuxième Bureau

Fouad Shehab was the son of an aristocratic family whose roots extend back to the Shehab dynasty that ruled the area of Mount Lebanon from 1697 to 1840. He trained in the military academy starting in 1921, and after graduating he rose rapidly through the ranks of the army. Shehab was promoted to general and named commander in chief of the Lebanese Army in 1945, a post that he held until 1958, when he was elected president. This election was surprising, as the Middle East was known for frequent military coups (at least three dozen such coups occurred in the Arab world between 1940 and 1960).[14] Shehab was initially reluctant to accept the presidency and did so only when he came to feel that it was absolutely necessary in order to stabilize the country after the civil war of 1958.[15]

The military career of President Shehab and the tours he served in the country provided him with an excellent knowledge of the different Lebanese regions, especially of their economic and social needs. He was more aware than other elites of the realities in peripheral regions (the North, the South, and the Beqaa valley), which generally have a majority Muslim population.[16] This understanding led Shehab to believe that the creation of a just and modern state in Lebanon was necessary in order to preserve the coexistence established by the National Pact. Indeed, Shehab considered the socioeconomic inequalities of Lebanon to be the principal source of social problems and of political tensions in the country.

Influenced by his military training and by political changes in France after World War II, Shehab saw planning as the main step in the construction of an effective state. He started a movement of top-down modernization, which American political scientist Michael Hudson contends was influenced by the examples of Charles de Gaulle and Gamal Abdel Nasser: "Shehab shared with them an attitude of distaste for civilian politicians, which he had acquired during his military training in France. As De Gaulle was repelled by the incompetence of French politicians during the 1930s and Nasser was indignant at the decadence of Egyptian politics under King Farouk, so too Shehab may have felt contempt for the corruption and lack of direction in Lebanon's political life."[17] To help modernize the state, Shehab sought the expertise of Father Louis Joseph Lebret, the head of the Institut International de Recherche et de Formation en vue du Développement.[18] The IRFED mission's report on its activities in Lebanon provides evidence that social issues were the principal worry of President Shehab and that he was especially concerned about their manifestation in the exodus of rural populations to the city. Shehab therefore promoted a social policy aimed at developing rural areas and convincing their inhabitants to remain. This development project also extended to improving the impoverished urban areas to which the rural population had fled, most notably the southern areas of Beirut.[19]

Shehab also started a program of administrative reform, using legislative decrees to accelerate the changes. He despised the sections of the political elite that he dubbed as the *fromagistes* (cheese eaters), a scornful reference to their practice of taking advantage of the system and maybe to their habit of conducting politics in posh surroundings. To limit corruption and eliminate the endemic patrimonial character of the administrative system, he created two new institutions: the Civil Service Council, which recruited and trained public officials, and the Central Inspection Board, which supervised public servants. In addition, to secure Lebanese national unity, he instituted a policy in which all major sectarian groups were represented equally within the administration.[20] Among his other contributions were the creation of a central bank to issue currency and manage the economy[21] and the pursuit of a policy of Lebanese neutrality in inter-Arab conflicts.

To implement these economic and social policies, the president, who did not have a political base, relied on the military. He appointed officers to sensitive positions in state apparatuses such as the Internal Security Forces, the Sûreté Générale, and the National Police. Shehab also appointed technocrats rather than political lackeys to key positions in the civil service and used the intelligence apparatus of the army known as the Deuxième Bureau to keep tabs on political activity in the country. Shehab's intention seems to have been to use the efficiency of the armed services to support his civic-minded projects, to create an arrangement in which the army "would back his efforts strongly but behind the scenes,"[22] or, less charitably, in which "military authority concealed itself behind the official façade of civilian government and democratic institutions."[23] The opposition in Lebanon, as well as many supportive army officers, believed that Shehab was implementing a new direction toward military involvement in the Lebanese state, following in the footsteps of other regional leaders such as Nasser of Egypt. This interference, or alleged interference, of the army became infamous in the 1960s and 1970s. It is difficult to ascertain the actual extent of the army's intervention in politics under Shehab, especially as it was forbidden at the time to print news about military activities. There were rumors, however, of military pressures on administrative appointments at all levels, of officers receiving kickbacks for influencing budgetary decisions, and of widespread influence peddling: "Opponents of the regime claimed that good connections with the army would help one to obtain a license, settle a dispute, or to obtain a government job."[24]

The Deuxième Bureau bore the brunt of the accusations of political interference under the regimes of Fouad Shehab and his successor, Charles Helou. The bureau was created in November 1945 when Shehab, then the commander in chief of the LAF, asked Émile Boustani to establish a new apparatus for military intelligence. Boustani's mission consisted of two main tasks: gathering information needed for the security of the country and analyzing and cross-referencing this information to verify the credibility of its sources. The organization was also given a broad mandate to conduct counterespionage operations, prevent sabotage by enemy states, and investigate internal threats ranging from revolutionaries to riots, smuggling, and thievery. Despite this extensive mandate, the budget and manpower of the new organization were at first rather small. It grew somewhat during the following decade, but by and large the Deuxième Bureau remained unknown and unregulated, reporting only to Shehab. When Shehab ascended to the presidency, this relationship took on a new aspect, and from that time on it became a custom in Lebanese politics: the head of the Deuxième Bureau would answer directly to the president. This special relationship gave the head of the bureau prerogatives that he was not officially entitled to by law.[25]

It was only after 1964 and the election of Charles Helou, however, that the Deuxième Bureau became a real "parallel power." The duality of the two powers, military and civil, reached its apogee between 1965 and 1968, declined after the legislative elections of 1968, and disappeared after the election of Suleiman Frangieh to the presidency in 1970.[26] The abuses committed by the Deuxième Bureau lent an unfortunate tarnish to the reputation of Fouad Shehab and to his progressive school of thought, which came to be known as "Shehabism." Without these excesses—and even to some extent despite these excesses—the period from 1958 to 1970 could be considered the golden age of Lebanon.[27]

General Michel Aoun

Michel Aoun was born in February 1935 in a Christian-Shi'i area of the southern suburbs of Beirut. He entered the military academy in 1955 and, like his predecessor Shehab, climbed quickly through the ranks after his graduation. From 1978 to 1980, Aoun studied at the École de Guerre (Higher War School) in Paris, France. In August 1982, in the wake of the Israeli invasion of that year, Aoun was appointed as chief of staff of the LAF and was charged with upholding security in Beirut as the Israelis retreated. In June 1984, he was appointed by President Amin Gemayel as the commander in chief of the army.[28]

Lebanese columnist Sarkis Naoum has suggested that Michel Aoun's political thinking began to crystallize in 1969, the date of the first military clash between the LAF and the Palestinian fedayeen. The Palestinian presence in Lebanese territory became Aoun's obsession and regaining the Lebanese state's sovereignty and domination over its territory his primary goal.[29] In the 1970s, Aoun began to participate in meetings with the Tanzim, a nationalist group organized by right-wing Christians and headed by George Adwan. This collaboration lasted until October 1990, when Aoun was forced out of the presidential palace by the Syrian and Lebanese forces.

Aoun believed that the army could not be composed of multiple confessions and still remain united; he also believed that the unification of the army would lead to a unification of the country as a whole (and not the other way around). When he became commander in chief of the LAF, Aoun established relations with handpicked junior officers and convinced them that political decisions could not be allowed to create discord within the army. He positioned the army against the various militias, including the Maronite Lebanese Forces, emphasizing the struggle between the state and those individuals who would act outside it. Aoun apparently never considered that disunity might escalate within the army itself. He placed the blame for any dissension or military weakness at the feet of the conflicted civilian leadership, and thus he came to believe that these problems could be solved with him at the helm of the government.[30]

Upon his appointment as the head of the interim government in September 1988, Aoun began to reorganize the army and to implement his vision of Lebanon. An army booklet published in 1988 and titled *The Army Remains the Solution* is indicative of the institutionalization of Aoun's views at the height of the civil war. According to Israeli scholar Oren Barak, this pamphlet very succinctly declared that "in developing states the role of the army is to fill the void when the political rule collapses."[31] It indicated that any weakness or discord in the LAF had been instigated by external pressures: the insidious influence of traditional leaders, or foreign armies, especially the Israeli and Syrian armies and militias. The pamphlet also described the latter as a "great obstacle" to the resurrection of the Lebanese state and contended that they must be disbanded. The solution that was offered to Lebanon's predicament was either a military government or military political leadership. To implement this solution, Aoun and his colleagues envisaged suspending the constitution and declaring a state of emergency. When a return to normalcy was ensured, the army would retreat to the barracks, new elections would be held, and a new government would be elected. According to Barak, the period for military rule was envisioned to not exceed three years, so as to avoid alienating the population and to prevent power from corrupting the officer corps.[32]

As Barak has pointed out, this reorganization shows that Aoun's actions in the period between 1988 and 1990 were premeditated. Aoun intentionally planned to exert military control over the state. This politicization of the army was unprecedented in Lebanese history. Even under Shehab, the army had accepted civilian rule, but Aoun sought to do away with traditional politics and the consociational system of elite accommodation. In an interview with French journalist Frederic Domont, Aoun said that he always "aspired to the symbiosis of the couple, army-nation."[33] In his view, the army is not only a vital function of the state, but also coextensive with the most enduring aspects of the national polity:

> [The army is] the backbone of national cohesion. It is the cement of society, as it sensitizes its soldiers to respect the State and its institutions, and executes the orders of the government. Its role was primordial in the defense of the survival of the State. The army is the institution that defends the country and protects the Lebanese citizens. It does not enter into internal conflicts and is the guarantee of the unity of the country. It must remain neutral in internal conflict. . . . [I]t is not there to make or break regimes. On the contrary it is guarantor of the democratic system. . . . It must be at the service of the citizen and

defend values such as freedom of expression or freedom of opinion. It is not an oppressing army, rather a benevolent army.[34]

This statement is an expression of the patriarchal vision that Aoun had of the relationship between the army and society. It also gives us an insight into Aoun's vision of himself as the benevolent dictator in Lebanon.[35] Sarkis Naoum suggests that Aoun had "a great project for Lebanon . . . a national project . . . [a vision of] a liberated nation." Naoum also contends that this liberty was more important to Aoun than was power.[36] These ideals, however, proved hollow, as Aoun did not live up to them. He did not hesitate to act unilaterally and to participate in the destruction of Lebanon during the course of his failed attempt to ascend to the presidency.

The Influence of the Military During Émile Lahoud's Regime

After the Ta'if Agreement and the end of the civil war, the LAF was reunified under the leadership of a new commander in chief, Émile Lahoud. During this era, the army acquired a renewed corporatist spirit, and the ranks of the officers became more confessionally balanced. In addition, however, by the late 1990s the army's manpower had quadrupled, expanding to include nearly one-tenth of the total Lebanese workforce.[37] In such an environment, the man who controlled the army had a greatly expanded capacity to influence public opinion and to start a political program.

After being elevated to the presidency (see the discussion in chapter 4), Émile Lahoud expressed an intention to imitate his predecessor, Fouad Shehab. While taking the oath of office, he delivered a speech focusing on the need to eliminate corruption and to replace clientelism with transparency. Although the hopes of the Lebanese were galvanized by what became known as the "Oath-Taking Speech," Lahoud's actual practices of governance were quickly criticized. Among his strongest opponents were the followers of Rafiq Hariri, whose neoliberal economic perspectives were at best tangential to Lahoud's vision of an authoritarian and proactive state. Indeed, the arrival of Lahoud to the presidency in 1998 signaled a renewed military involvement in Lebanese politics. One notable aspect of this change was the unprecedented intrusion of the military into the work of the judiciary. The nomination of Nasri Lahoud, Émile's brother, to the position of president of the Higher Judiciary Council illustrates not only the nepotism of President Lahoud but also the militarization of the judiciary system. Nasri Lahoud retired in November 2002, but his role as the president's man in the judiciary was taken up by public prosecutor Adnan Addoum. This militarization of Lebanese state institutions and the slide toward authoritarianism received the benediction of Syria.

Mohsen Dalloul, a former Shi'i minister and parliamentarian, has written a book highly critical of the Lahoud regime, in which he contends that the military institution took the opportunity during Lahoud's presidency to create a shadow power that threatened civil authority.[38] Dalloul asserts that the military attempted to strangle the political life of the country, disrupting the potential for consociational cooperation in order to create a need for expanded military authority. Furthermore, Dalloul accuses the regime of using intelligence and security agencies to curtail political dissent, and he contends that these agencies controlled a number of cabinet ministers. In short, he suggests that the executive obeyed the instructions of the military, rather than the other way around. Dalloul also criticizes the personalized rule under Lahoud—claiming that the president's personal interests governed his political life—and posits that under Lahoud, the confessional system became more important than the rule of law. I believe this assessment of Lahoud's term to be accurate, despite the fact that this militarization has been denied by some. One of my informants, a retired general, contended that the military actually lost influence under Lahoud.[39] However, as the following sections indicate, the reality of the regime belies such denials.

Arrests, Torture, and Military Trials

The Lahoud presidency became known for the arbitrary arrest of human rights activists, students, and opposing politicians, leading many to fear that Lebanon was becoming more like Syria in its lack of respect for human rights. For example, in April 2000, a demonstration of students belonging to the Free Patriotic Movement was violently broken up by riot police. Several students were seriously injured, while others were detained, tried, and sentenced by the military court, when legally they should have been tried by ordinary criminal courts. Likewise in September 2000, Kamal al-Batal, the director of a Lebanese human rights organization called Mirsad, was arraigned before a military court. In August 2003, a lawyer and human rights defender named Muhammad al-Mugraby was held arbitrarily in detention.[40] In September 2003, Samira Trad, the director of the Frontiers Center for the defense of the rights of refugees in Lebanon, was detained overnight and charged with "harming the honor and integrity of the Lebanese state."[41] A particularly disturbing incident occurred in August 2001, when about two hundred teenagers and students belonging to the Free Patriotic Movement and the Lebanese Forces were arrested.[42] The crisis escalated when demonstrators gathered in front of the Justice Palace in Beirut, demanding the release of their comrades, only to be confronted by security forces in plainclothes who beat up and arrested the demonstrators.

In the wake of these events, and under advisement from Syria, Lahoud pressured the parliament to amend a law that it had adopted only a few weeks earlier. Ironically, the original law was designed to protect citizens from arbitrary detentions by the military. The amended code of criminal proceedings, however, gave absolute power to public prosecutors at the expense of civil liberties and human rights. Public prosecutor Adnan Addoum, in particular, was granted a free hand to detain anyone of whom the Syrian regime and its Lebanese allies disapproved. The amendments authorized Addoum to launch an investigation without filing charges, which created the possibility of turning a simple legal process into a political weapon. In addition, the law provided the judiciary with the right to detain suspects without trial for periods of up to a year if they were believed to be a threat to state security.[43] The impact of these legal changes was far reaching; Bassem Saba', a former information minister, called the amendments a prelude to "the militarization of the judiciary," while Maronite parliamentarian Boutros Harb declared that the country was already run by a "totalitarian military regime."[44]

Arbitrary arrests and prosecutions in military courts for vaguely worded offenses like "threatening national security" or "insulting a friendly state" were not the only hallmarks of the coercive influence of the security and military apparatuses in the affairs of the Lebanese state. Even more alarmingly, these arrests were often accompanied by the torture of detainees. According to Amnesty International, members of the Lebanese Forces who were arrested in August 2001 were reported to have been "subjected to torture and ill-treatment and held incommunicado for prolonged periods during pre-trial detention." The accused "were reportedly denied contact with their families, lawyers or doctors and were allegedly subjected to beatings, sleep deprivation, [and] listening to voices of people being tortured."[45] In a separate case, twenty-three Islamist activists accused of clashing with Lebanese security forces were held in detention from early 2000 to the end of Lahoud's term in 2007. According to Amnesty International, "They were subjected to torture by electric shocks and to verbal abuse, denigration of their religious beliefs, deprivation from prayers, [and] threats of sexual abuse of their female relatives," among other offenses.[46]

Furthermore, it is likely that the abuses under the Lahoud regime did not stop at torture. Ramzi Irani, the leader of the Lebanese Forces at the Lebanese University, was found dead in the trunk of his car in May 2002 after having disappeared two weeks earlier. The Lebanese government—or, more accurately, the Lebanese security apparatuses—are suspected of being behind his death. Irani had organized demonstrations against Syria's continued presence in Lebanon only a few weeks before his disappearance; he had long been under the surveillance of the security apparatuses and was frequently called in for questioning. According to the Lebanese Forces, the autopsy on Irani showed that he had died of two bullet wounds. It is likely that he was killed to prevent him from identifying his abductors.[47]

Edouard Belloncle, a former adviser to the European Commission in Lebanon on prison, police, and the justice sector, has argued that the actions of the Lebanese military and security forces during Lahoud's regime were the result of a too close affiliation with the Syrian military presence, leading to an "internalization" or "neighborhood effect" in which the Lebanese institutions came to adopt Syrian methods. Further-more, he suggests that during the course of this affiliation, the Lebanese military and security apparatuses became a tool of Syrian control of Leb-anese political life.[48] In addition to the flouting of some citizens' basic human rights, many other individuals suspected of being against Syria were kept under surveillance and their right to privacy violated. Even for-mer prime minister Rafiq Hariri did not escape this illegal surveillance; the report of UN investigator Detlev Mehlis verified that Hariri's phone was tapped for five years prior to his assassination. Mehlis suggested that transcripts of Hariri's phone conversations were made by Colonel Ghas-san Tufayli, the head of a military intelligence surveillance unit, who then delivered them to General Raymond Azar (the military intelligence chief), General Jamil Sayyed (the head of the Sûreté Générale), President Émile Lahoud, and Rustum Gahzaleh (the head of the Syrian military intelligence in Lebanon).[49]

The Proliferation of Security Apparatuses

There are a number of different security apparatuses in Lebanon whose functions overlap. The role of these institutions, and their involvement in political affairs, was greatly expanded during the Lahoud regime. The Direction Générale de la Sûreté de l'État (General Directory for State Safety, known as the Sûreté Générale) has been in existence since 1945, making it one of the longest-standing coercive apparatuses of the state. Although traditionally controlled by a Maronite, it came to be headed by Jamil Sayyed, a Shi'i, in the postwar period. Its main mission has always been the surveillance of Lebanese political life. Many would argue, how-ever, that in the Lahoud regime the Sûreté Générale became the principal instrument of Syrian manipulation and censorship in Lebanon.[50] Sayyed was one of the most influential and most feared intelligence officers of the Second Republic. Before taking the helm of the Sûreté Générale, he had served in the army for thirty years. He was the chief of security for President Elias Hrawi from 1989 to 1990, played a key role in reor-ganizing the army's intelligence services from 1990 to 1992, and was appointed deputy chief of military intelligence in 1992, before ultimately being chosen by the newly elected Lahoud to head the Sûreté Générale in 1998. It was rumored that Sayyed was planning to run for parliament in 2005 and that he was being groomed by Syria to take over Nabih Berri's seat as Speaker of the house. Sayyed was also suspected of direct or indirect involvement in Rafiq Hariri's assassination. In April 2005, on the eve of the Syrian withdrawal from Lebanon, Sayyed submitted his resignation. He was arrested along with three other security chiefs in September 2005, but was later released in April 2009 on the grounds that there was insufficient evidence to indict him and his colleagues.

Another of the Lebanese security apparatuses is the Direction Générale de la Sécurité de l'État (General Directorate for State Security, also known as the Sécurité Générale—and not to be confused with the Sûreté Générale). This institution was created in the early 1990s at the request of Nabih Berri and was given the mission of protecting politicians and magistrates. After the Sûreté Générale came under Shi'i control, the Sécurité Générale came under Christian control. From 1998 to 2005, it was headed by Brigadier General Edward Mansour, the brother of the parliamentarian and minister Albert Mansour. Edward Mansour was one of the four generals dismissed from their positions and imprisoned in May 2005 on suspicion of being accessories in the assassination of Rafiq Hariri. He was released in April 2009.

The Deuxième Bureau (military intelligence) has come to be the largest of the state security apparatuses, employing an estimated thirty-five thousand personnel in the 1990s.[51] Its main mission is to keep track of political opposition to the regime. As was noted above in the discussion of Shehabism, the Deuxième Bureau has a long history of political involvement. During the Lahoud regime, it was directed by Raymond Azar, and it is through the agents of this intelligence service that the surveillance of Rafiq Hariri and other politicians was carried out. Azar was dismissed from office in May 2005 and was one of the four security chiefs arrested in association with the Hariri assassination and then released in 2009, following a ruling by the Netherlands-based Special Tribunal for Lebanon.

Other important security apparatuses in Lebanon include the Internal Security Force and the Presidential Guard. The former is the local police force. Under Syrian tutelage, its primary mission of maintaining order was taken over by the army, leaving the purpose of the organization somewhat in doubt. From 2004 to 2005, the Internal Security Force was directed by Ali al-Hajj, a Sunni originally from northern Lebanon. Al-Hajj was originally the commander of the Prime Ministerial Guards Brigade (yet another security apparatus), but he was promoted by the president to head of the Internal Security Force when his charge, Prime Minister Hariri, discovered that al-Hajj was also working for Syrian intelligence. Al-Hajj was another of the security chiefs arrested and released for suspicion in the murder of Rafiq Hariri.

The Presidential Guard is an elite unit composed of four thousand soldiers. During Lahoud's regime, it was placed under the direction of Lahoud's close aide-de-camp, Brigadier General Mustafa Hamdan. Because of his close relationship to Lahoud, Hamdan was one of the most influential people in Lebanon in the period between 1998 and 2005. Hamdan is also the nephew of Ibrahim Qoleilat, who headed the Sunni militia known as the Mourabitoun at the beginning of the civil war. It was rumored that Hamdan reactivated the Mourabitoun during Lahoud's term and used it as an intelligence service in Beirut. Hamdan turned himself in for questioning after Hariri's assassination—and like the other security chiefs he was later released without charges.

In summary, the army and the state security apparatuses became important players on the Lebanese political scene during Lahoud's regime. Beyond their more subterranean role in gathering information and applying coercion, violence, and political pressure, these institutions also played a more outspoken role in the elections, pushing vocally for the regime's candidates. It seemed as though Lebanon in the Lahoud era was getting closer to the paradigm of the *Mukhabarat* state (security state) that is characteristic of many other Arab regimes. During the prewar period, Lebanon was regarded as the only democracy in the Arab world, in contrast to the rule of military juntas that was standard throughout the region. After the Ta'if Agreement, Lebanon has retained some of the trappings of democracy, including a relatively free press, which will be discussed at the end of this chapter. Nevertheless, after Lahoud's accession to the presidency, Lebanon came to adopt a greater amount of institutionalized militarism than at any other point in its history. The larger trajectory of Arab politics in the region, and in particular the Syrian influence on the Lebanese Army and intelligence services, was the greatest contributor to this change.

The Role of the Clergy in Politics

The clergy has always had an impact on political life in Lebanon owing to the confessional nature of the country's political allegiances. Indeed, the concept of national citizenship has not taken hold in Lebanon in the same way that it has in Western nations. Loyalty to the family, the clan, and the religious community overrides other allegiances, leaving little room for national patriotism. In addition, the legislative system gives religious leaders a formal influence on the personal lives of the Lebanese: the Personal Status Code is still confessionalized, meaning that religious courts are the only authority that rules on issues of marriage, divorce, and inheritance. The constitutional amendment of 1990, which initiated the Second Republic, further increased the role of the clergy in political life by establishing the Constitutional Council that officially solicits the input of religious leaders on topics such as personal status, religious practices, and education.[52]

There are a number of complex historical and sociological factors that have contributed to the political influence of particular religious leaders at various times in Lebanese history. This influence cannot be explained merely by individual charisma or by the basic fact of sectarianism in Lebanon. In this section, I propose that there is a marked difference between, on the one hand, traditional Lebanese religious leaders who have for one reason or another become politicized and, on the other hand, politicians who cultivate a religious persona. The former kind of religious leader tends to emerge only when there is a void, a lack of unifying political leadership in the community. The presence of strong political elites generally shuts traditional religious leaders out of the government, confining their importance to the religious sphere, where for the most part they are happy to remain.[53] Unlike charismatic political leaders, who may emerge from "below," traditional religious leaders usually belong to an established, elite power structure, and they are generally uninterested in taking on the risks of political office. Indeed, many of them exhibit a notable lack of charismatic leadership.[54] In Lebanese history, most religious leaders have been of this type and have become politically outspoken only in times when they felt that their community was under attack. My interpretation concurs with and completes the arguments of German scholar Thomas Scheffler, who suggests that religious leaders in Lebanon were forced to cultivate a more militant mood among their disciples as a response to the deteriorating security conditions in the country during the civil war.[55] I suggest that established religious elites welcomed neither the militarization nor the politicization of their creeds.

In postwar Lebanon, however, we see the emergence of a new type of leader who is first and foremost a politician, but who wears religious garb and claims religious capital. Such leaders borrow the symbolism of religion in order to legitimate and implement their political objectives. These leaders tend to be charismatic personalities, not traditional clerics committed to a time-honored religious hierarchy. As outlined in chapter 3, Hassan Nasrallah epitomizes this new trend.

The Shiʻi Community and Musa al-Sadr

The first community to experience politicized leadership was the Shiʻi community under Musa al-Sadr. Until the 1960s, Shiʻa lived under the rule of several political families, most of whom were important landowners such as the Asʻad of southern Lebanon or the Hamadeh of the Beqaa region. These families monopolized political representation and were completely disassociated from the masses. This state of affairs changed after the 1959 arrival in Lebanon of Musa al-Sadr.

In every discussion of al-Sadr, a recurrent theme seems to appear: his physical beauty, charm and charisma, piercing green eyes, Christ-like face and tall stature, enigmatic smile, and elegance and good manners.[56] American scholar Augustus Richard Norton describes him as one of the most intriguing personalities of the twentieth-century Middle East, pointing out that al-Sadr's admirers describe him as a tolerant, sensitive man, a visionary with a finely honed political instinct, while his detractors speak of him as a cunning manipulator and a political chameleon.[57] Some of the Christians who were the first to compare him to Christ ended up calling him the "Rasputin of Lebanon."[58] In all accounts, though, one unavoidable factor is al-Sadr's charisma or magnetism.

Al-Sadr's work was the political and social awakening of the Shiʻi community. In 1963, barely four years after his arrival, he obtained Lebanese citizenship and a diplomatic passport by presidential decree from Fouad Shehab. This speedy naturalization is an indication of al-Sadr's rapidly acquired influence in Lebanese political circles. For most people, Lebanese citizenship is almost impossible to acquire: it can be ensured only through the Lebanese citizenship of one's father. Birth on Lebanese soil, residency, and even marriage to a Lebanese woman[59] do not guarantee citizenship. Therefore, such a mark of favor indicates al-Sadr's close relationship with the Shehab regime, a relationship that led some to see him as a vassal of Shehab. In addition, al-Sadr's work on behalf of his community brought him into contact with other Lebanese religious figures. He often visited the Maronite patriarch and collaborated with progressive Christian groups. He also spoke in Christian churches. An iconic photograph of the time shows al-Sadr speaking in front of the altar at the Saint Louis the Capuchin Church in Beirut in February 1975; the crucified Christ on the altar behind the turbaned Shiʻi cleric struck the imagination of observers who were awed by this example of intersectarian cooperation and tolerance.

In the course of a single decade, al-Sadr was able to politically mobilize the Shiʻi masses by orienting their socioeconomic aspirations along the lines of sectarian identity. He would not have been able to do so were it not for the gulf between the traditional political leadership and the ordinary believer. This gap had led to a quasi void of political representation, as the majority of Shiʻa did not truly feel that their political leaders spoke for their interests. Al-Sadr rapidly filled this void and simultaneously managed to play a religious leadership role that was accepted and recognized as such by the other religious communities. However, although al-Sadr wanted to be perceived as primarily a religious leader, his conception of the role of the cleric was quite different from the vision of traditionalist ulama (religious scholars). Al-Sadr believed that the clerics should strive to reform society and engage in politics.

In 1967 al-Sadr managed to obtain parliamentary approval for the creation of the Supreme Shi'i Council. Prior to that date, the Shi'i community was subject to the edicts of the Sunni Islamic courts. For al-Sadr, the formation of this new council was a way to put an end to the discrimination suffered by the Shi'i community and to give his community an official voice to express its political and social demands. The Supreme Shi'i Council elected al-Sadr as its chairman, first for a six-year term and then for an extended twenty-five-year period, ending in 1993. For al-Sadr, the Shi'i council became a personal platform, establishing him as a prominent voice of the Shi'i community.

In 1974 al-Sadr joined with the Greek Catholic bishop Grégoire Haddad to create the Movement of the Deprived. The organization was populist in spirit and was initially cross-confessional; it employed the rhetoric of third worldism that was popular at the time among the Shi'i intelligentsia and among leftist Lebanese more generally. A year later, in July 1975, al-Sadr was obliged to acknowledge the existence of a military branch of his organization, which came to be known by its acronym, AMAL.[60]

In 1978 al-Sadr disappeared during a trip to Libya. It is suspected that he was assassinated by Qaddafi's regime.[61] Nonetheless, as his followers refused to accept his demise, he officially remained as the nominal president of the Supreme Shi'i Council until the end of his term in 1993. Al-Sadr's second in command, Muhammad Mahdi Shams al-Din, took over his duties as "acting chairman." Shams al-Din was a scholar who lacked the charisma and political influence of his predecessor. Under his watch, the political mantle of al-Sadr was inherited by AMAL, and especially by its new strongman, Nabih Berri. With al-Sadr missing in action, Berri was able to capitalize on his legacy and control Shi'i political representation until the mid-1980s.

The appearance of Hezbollah in the mid-1980s posed a challenge to Berri's position as the leader of the Shi'i community. First, Ayatollah Muhammad Hussein Fadlallah, who is often associated with Hezbollah and is thought by some to be the organization's spiritual leader (despite his vigorous denials), tried to vie with Berri for his position as the Shi'i spokesman. Fadlallah managed to appeal to a large audience on the national and international levels, but his influence did not continue into the 1990s. At that time, the arrival of the charismatic Sayyed Nasrallah as the general secretariat of Hezbollah further weakened Berri's position. Nasrallah is not a religious leader, but his religious garb, language, and personality appeal to a large faction of the Shi'a. Today the Shi'i community in Lebanon is divided among two factions, one represented by Berri, the other by Nasrallah, both claiming Musa al-Sadr's political legacy. Al-Sadr's social legacy, on the other hand, is continued primarily by his family through the Imam Sadr Foundation.

The Sunnis and Mufti Hassan Khaled

The office of the mufti of Lebanon is a Sunni institution that was created under the French Mandate.[62] The mufti is the religious leader of all Sunni Muslims in Lebanon and their representative before the official authorities. In 1955, under Mufti Muhammad Alaya, a new Supreme Legal Council was created to organize Sunni religious and internal affairs. The council is headed by the mufti but also includes important Sunni political leaders. As a result, political and ideological rivalries within the Sunni community tend to play out around membership in this council. Most important is the office of the mufti itself, which is a lifetime appointment.[63]

In 1966 a heated election resulted in a previously unknown religious leader, Hassan Khaled, ascending to the office of the mufti. Khaled was chosen over a more popular, Nasserist religious leader, Shafiq Yamut, who was not approved of by conservative Sunni politicians. As a relatively unknown religious leader, Khaled was seen as someone who would not threaten the power of the political leaders. After the breakdown of the Lebanese state, Khaled chose to play an increasingly political role in his community. The mufti's office, and sometimes his private residence, became the focal point of Sunni political decisions. Khaled would gather Sunni leaders for weekly discussions of political affairs, a practice that proved irritating to the various combatants in the war. Mufti Khaled paid for this political involvement with his life: he was assassinated in May 1989, allegedly by Syrian operatives. Others who attended his weekly meetings were also assassinated during the last years of the civil war.[64]

Thomas Scheffler suggests that the Israeli invasion of 1982, the departure of the PLO from Lebanon, and the elimination of the Sunni Mourabitoun militia left a void in the Sunni community. In his view, this void was partially filled by the ascendancy of armed movements headed by local religious leaders, such as the Tawhid movement in Tripoli headed by Sheikh Said Sha'ban.[65] However, I contend that this void in official Sunni leadership in the 1980s was largely filled by Hassan Khaled and his independent deliberations. After Khaled's murder, the office of the mufti was filled on a temporary basis by his deputy Muhammad Qabbani, a scholarly and rather lackluster cleric. By that time, however, a new star had begun to emerge in the Sunni Lebanese political scene. With the advent of Rafiq Hariri in the early 1990s, the need for a politicized Sunni religious leader was diminished. Hariri's ascent to the newly strengthened position of prime minister at the end of the civil war ensured that the Sunni community would have a strong voice in the government. Qabbani's eventual election as the new mufti of Lebanon did not occur until 1996, and by that time the office of the mufti had lost the importance that Hassan Khaled had given to it. Rafiq Hariri was well settled as leader of the Sunni community and had no fear of competition from the mufti.

The Druze and the Sheikh al-'Aql

The Druze are an esoteric sect found primarily in Lebanon, Syria, and present-day Israel, with a large diaspora in North America. The Druze faith began as a movement in Ismaili Shi'ism that was mainly influenced by Greek philosophy, especially Neoplatonic thought, and by Gnosticism. It was founded in Egypt in the eleventh century by Hamza bin Ali, an Ismaili mystic of Persian origin. The religious practices of the Druze are something of a mystery—even to the large majority of the Druze. The Druze community is divided between a minority group called the 'Uqqal (the sages/initiated), who spend their life studying scriptures, and a majority group called the Juhhal (the "ignorant of the faith").[66]

The total number of Druze in the world is estimated at one million; the oldest and until recently the most concentrated Druze population is found in Lebanon.[67] Since the eleventh century, the religious authority of the Druze has been held by the 'Uqqal. Around 250 years ago, however, a functional division began to crystallize in Lebanon between this spiritual leadership and a separate class of political representatives. Judith Harik, an American scholar in Lebanon, points out that the political representatives of the Druze "are not drawn from the highest religious rank, nor are they especially known for their wisdom or piety. Instead, they are chosen from a *subordinate* class of holy men."[68]

In contrast to other communities in Lebanon, then, Druze religious leaders have not played a direct role in politics. The Druze traditionally had two religious leaders representing the two main factions of the community, the Jumblatis and the Yazbakis. In 1962, as part of his reform plans, President Shehab tried to reach out to the Druze community by promulgating new laws to regularize its religious organization and formalize its place in the Lebanese confessional system. These laws officially enshrined the practice of nominating for life two spiritual leaders, and they created the Druze Community Council, charged with administering the temporal and financial affairs of the community. In regard to political leadership, the representation of the Druze has over the past fifty years centered mainly on two members of the Jumblat family—Kamal Jumblat, until his assassination in 1977, followed by his son, Walid Jumblat.

An interesting political skirmish occurred among the Druze starting in 1991. Before his death, Sheikh al-'Aql Muhammad Abou-Shaqra appointed a deputy, Bahjat Ghaith, as a temporary replacement.[69] This assignment created a controversy in the community, as most Druze expressed their unhappiness with Ghaith's appointment and the manner in which it was made. The problem was as much political as it was religious. Ghaith was a wealthy man who had made his money in the Persian Gulf. Upon his return to Lebanon in 1980, he funded a hospital established by Abou-Shaqra, as well as additional charitable causes. His deputization was met with opposition because he was not considered a spiritual leader and because many felt that his appointment circumvented the electoral mechanisms established by the 1962 laws. In addition, Ghaith made it clear that he did not see his appointment as a temporary or humble role; indeed, strengthened by his international network and his excellent relations with Syrian leaders, Ghaith expressed a desire to expand the political import of his new office.[70] In particular, he saw it as an opportunity to oppose the political centrality of Walid Jumblat, and he made use of the monthly Druze Community Council newspaper, *al-Duha*, to mark his opposition.[71]

An agreement between Walid Jumblat and Talal Arslan (the leader of the Yazbaki faction) stipulated that Ghaith would remain as interim *sheikh al-ʿaql* until a permanent candidate was found for the position. Ghaith continued his attacks on Jumblat, however, and eventually Jumblat decided to counter with the resources of the Lebanese state. In 1995 he persuaded Rafiq Hariri to name Jumblat's ally Salman Abdul Khaliq as the new interim *sheikh al-ʿaql*. Ghaith, however, refused to leave his seat on the Druze Community Council and appealed to the State Council, arguing that his removal was unconstitutional. In January 1996, he lost the appeal. Nevertheless, Ghaith was reinstated in 1998, under pressure from Talal Arslan and other Druze religious leaders who resented Hariri's interference. Then, in 2000, Syria exerted influence to push a bill through the parliament mandating that the *sheikh al-ʿaql* be appointed by a parliamentary committee. The Druze parliamentarians who were declared responsible for the appointment under the new legislation all had close political ties to Syria. Jumblat, in response, managed to push through a revision of the 1962 law, which had stipulated life tenure for the spiritual leader, in order to reduce the term of the *sheikh al-ʿaql* to ten years. This change meant that Ghaith's term was due to expire in 2001; however, through further political manipulation, Ghaith managed to survive in the position until October 2006, when he was finally replaced by Naʿim Hassan, a Jumblat ally.

The Maronite Community and Its Patriarch

The Maronites are a large Eastern Christian denomination that has been affiliated with the Catholic Church in Rome since the sixteenth century. The Maronite Church was established on the banks of the Orontes River in present-day Syria in the sixth century and traces its authority and origins to the apostle Peter. The Maronites are led by a patriarch, who has historically acted as both a spiritual guide and a political figurehead.[72]

Since the nineteenth century, Maronite patriarchs have occupied an increasingly important political role, defining the stance of the community toward other sectarian groups and acting as public spokesmen.

In the early twentieth century, Patriarch Elias Howayek played a crucial role in the creation of Greater Lebanon. He reconciled opposing Maronite groups and formed alliances with the other Lebanese communities. Howayek was asked to lead the Lebanese delegation to the Versailles Peace Conference in 1919, where he presented the assembly with a memorandum expressing Lebanon's right to independence and its ability to exercise national sovereignty. The claims of the patriarch were recognized and approved by the French government, which then created "Greater Lebanon" in 1920. Upon his return to Lebanon, Howayek was welcomed like a chief of state. His successor, Patriarch Antoun 'Arida, did not play as important of a political role during his tenure (1932–55), though he was notably active in supporting the movement for Lebanese independence in 1943 and in opposing (unsuccessfully) Lebanon's participation as a founding member of the Arab League in 1944. After 'Arida's death in 1955, the Vatican appointed the archbishop of Tyre, Boulos (Paul) Meouchi, as the new patriarch, bypassing the customary election process in which the leader is selected by the Maronite bishops. Patriarch Meouchi was a strong leader who became deeply involved in Lebanese political life. In 1965 he was the first Maronite religious leader to become a cardinal of the Roman Catholic Church. He was also the first Maronite patriarch to visit the United States, and the highlight of his six-week tour in the country was a meeting with President John F. Kennedy in August 1962. The patriarch handed President Kennedy a memorandum outlining the Maronite Church's position on important issues, and he appealed to the president to work for a solution to the Palestinian problem that would not be at Lebanon's expense.[73] The patriarch was concerned that the Palestinians would be naturalized in Lebanon. He believed this action would disrupt the demographic balance of the country, as most Palestinian refugees were Sunni.

Meouchi was a force for unity in Lebanon. In addition to maintaining the solidarity of the Maronite community, he reached out to Muslim leaders and cultivated the respect of the Muslim masses. He received

Muslim politicians at Bkerke (the seat of the Maronite patriarch) and paid visits to the Sunni areas of Beirut. Furthermore, his speeches stressed Lebanon's "Arab character," the importance of integration into the Arab-Muslim environment, and the need to maintain friendly relations with Arab countries. Meouchi shocked the Maronite community in March 1957 when he encouraged a visiting delegation of high-ranking Sunni clerics to conduct their evening prayers in Bkerke's main reception hall.

Whereas other Maronite patriarchs have generally avoided criticizing the various ruling regimes in Lebanon, out of fear of having their criticism mistaken for an attack on the Lebanese state, Patriarch Meouchi gave a freer expression to his political views and in particular to his disapproval of (Maronite) President Chamoun's hard-line policies during the 1958 crisis. This position did not endear him to the more conservative members of his community, but Meouchi believed that the political leadership was pursuing a course that would be disastrous for the stability of the region, and he did his best to turn his flock away from such a dangerous course. Unfortunately, the majority of Maronites did not heed his call, and the community largely supported Chamoun's illegal bid for reelection. It led to the results that Meouchi feared: a mini–civil war in 1958 that presaged the conflict that would rock Lebanon from 1975 to 1990. The 1958 crisis ended with a compromise that saw the elevation of General Shehab to the presidency. Meouchi initially supported Shehab, but the patriarch did not hesitate to turn against this president as well when the first signs of military interference in politics started to appear.[74]

After Patriarch Meouchi's death in February 1975, Monsignor Pierre Antoine Khuraish was elected as patriarch by the Maronite Synod. Khuraish was considered to be a compromise candidate, and during the escalating civil war he tried to live up to this reputation by resisting calls to violence and promoting equilibrium in the Maronite community. The expanding Christian militias, however, reproached the patriarch for his unwillingness to take their side, which led to a decline in the patriarch's influence. More strident voices in the Maronite community, such as those of the monks of the Lebanese Maronite Order, came to overshadow the patriarch. The leaders of the Lebanese Maronite Order, Charbel Qassis (1980–86) and Boulos Naaman (1986–92), viewed their institution as the defender of their community.[75] The monks saw involvement in politics as their moral obligation, and in collaboration with Bashir Gemayel's Lebanese Forces militia, they pursued the idea of a Maronite state based on the model of Israel.[76] The militant stance of the monastic order effectively undermined the authority of the patriarch and made possible the growing militarism of the Maronite community as a whole.[77] In 1986 Khuraish resigned from his position under pressure from the Apostolic See in Rome, while the Maronite monks went on to participate in the civil war to defend the Christian identity of Lebanon.

After Khuraish's resignation, Mar Nasrallah Boutros Sfeir was elected as the new patriarch. Sfeir was also a compromise candidate, known at the time for his moderate and noninterventionist political views. He was a scholarly and uncharismatic leader who played only a minor political role in the 1980s. Sfeir's lack of enthusiasm for violence and his continuation of policies of compromise and reconciliation were a disappointment to the monastic orders and the Christian militias, who had hoped that a more sympathetic patriarch would be elected after Khuraish was forced out of the position. Sfeir, however, remained largely silent on political issues until close to the end of the civil war, when he finally spoke out to oppose Michel Aoun's interim government and its vendetta against Syria. Sfeir played a central role in encouraging the Maronite delegates to accept the formula for peace that was proposed at Ta'if. This position was not without consequences, however, as it enraged many of Aoun's supporters. In November 1989, a group of young Maronite partisans attacked Bkerke and assaulted the patriarch, forcing him to kiss a picture of Aoun.

With the Christian leadership in disarray at the end of the war, it appears that Sfeir felt obligated to take on a broader role in the political life of his community. Furthermore, as the Ta'if Agreement's provisions for the withdrawal of Syrian troops failed to materialize, he became an increasingly vocal critic of the new regime. Sfeir endorsed the Christian boycott of the 1992 legislative elections (discussed in chapter 2). His growing prestige as a leader of the Christian community was reinforced in 1994, when he was promoted to the rank of cardinal by Pope John Paul II, and again in 1997, when the pope paid a visit to Sfeir in

Lebanon. These events helped to eradicate any loss of face that remained from Sfeir's 1989 humiliation at the hands of Aoun's supporters.

In the late 1990s, Syria began to indicate a desire for reconciliation with the patriarch and an increased dialogue with Christians in general. Sfeir, frustrated with the continuing entrenchment of Syrian influence in Lebanese political life, largely rebuked these overtures. From 2000 to 2005, he headed a movement that demanded a more accurate application of the Ta'if Agreement and the withdrawal of Syrian troops from Lebanon, going so far as to describe the Lebanese government as a "creature of Syria."[78]

In February 2001, Sfeir went on a six-week pastoral visit to the United States and Canada. Sfeir gave a speech at a congressional luncheon in Washington, DC, in which he openly criticized the Syrian presence in Lebanon and stated that "Lebanon lacks sovereignty, independence, and freedom in its decision-making."[79] Upon his return to Lebanon, Patriarch Sfeir was greeted by a gathering of an estimated one hundred thousand believers, a scene that recalled Patriarch Howayek's triumphant return from the Versailles Peace Conference in 1919. This popular reception consecrated Sfeir's status as a politico-religious leader. After his North American trip and exuberant return, pressure was exerted on the patriarch by President Lahoud and other Syrian allies to accompany the pope on his four-day visit to Syria in May 2001. Sfeir rejected these pressures and refused to go to Damascus. In the following years, Sfeir was involved in a number of anti-Syria organizations, including the Qornet Shehwan Gathering and the Democratic Forum, and he worked to maintain the unity of the opposition in the face of Syria's divide-and-conquer tactics.[80] During the time of the Syrian domination of Lebanese political life, the previously quiet Patriarch Sfeir emerged as a voice of the Christian community, using his office as a platform to organize opposition that could not otherwise be voiced. Patriarch Sfeir resigned from his position in June 2010, but his resignation was accepted by Pope Benedict XVI only in February 2011.[81]

The changes in the role of the patriarch were the result of a long process that took place in Lebanon during and after the civil war: the disintegration of the Christian political leadership led the religious authority to assume a more prominent political role. The prominence of Rafiq Hariri did not allow for such an increased role for the Sunni mufti, while the *sheikh al-'aql* was embroiled in a dispute with Walid Jumblat. In the Shi'i community, the division of roles between politicians and religious leaders continued until 1992, despite the increased activism of religious leaders such as Ayatollah Muhammad Hussein Fadlallah. The election of Sayyed Hassan Nasrallah as secretary-general of Hezbollah shows that, like the Maronites in the civil war, a community that feels threatened will lean toward trusting warrior-priests with their safety.

The Influence of the Press

A third group of unelected or strategic elites in Lebanon is the journalists of the printed press and broadcast media. Their importance as trendsetters in politics is indicated by the price that they paid in blood after the 2005 Syrian withdrawal: Samir Qassir and Gebran Tueni, two prominent journalists at the daily paper *an-Nahar,* were assassinated, while May Chidiac, an anchorwoman with the Lebanese Broadcasting Company, lost both a leg and an arm in another attempted assassination. These attacks were, by all indications, reprisals for these journalists' role in voicing opposition that contributed to the Syrian withdrawal.

The Printed Press

The Lebanese press is known throughout the Arab world for its relative diversity and freedom. The first Lebanese newspaper began weekly publication in January 1858. In the following decade, journalists would see both times of freedom and times of increased restriction, and this pattern seems to have continued into the present day. When the Ottoman Empire increased its restrictions on the press in 1864, many Lebanese journalists fled to Egypt, where they helped to found some of the most important newspapers of the country. *Al-Ahram,* currently the leading newspaper in Egypt, is one of the publications started by those early Lebanese expatriates.

Through the period of the French Mandate and the First Republic, Lebanese journalism continued to flourish while negotiating a regular cycle of greater or lesser governmental restrictions. In 1962 a systematic press law was adopted. It established that there would be a minimum of formal censorship to prevent abuses, including a prohibition on material clearly intended to inflame sectarian hatred, but that the press's freedom of expression would generally be respected. Nonetheless, journalists since that time have often found it prudent to impose an additional degree of self-censorship, in order to avoid conflict and to prevent a return to greater state control of the press. This tendency toward self-censorship, along with the widespread editorial prejudice exerted by the papers' owners and the occasionally heavy-handed implementation of the state's censorship laws, has made the freedom of the press both a conflicted and a treasured aspect of Lebanese society.[82]

In a 2006 review, Lebanese scholar Ziad Majed found that there were twelve national daily newspapers in Lebanon with an estimated distribution of eighty thousand copies per day. Ten of them were published in Arabic and two in Western languages: the *Daily Star* in English and *L'Orient le Jour* in French.[83] The most important of the Lebanese newspapers is *an-Nahar,* which has been continuously owned by the same family, the Tuenis, since its establishment in August 1933. *An-Nahar* is widely respected for the fact that it employs journalists of diverse backgrounds and political views, and it maintains the highest circulation of any Lebanese paper. Indeed, whereas certain daily newspapers belong to politicians, such as *al-Mustaqbal,* established by Rafiq Hariri in the 1990s, or have an editorial policy close to a political vision, the main daily, *an-Nahar,* has preserved its reputation as a serious and objective newspaper.

The work of *an-Nahar*'s respected columnist Samir Qassir is an outstanding example of the independent spirit that remains alive in the Lebanese press. Qassir was a staunch critic of Syrian involvement in Lebanon, and he had been calling for Syrian withdrawal since the year 2000. Qassir himself was born in Lebanon to a Palestinian father and a Syrian mother. He received a doctorate in history from the Sorbonne in 1990 and then came back to Lebanon, where he worked both as a lecturer at the University of St. Joseph and as a columnist.[84]

It would be too simple to classify Qassir's views as "anti-Syria"; his arguments were much more nuanced. He was adamant in his call for

Lebanese freedom from Syrian interference, but he also cared greatly about Syria and its people. Qassir called for a change in the way the Syrian regime dealt with its own people, raising questions of democracy, freedom of the press, and the freeing of political prisoners in Syria.[85] He lauded the work of Syrian intellectuals who were pursuing these same goals and stood by those who were being assaulted or imprisoned.[86] Qassir saluted the Petition of the Thousand (intellectuals) that was presented to the Syrian Parliament in March 2004, seeing in it a revival of Syrian civil society and an opportunity for Syrian reform that would not give the appearance of a concession to American threats.[87] Nevertheless, he criticized the Syrian opposition for failing to raise the Lebanon question, a silence that Qassir found rather strange.[88]

Qassir was also critical of the pro-Syria regime in Lebanon, and especially of its militarization under Lahoud. He excoriated the security apparatuses for "censoring ballet shows, banning movies and periodicals, surveillance of opposition members, spying on student organizations and penetrating civil society organizations, influencing the media and other flawed actions often found in the semi-military regimes of the third world."[89] He did not hesitate to mention the close relationship between the security apparatuses and Lahoud, thereby holding the president responsible for this state of affairs.[90] Among Qassir's other pet peeves were the absence of the reform promised by Lahoud in his "Oath-Taking Speech,"[91] the decline of the freedom of the press under the regime,[92] and Lahoud's efforts to extend his term beyond the constitutional limit.[93]

This review of Qassir's ideas about the Lebanese and Syrian regimes indicates how much of a gadfly this courageous journalist had been. It is no wonder that the intelligence services chose to dispose of him. Qassir had been under surveillance since at least 2001. At that time, in the wake of a series of scathing articles critical of the Syrians and pro-Syria Lebanese intelligence operatives, agents of those same security apparatuses tailed him, harassed his neighbors, and had his passport confiscated on spurious grounds.[94]

Robert Fisk, of the British daily the *Independent*, has called Qassir "one of Lebanon's most prominent journalists and one of the most vociferous and bravest critics of the Syrian regime."[95] Adam Schatz of the *Nation* described Qassir as "an unflagging advocate of democracy, an opponent of Arab dictatorships and of Western double standards, a champion of Palestinian rights who was also a scathing critic of anti-Semitism."[96] In 2004 two volumes collecting Qassir's editorials were published by Dar an-Nahar, the newspaper's publishing house. The first, *Dimuqratiyat Suria wa istiqlal Lubnan* (The Democratization of Syria and the Independence of Lebanon), contains essays that discuss Syria and its relationship with Lebanon, while the second, *ʿAskar ʿala meen?* (The Military Against Whom?), contains essays that examine the pro-Syria military regime that emerged under Émile Lahoud.

Gebran Tueni, the second of the murdered *an-Nahar* journalists, was the paper's editor in chief. He was born into a family of intellectuals and carried the name of his grandfather, who founded *an-Nahar* in 1933. His father, Ghassan, was a well-respected journalist and a former representative of Lebanon at the United Nations, while his late mother, Nadia, is known as one of the greatest Lebanese poets of the twentieth century.[97] In the year 2000, after a distinguished career in Lebanese journalism, Tueni inherited the responsibilities of the newspaper that his grandfather had founded. He became the publisher, chairman of the board, general manager, and one of the editorialists of *an-Nahar*.

In March 2000, in an open letter to then heir apparent Bashar al-Assad of Syria, Gebran Tueni broke a standing taboo in Lebanese politics by making a vocal criticism of Syria. While hailing Bashar al-Assad as the "representative of a new young and progressive generation" in Syria, Tueni's letter politely expressed a desire for the full implementation of the Ta'if Agreement and the withdrawal of Syrian forces from Lebanon.[98] This letter created ripples within Lebanese society and paved the way for other critiques, including a similar declaration by the Maronite bishops in September 2000. Asked about Syria and its relations with Lebanon after this open letter, Tueni said that speaking out about the problem was a first step toward finding a solution.

Tueni ran in the May 2005 legislative elections and won a seat as the Greek Orthodox representative of Beirut. He would not, however, have the opportunity to pursue his ideals in the parliament, as he was assassinated just a few months later. Upon his death, his father, Ghassan

Tueni, took over his parliamentary seat as a placeholder, and in the 2009 elections his daughter Nayla Tueni ran for and won the same seat. Thus, despite his affirmation to the contrary, part of Gebran Tueni's legacy was to show that politics in Lebanon is still a family affair.

The Broadcast Media

One reason for the relatively large margin of autonomy enjoyed by the printed press in Lebanon is that its impact is generally limited to the privileged domain of the intelligentsia. The broadcast media, on the other hand, are more accessible to the masses and receive a correspondingly greater degree of political oversight. In fact, the majority of television stations in Lebanon are privately owned by politicians. In the period from 1989 to 2005, there were seven such stations, each of which provided a different perspective on politics. Although this description might give the impression of a healthy diversity emerging from freedom of expression, any such impression would be an illusion. The majority of these television stations were completely controlled by political actors. The station called Future TV belongs to the Hariri family, the National Broadcasting Network (NBN) belongs to Nabih Berri, and the Lebanese Broadcasting Company International (LBCI) is run by a coalition of Christian businessmen that includes parliamentarians and cabinet ministers. Murr TV, which existed until 2002,[99] was rather obviously controlled by Michel Murr's brother Gabriel. The station called New TV (al-Jadeed) belongs to a Sunni businessman named Tahseen Khayat, who is a close ally of the former president Émile Lahoud. Two other stations are explicitly controlled by religious groups: al-Manar is owned and operated by Hezbollah, while Télé Lumière is controlled by the Maronite patriarchate.

During the civil war, broadcast media proliferated in Lebanon. Television and radio were seen by many different actors as important weapons in the struggle for political hegemony, as well as a means of communicating the instructions of sectarian leaders to their followers.[100] After the war, however, this proliferation of private stations was quickly reined in under a strict state licensing system. Organizing the broadcast media became a government priority as a way to control any opposition to the regime. In October 1994, the government issued the new Audiovisual Law, which created a National Council for Audiovisual Media to oversee the airwaves. The law also divided television and radio programs into four categories. Category 1, which allowed the broadcasting of news and political programs, was the most important. Originally, provisions were made for up to sixty Category 1 television stations. In 1996, however, the number of available Category 1 stations was reduced to four. Licenses were granted to three stations already linked to regime members: Future TV, Murr TV, and LBCI. The fourth license was granted to a station that did not yet exist: Nabih Berri's NBN. Some people began to ironically refer to this station as the "Nabih Berri Network" or the "No Broadcasting Network"—though NBN did eventually start broadcasting, in August 1997. The audiovisual cabinet also deigned to grant three exceptional licenses, which led to the establishment of Télé Lumière, al-Manar, and New TV. Hence, as Marwan Kraidy notes, "this media monopoly suggests that the Lebanese regime indeed [had] become an oligarchy where political power and media ownership converge."[101]

Each of the seven stations that were granted a license had been careful to rein in any semblance of criticism of government policies. In the following years, however, with the breakdown of the taboo against criticizing Syria, the Christian-run station LBCI started to become more critical of the regime. The station came to express a measure of the Christian anger that was pervasive in Lebanon in the post-Ta'if era. This dissatisfaction was often apparent in political talk shows, and especially in the ones conducted by May Chidiac. A prominent journalist with LBCI, Chidiac had studied journalism at the Lebanese University, and during the civil war worked for the "Voice of Lebanon," one of the illegally operating Christian radio stations. In September 2005, after conducting a morning interview with another journalist from *an-Nahar* regarding Hariri's assassination and the pressures on the Syrian regime by the international community, Chidiac returned to her car. A bomb had been placed under the driver's seat, and the explosion almost took her life.

In her autobiography, *Le ciel m'attendra* (Heaven Will Wait), Chidiac says that as the star journalist of LBCI she had been placed along with two dozen other people on a black list that was circulating among the secret services of Western embassies. The list contained the names of politicians, journalists, and leading members of civil society who were critical of Syria's influence in Lebanon. After Rafiq Hariri's assassination, Chidiac says that she was advised by Pierre Daher, the chief executive officer of LBCI, not to be emotional on television, to be less vehement, and not to repeat anti-Syria slogans. Nonetheless, she believed that she was safe because she was a journalist and because women had never been deliberately targeted during the civil war.[102]

Chidiac lost her left arm and her left leg in the assassination attempt.[103] In May 2006, UNESCO awarded her the World Press Freedom Prize in recognition of her courage in defending and promoting freedom of the press. She was also honored with the Courage in Journalism Award, given by the International Women's Media Foundation, and was inducted into the Legion of Honor by French president Jacques Chirac. She went back to LBCI ten months after the murder attempt to star in a new prime-time program titled *With Audacity*. Chidiac resigned from the media in February 2009, and there were rumors that she was considering running for parliament in the next elections. She ultimately chose not to run for office, however, electing instead to retreat from the political scene.[104]

Although journalists such as Chidiac can at times be elected or appointed to the political system, their primary role as opinion makers marks them as members of the strategic elite in Lebanon. During the period of Syrian influence, journalists were among the first to cross the so-called red lines imposed by the security agencies, and they were thereby pivotal in opening the national debate that led to the Syrian withdrawal in 2005. Although the immediate cause of the 2005 Cedar Revolution was the assassination of Rafiq Hariri, the groundwork of this revolution was at least five years in the making. The committed work of Lebanese journalists is a large part of what made it happen.

In the post-Syrian period, journalists have become polarized between supporters of the government and supporters of the Hezbollah-led opposition. This polarization reflects the divisions in society and is indicative of the pervasive influence of politics on the media. Although the media in Lebanon are free and diverse compared to other Arab countries, they are fractured along political and sectarian lines. In addition, self-censorship persists for many journalists, who confront legal and bureaucratic hurdles, including tough press laws that stipulate jail time and heavy fines for libel and other press offenses. It is still common for journalists to be prosecuted under criminal defamation laws in Lebanon, and a number of my informants spoke of the continuation of a tense in-the-field relationship between journalists and the army and security services.[105]

Conclusion

In the wake of the Ta'if Agreement, new players, including military commanders and religious leaders, were able to emerge onto the political scene and then officially enter the consociational system. At the same time, other strategic elites were permitted or compelled to apply their influence outside of the formal political system. During Lahoud's regime, military officers showed an increasing willingness to embrace Syria's presence and to adopt Syrian patterns of behavior, especially authoritarian rule. Meanwhile, a new kind of religious leader came to prominence in Lebanon, combining political and spiritual roles, and some traditional religious leaders felt called to increase their political activism. Journalists began to rebel against a tradition of self-censorship, seizing in particular on the change of leadership in Syria as an opportunity to shape national discourse and call for a Syrian withdrawal from Lebanon.

6

Emerging Elites and the Absence of Women from Politics

In this chapter I argue that in the postwar era, there has been little change in the behavior of Lebanese political elites. This stagnation is largely owing to the fact that there was no fundamental regime change after the Ta'if Agreement, but only a modification of the power-sharing structure.[1] Despite the rebalancing of power between Muslims and Christians, the central characteristics of the prewar Lebanese political system are still intact. The continuation of long-standing power-sharing traditions has led to a return to prewar political behavior, including a resurgence of the clientelism that was noted in the Lebanon of the 1960s and 1970s.[2] Patron-client relations have remained central to the political culture and continue to determine how elites are recruited into the political system. In addition, women's participation in Lebanese politics remains symbolic at best. Despite the events of 2005, these ingrained features of the Lebanese political scene have proved extremely resistant to change.

By 2005 the Lebanese system was becoming increasingly closed to the entry of new elites. Nevertheless, it was still possible to identify a certain number of new actors who were emerging on the political scene. Their entrance into the political system through election or appointment depended on several variables, the most important of which—in addition to the obligatory Syrian approval—is clientelistic relations with members of the established elite. It has become clear that no new political elites could emerge and persist in the political system without the support of a strong incumbent elite member. The 2005 elections, which took place after the Syrian withdrawal and resulted in a high rate of political turnover, verified that political inheritance and clientelism are firmly entrenched in Lebanon. Of particular note in this election was Saad Hariri's ascension to his slain father's parliamentary seat and the election of numerous unknown politicians based on little more than political loyalty to the Hariri and Aoun parliamentary blocs. This chapter will show how clientelism shapes elite recruitment in the postwar period. Findings from my fieldwork in Lebanon will be presented in the form of a typology of emerging elites; seven "ideal types" of emerging elites are identified, with examples, in order to map the characteristics of the current political scene. The reasons for the glaring absence of women from the political elite are also analyzed.

Clientelism in Lebanon

The Lebanese political system can be described as "neopatrimonial." As developed by Erdmann and Engel, this concept describes a system that is composed of clientelism and bureaucratic rationality in equal parts. Whereas a purely patrimonial or clientelistic system makes no distinction between personal and political relationships, a neopatrimonial system circumscribes the personal client-patron relationship within a framework of modern bureaucracy: "Neopatrimonial rule takes place within the framework of, and with the claim to, legal-rational bureaucracy or 'modern' stateness. Formal structures and rules do exist, although in practice the separation of the private and public spheres is not always observed."[3]

It is my contention that political clientelism in Lebanon is still based around a *personal relationship* between a political *za'im* and his protégé. It is the propensity of important politicians to adopt and bring into the elite clients who have social, political, or financial capital that the established politician might lack. The exchange is generally not a tenuous one in which the client provides electoral support in exchange for the patron's attention. Rather, it is a more concrete relationship in which the client receives access to state resources in exchange for supporting the patron's power within the parliament. The political boss marshals his [*sic*] political weight and social prestige on behalf of the client, helping the client to find his footing in the political world, and the client often reciprocates by lending local affiliation, youth, expertise, or advanced education to the patron's cause.[4] The patron expects obedience from the client and help in fulfilling the patron's political agenda. Following Erdmann and Engel, we can make an important distinction between this concrete, personalized clientelism and the more amorphous concept of "patronage" as that term is usually understood. Whereas clientelism indicates a personal relationship between elites, the latter term is used more broadly—and more innocuously—to describe support that a politician lends to constituents: "[Patronage] is the politically motivated distribution of 'favours' not to individuals but essentially to groups. . . . The difference between clientelism and patronage is essentially a distinction between the recipients, between 'individual' (land, office, services) and 'collective' benefits (e.g. roads, schools)."[5]

The phenomenon of clientelism has been pervasive in Lebanese politics since the time of the country's independence. Analysts of prewar Lebanon have shown that the patron-client relationship is a long-established model, not only in politics narrowly conceived but throughout Lebanese social and economic life. Lebanese sociologist Samir Khalaf, for example, pointed out that the clientelistic system developed out of long-standing ties of family and creed and that the basis of patronage remained personal and tightly circumscribed. In supporting a political leader, the clients have long been understood as pledging their allegiance to a person and not to a program.[6] Clientelism was thus expected within the prewar political system, and it was customary for a political boss to retain power by promoting new candidates to the elite, thereby obtaining their loyalty.[7] An ambitious young man with symbolic capital could attach himself to one of the political bosses and could hope in return for a nomination to a cabinet position. An exemplary case of such arrangements was seen in 1970 when Sa'ib Salam, an important Sunni leader from Beirut, formed an extraparliamentary government of young technocrats. The oldest member of that cabinet was forty-five, while Salam was sixty-five. The younger technocrats were recruited as clients by the leading political bosses under Salam, though many of them were later abandoned when political expediency demanded that the bosses distance themselves from the new cabinet. This example shows the precarious role of the client in the patron-client relationship.

British scholar Michael Johnson has argued that the clientelist system in Lebanon partly broke down at the beginning of the civil war, in the period between 1970 and 1976, but then quickly reasserted itself in a different form in the period between 1976 and 1985.[8] I agree with Johnson that the clientelist system was in operation during most of the civil war, and I want to further suggest that it continued unabated in the Second Lebanese Republic (albeit in a slightly different form). During the civil war, the system split into two parallel structures: one set of client-patron relationships existed within the state itself, while a second set of relationships operated within the militia system. This situation mirrored the larger fragmentation of power in Lebanon, with civilian administrative structures operating in parallel with the increasingly autonomous power of military units. A patronage system developed within the militias as they—or, more precisely, their leaders—began to take on political functions and to provide services that the state was unable to offer.[9]

After the Ta'if Agreement, many of these militia leaders and their clients were absorbed into the Lebanese political system. The militia leaders who refashioned themselves as major politicians reverted to the more classical form of clientelism, and the integration of their expanded networks with the civilian system bloated the state apparatus with numerous minor clients. Former militia leaders were successful in bringing important clients into the executive and sometimes the legislative institutions. In more recent years, clients' entry into the political scene came to take the form of a ministerial portfolio and rarely one of elections—as will be shown below. The notable exception to this rule is to be found in the 2000 parliamentary elections, when Rafiq Hariri managed to bring seventeen relative newcomers into the political elite on his electoral ticket. Despite their status as elected officials, however, my interviews with four of these parliamentarians demonstrated their awareness that their chances of remaining in politics or being reelected without Hariri's backing were almost nonexistent. They expressed their complete dependence on their political patron.

The reliance on clientelism in Lebanon is associated with an absence of political institutions where elites can be formed and recruited, such as elite schools (for example, the École Normale Administrative and the

École Polytechnique in France)[10] or recruitment clubs associated with political parties (for example, the Young Republicans in the United States). The absence of such institutions impels young people who are interested in politics to enter into a clientelistic relationship with a political boss. Although the emerging Lebanese political elite may be highly educated, their degrees do not usually come from local institutions. The name of the American University of Beirut often appears in the biographies of older Sunni elites and the name of St. Joseph University is often associated with older Maronite elites, but these schools were never an important recruiting ground, and today their association with the elite is increasingly tenuous. In regard to political parties, they exist in Lebanon but with a very different character than in Western democracies. Parties were first created in Lebanon in the early twentieth century to give a modern aspect to older political structures that were based on primordial ties of kinship or religion; consequently, the majority of parties have a sectarian character (see the discussion in chapter 3). These political parties continue to act predominantly as an expression of clientelistic relationships, rather than as an alternative to the clientelist model.

In many Western democracies, the development of the political elite could be most effectively pursued by a study of political parties. But in Lebanon, such a study would yield an incomplete and asymmetrical view. The study of the developing Lebanese elite must therefore remain focused on the key figures that dominate political life and the clientelistic networks that they have developed. Such relationships are the only channel for access to the elite that is available to ambitious Lebanese youths. The youths who are entering into such clientelistic relationships today remain preponderantly male, and it is to this issue of gender imbalance that I will turn in the next section.

Women's Absence from the Political Elite: A Result of Patronage

One of the most notable features of the emerging elite in Lebanon is the near absence of women from the political sphere, despite Lebanon's reputation as a relatively modern, Westernized country. The fact that women are acutely underrepresented, not only in the established political elite but also in the emerging elite, is quite remarkable, especially as Lebanese women are highly educated and have been described as more emancipated and more "modern" than women in other Arab countries. This underrepresentation is perhaps not entirely surprising, given the continuing obstacles encountered by women in politics worldwide; however, I will suggest that clientelism in the Lebanese system presents a particularly daunting barrier to women's entry into the political elite.

In his seminal work of 1976, *The Comparative Studies of Political Elites*, Robert Putnam affirmed that women were pervasively underrepresented in the elite.[11] Today, more than three decades later, that situation remains largely unchanged. Women constitute only 15.7 percent of legislators worldwide and only 6.4 percent of legislators in Arab countries.[12] Sheri Kunovich and Pamela Paxton have argued that the visibility and prestige of political positions are the most important reasons for the relative slowness of women's integration into these positions—and that the traditional political elite are the "gatekeepers" of this disparity.[13] Whereas Kunovich and Paxton focus on political parties as the locus of obstacles to women's advancement, in Lebanon the role of gatekeepers is played by the political bosses.

It is notable that although women have had the right to vote in Lebanon since 1957, very few women have been elected to the parliament. The majority of the women who were elected have been relatives of established politicians.[14] Others seemed to arrive in parliament almost by accident: Maha Khoury As'ad received forty-one votes in the boycotted elections of 1992, while Ghinwa Jalloul filled an empty spot on Rafiq Hariri's electoral list in the 2000 elections. Women parliamentarians in Lebanon have never exceeded 4.7 percent of the legislature, and that higher number occurred only recently, after the 2005 legislative elections.[15] In addition, until 2004 no woman had ever been appointed to a ministerial position in Lebanon. Sofia Saadeh explains that such an appointment would be seen as an embarrassment to the traditional sectarian elites who control the offices: "The reason is obvious. The Cabinet has always been formed on the basis of the Grand Coalition between the major sects. It becomes understandable under these conditions that no sect would want to be represented by a woman. A woman at the head of a sect would mean in a traditional set-up the lowering of status of that sect vis-à-vis the other sects headed by male ministers."[16]

When women did finally break the glass ceiling that kept them out of ministerial positions, the pattern of appointing the relatives of established politicians was again observed. Leila al-Solh, nominated in 2004 as minister of industry, is the daughter of Riad al-Solh, one of the founding fathers of the Lebanese state. Nayla Mouawad, who was appointed as a minister for social affairs in 2005, is the widow of President-Elect René Mouawad. Bahia Hariri, appointed in 2008 as minister of education and higher education, is the sister of the assassinated prime minister Rafiq Hariri.[17] This pattern, in which the political success of women is almost always based on their association with a well-known male relative, reaffirms the difficulties facing women in Lebanese politics: it is only when they are seen as standing in for powerful male figures that women come to be seen as acceptable representatives of their communities.

All of the women who have ended up in the Lebanese political elite came from privileged backgrounds. This fact verifies the conclusions of American scholars Joanna Liddle and Elizabeth Michielsens, who have shown that social class has a relatively greater effect on women's access to political power in comparison to its effect on male aspirants. Liddle and Michielsens confirm that radical changes in women's conditions during the past fifty years have had only a limited effect on women's access to political power, except in Scandinavian countries, and they maintain that the women who have been able to get into this traditionally male-only club have done so by leveraging their backgrounds as members of the privileged classes (a concept that includes Bourdieu's categories of cultural and social capital as well as economic wealth).[18] It is not only these few privileged women, however, who express political ambitions in Lebanon. Whereas in the 2009 legislative election, only 12 women out of 587 candidates—a figure that translates into a mere 2 percent—ran for office, figures for municipal elections were more encouraging. Indeed, 353 female candidates ran in the 1998 municipal elections, and about 50 percent of them were elected.[19] In the 2004 municipal elections, 230 women were elected. In recent years, women have been pushing for the adoption of a quota system to guarantee female representation on all municipal councils. The decision was made in the Lebanese cabinet in early 2010 to allocate women a quota of 20 percent. Although the law was not passed on time for implementation, it led to a slight increase (from 2 percent to 4.7 percent) in the number of women in municipal councils.[20]

The desire of women to participate in Lebanese politics should not be surprising, as there is plenty of evidence to indicate that the political ambitions of women are not inherently less developed than they are in men. As Susan Caroll concludes in her study of American women's political ambitions, scholars should examine discrimination and structural limitations, not a perceived lack of ambition, in order to explain women's underrepresentation in high political circles.[21] The structural constraints that keep women out of Lebanese politics include a preference for male candidates in the recruitment process, an exclusion from established power networks, and a lack of role models. Ideology is a factor in all of these constraints: women's socialization into caretaker roles and negative perceptions of their professional capabilities hamper women's ability to overturn long-established arrangements of gendered power. Furthermore, religious teachings that confirm these stereotypical perceptions of women are commonplace in Lebanon.[22]

All of these factors help to ensure that even the most competent of female aspirants will have a difficult time entering the political arena. In addition to these more widespread constraints, however, the reliance on clientelism provides a further obstacle that is more specific to the Lebanese system. The underinstitutionalization of the political party system in Lebanon and the relatively heavy influence of sect, family, and patronage networks are major reasons for the absence of women from public offices. The personal relationships that make up the clientelistic system are more susceptible to the perpetuation of traditional biases and stereotypes than are the more strongly rationalized bureaucratic arrangements of other modern states. In an analysis of clientelistic arrangements in Senegal, Linda Beck has shown that women are constrained from entering the halls of real power in that country because of their limited access to patronage resources and because the nature of their personal relationships with male politicians perpetuates stereotypical assumptions about women's roles and abilities.[23] Likewise, in Lebanon, the clientelistic system helps to ensure that personalized obstacles to women's political success remain in place and that the true extent of their ambitions remains unrealized.

Lebanon has always been perceived as more Westernized than its Arab neighbors. However, the relative coexistence of different sectarian communities, the country's openness to the West, and the appearance of modernity do not mean that Lebanese women have enjoyed more access to decision-making processes than women in other Arab countries. Elite positions continue to be monopolized by men, whether in politics or at the management level in business. In the words of Dima Jamali and her colleagues at the American University of Beirut's school of business, "[Lebanese] women are still regarded as the custodians of cultural values and traditions, their roles are more privatized and their reproductive functions emphasized."[24] In an interview with Agence France-Presse, Lebanese sociologist and feminist activist Fahima Charafeddine explained that "Lebanon suffers from a kind of schizophrenia. . . . There is the façade of modernity which is reflected in appearances—go to any restaurant and the girls dress like they were in Europe." Yet in the context of political rights, "the Lebanese woman is a second-class citizen. . . . The Lebanese woman will be the last to secure her rights in the Arab world."[25] Unfortunately, the trappings of modernity in Lebanon have provided only an illusion of substantive equality.

It remains the case, though, that by 2002 the literacy rate of adult Lebanese women was as high as 81 percent, and women's economic activity rate was 30.3 percent.[26] In addition, by 1997 women represented 51 percent of students in Lebanese universities.[27] Lebanese women had also mobilized during the civil war, participating in female battalions in the Christian militias and providing vital material support for the male fighters in the Shi'i militias.[28] One wonders why they did not trade this war capital for political influence in the postwar period—after the Ta'if Agreement, women who had participated in the war simply went back to civilian life. One also wonders why the voting rights and the civil accomplishments of women in Lebanon have not been further leveraged as means of women's entry into the elite. In summary, this quasi absence of women from the political sphere when they are very present in the public sphere can be attributed to four factors:[29]

1. The patriarchal and personalized structure of the Lebanese political system, which relies heavily on the support of the clan or the confession for election into office, and the entrenched system of clientelism that has continued unabated in the Second Lebanese Republic. Alternative means of entry into the elite, such as a more generalized participation in political parties, are not viable under the current Lebanese system.[30]

2. The traditionally masculine connotations of patron-client relations, as established between ruling and emerging elites. Women are usually reluctant to enter such patronage relationships unless they are an actual relative of a prominent politician, as a woman in a client-patron relationship with a nonrelative will be quickly misconstrued as the mistress of the established politician. The lack of established precedent for client-patron relationships across gender lines thus becomes a self-perpetuating cycle.

3. The contempt that many women have acquired for politics in general, which they consider "polluting" or "dirty." Political dealing is part of the "man's world," and involvement in such activities can have drastic implications for the social perception of a woman's virtue—including her sexual virtue.[31]

4. Women's lack of experience and confidence in the political realm. Rola Ajouz, the only woman in Beirut's 1998 municipal council, said that "Lebanese women have trouble seeing themselves in positions of political power and responsibility." In the same interview, she declared, "We make up 52 percent of the votes, we are quite strong, but we are still unorganized and not united."[32]

In the late 1990s, when the idea of quotas for women's participation in the parliament was being debated in France, Rafiq Hariri floated a similar idea in regard to the Lebanese Parliament. Nothing came of this idea at the time, and it was argued that gender quotas overlapping with existing sectarian quotas would create an extremely unwieldy system.

Today, parliamentarian Setrida Geagea is putting forth the same idea for renewed debate. She argues that increasing female parliamentary representation cannot happen naturally in the Lebanese political context and that forceful measures will be required to institute change: "Though this is not the best way to promote women's rights because it's a kind of segregation towards them, we have to do it this way for perhaps two parliamentary terms so that people can get used to seeing women in government. . . . Then we can progress to a more natural political process."[33]

This approach may well be the best and only way to increase the number of women in Lebanese politics. Lebanon remains a deeply traditional society; the majority of elites whom I interviewed in my fieldwork were reluctant to admit that they would encourage, or even allow, their daughters to enter the political world. Women seem, for the near future at least, relegated to the margins of political life, or to the role of "decorations" of the political arena if they are able to access it.[34] This feature of the Lebanese political system cannot be placed at the door of any particular religious tradition, as both Christian and Muslim women are absent from the halls of power and from the democratic process more broadly. But the laws and norms of personal conduct in Lebanon are based on religion, and each of the various religious confessions is equally rooted in ancient patriarchal systems. The gender inequality enshrined in traditional religious teachings has thus to a large extent inculcated the current attitudes and structural obstacles that hinder women's entry into the political elite. Hisham Sharabi's concept of neopatriarchy seems to best convey the constraints experienced by Lebanese women in regard to political participation—Sharabi describes neopatriarchy as "a new, hybrid sort of society/culture" where traditional mechanisms of male power intertwine with the expansive hegemony of the modern state.[35]

A Typology of Emerging Elites

My fieldwork in Lebanon provided the basis for elaborating seven trajectories used by emerging elites. Five of these trajectories involve variations on the standard strategy of clientelism, that is, of entering into a patronage relationship with an important political leader. I describe these types as the civil society activist, the technocrat, the academic, the local representative, and the heir. The sixth type is constituted of young elites within the primary Lebanese political party, Hezbollah. These individuals are socialized into Hezbollah and rise through the ranks, usually based on their personal abilities and on the alliances that they form within the party. The seventh type, the nationalist militant, is composed of challengers, those individuals who object to politics as usual. The legislative elections of 2005 were a turning point for many such militants, allowing a number of them to more fully enter the system, after which they also seem to have adopted clientelism as a primary strategy.

These ideal types are composites of the biographies of different emerging elites whom I met during my sojourns in Lebanon, and the typology that I have compiled is thus a heuristic device or conceptual model that can help us to map the emerging political scene.[36] Some of the types that I identify have a long history in Lebanon and could be found in the various prewar and wartime cabinets: the heir, for example, has always been a part of the political game, as most Lebanese politicians desire to create *buyutat siyasiyya* (political dynasties).[37] Likewise, when veteran politicians could not reach an agreement in historical Lebanon, technocrats or academics were often recruited into the various ministerial cabinets. Other types that I identify did not exist or were not important in prewar Lebanon: the civil society activist, the nationalist militant, and the local representative are the products of the specific circumstances of postwar politics.

The War Generation and the Emerging Elite

Because of the civil war, legislative elections in Lebanon were postponed for twenty years, from 1972 to 1992. This delay meant that in the 1992 elections, young people were sidelined from political positions, as the older elites who had been leaders during the war lined up for the opportunity to hold office. These older contenders commanded resources, including money, Syrian backing, war credentials, or a combination of these resources. In the following years, however, young people with political ambitions began to achieve an important place in the political constellation. They waited on the fringes of the political elite for the opportunity to officially enter the system by assuming an elected or appointed position. Such positions came to be strongly dependent on clientelistic relations with the older generation, and they could be obtained only with Syrian approval of—or at least indifference to—the candidate. In more recent years (2005–9), the requirement of Syrian approval has become somewhat less than mandatory, even while there has been a gradual decrease in the rate of opportunity for emerging elites.

In his essay "On the Problem of Generations," published in 1928 and inspired by the angst of young Germans in the post–World War I period, Karl Mannheim argued that generations can be defined in terms of a collective response to a traumatic event or catastrophe. He maintained that a trauma will unite a particular cohort of individuals into a self-conscious age stratum.[38] Referring to the work of Mannheim, Robert Putnam later maintained that social conditions and events that take place during the formative years of a person's life (adolescence) leave an indelible mark, whereas these same events have a more ephemeral effect on people who are outside of the critical age category. As Putnam noted, difficulties can arise owing to the fact that states are generally led by people who were socialized two generations prior to the impact of current events.[39] In Lebanon we can identify three different political generations, as defined by their relationship to the traumatic events of the civil war:

1. A generation that was socialized prior to the civil war and later actively participated in the conflict. It is among this generation that we find the older elites who were established in power in the postwar period. The Pan-Arabism of former Egyptian president Gamal Abdel Nasser had a strong effect on this generation, especially its Sunni Muslim members.

2. The "war generation" born from the early 1960s to the mid-1970s and mainly socialized during the civil war. This generation is a cohort that grew up under local militia rule, and its members were generally isolated from each other along sectarian lines.[40] Their identity was forged by separation and strife. In the postwar period, members of the war generation were broadly characterized by disillusionment with

sectarian dogma and a desire to live life to the fullest, which was often manifested in an excess of materialism. The local and international press of the 1990s often touted this generation's excesses, consumerism, and search for meaning.[41]

3. A postwar generation, born in the late 1970s and early 1980s, that has no real memory of the war. In comparison with the war generation, the members of this postwar cohort have displayed a renewed willingness to embrace divisive rhetoric and to threaten to take up arms against their compatriots from other sectarian groups.

It is among the members of the war generation that the currently emerging elite is to be found. While universally marked by the war, their behavior takes a number of different directions as determined by their social and sectarian origins as well as their personal views. These various pathways to power can be summarized in a description of ideal types.

Emerging Elite Type 1: The Civil Society Activist

He is a male, between thirty and forty-five years old, and he comes from a middle- or upper-middle-class family. At least one member of his extended family (an uncle or a cousin) is or has, in the past, been a member of the political elite. The civil society activist is highly educated and frequently holds a PhD in political science or law from a prestigious Western university. He often has a background as an educator or as a member of a similarly liberal profession. He has only tenuous political connections, but he cares passionately about politics. The typical civil society activist has tried to run for parliamentary elections but has failed in his attempt owing to lack of funds or insufficient political support. He often is the leader of a nongovernmental organization (NGO) or civil association, as such groups in Lebanon are beginning to take on a role that is functionally equivalent to the role of Western political parties.[42] To enter the political sphere, the civil society activist allies himself with an important political leader, usually the representative of his religious community. Former minister of interior Ziad Baroud is a perfect representative of this generation.

Ziad Baroud. Born in 1970, Ziad Baroud is a lawyer and a human rights activist. He is a lecturer at St. Joseph University, where he received his master's degree in law in 1992. Since 2001 he has worked as a consultant for the United Nations Development Programme, offering advice on local governance and decentralization. Baroud is a very active member of civil society and has been on the board of several NGOs. He served as secretary-general of the Lebanese Association for Democratic Elections in 2004–5 and was a member of the National Council for a New Electoral Law. He was also a member of the Lebanese Transparency Enhancement Association (La Fasad), and he participated in the Saint Cloud Conference in France at the invitation of the French Foreign Ministry.[43]

In July 2008, Baroud was appointed as the minister of the interior and municipalities in the cabinet under Prime Minister Fouad Siniora. His was one of three appointments made by President Michel Suleiman to constitute the president's bloc following the signing of the Doha Agreement. His post was considered key, as the Interior Ministry was tasked with organizing legislative elections in 2009.

Baroud is probably one of the most popular ministers ever in Lebanon. His appointment lasted until January 2011, when Saad Hariri's government was toppled. He remained as caretaker minister until a new government was formed in June 2011. Despite his popularity, Baroud was not asked to participate in the new cabinet.

Emerging Elite Type 2: The Technocrat

The typical Lebanese technocrat, also a member of the war generation, belongs to the middle class. His parents were civil servants, and it is unlikely that any of his family members have ever been part of the political elite. He has studied finance or engineering in one of the best universities in Europe or North America. The technocrat is perfectly trilingual (Arabic, English, and French) and has worked abroad for five to ten years before returning to Lebanon as an expert or a consultant. He now occupies an important managerial position in the Lebanese state apparatus. He has also established a relationship with his religious community's political leader, and he acts as a consultant in technical affairs for the political leadership. He has tried his own luck in popular elections, but unlike the civil society activist, he chose to run for a municipal position rather than for a seat in parliament. He has so far been unsuccessful on the political stage and has not yet emerged as a public persona.[44]

Emerging Elite Type 3: The Academic

Like the civil society activist and the technocrat, the academic is of a middle-class background and has studied abroad at prestigious universities. He has likely worked in international institutions such as the United Nations, the International Monetary Fund, or the World Bank. He could specialize in one of many fields; he might be a political scientist, an economist, or an engineer. After returning to Lebanon, he taught at a university—usually the oldest and most prestigious, the American University of Beirut—and managed to attract the attention of an established political leader. In all of these ways, the academic might look like a combination of the two previous types, but one important trait distinguishes him from other aspirants to politics: the patron-client relationship that he enters is *not necessarily with the politician who represents his confession or sect.* The profile of the academic among young emerging elites was mainly found in the network around Rafiq Hariri prior to that leader's assassination. Hariri's experience as an international businessman seems to have led him to choose clients first and foremost on the basis of their abilities and without concern for the client's religious affiliation. The academic's relationship with his political patron can therefore take on a somewhat untraditional inflection, being composed of a relatively greater portion of professional respect and a relatively lesser portion of shared ideological or religious background. Basil Fuleihan, who was wounded in the blast that took Hariri's life, is a perfect example of the academic.

Basil Fuleihan. Described as a "scholar, gentleman, and gentle man,"[45] Basil Fuleihan was born in 1963. He received a bachelor's degree from the American University of Beirut (1984), a master's degree from Yale University (1985), and a doctorate in economics from Columbia

University (1990). Fuleihan obtained positions with the International Monetary Fund and the United Nations Development Programme and taught economics at the American University of Beirut. He was elected to the Lebanese Parliament in 2000 on Rafiq Hariri's list and became the minister of the economy and trade.

Fuleihan's wife, Yasma Fuleihan, explains that her husband met Rafiq Hariri in 1994, when Fuleihan was the head of a United Nations development project at the Finance Ministry. "Hariri got to know Basil because of his ability in negotiations, and the way that he could come up with solutions to complicated problems. Hariri found that by talking to Basil he would find that somehow the thing was not a problem, that the solution was there. . . . They started to have a close relationship. Hariri would call him early in the morning and they would talk," she said.[46]

Lebanese American journalist Michael Young described Fuleihan as "an embodiment of the best that Hariri had managed to attract in the early 1990s: the 30-something university graduate, preferably with a degree from a foreign institution, devoted to the art of making money, and crafted in the best ateliers of urban mobility in London, Paris, or New York."[47] Fuleihan's many achievements as the minister of the economy and trade include his lead role in Lebanon's negotiations with the European Union, culminating in the signing of the Euro-Mediterranean Association Agreement in June 2002. He was also the chief architect of Lebanon's economic and financial program, presented to the Paris I and Paris II meetings on February 1, 2001, and November 23, 2002, respectively.[48] During both meetings, the international community endorsed Lebanon's macroeconomic policy, and as a result Lebanon was able to solicit loans in excess of four billion US dollars at favorable market rates. In addition, Fuleihan worked on the development and modernization of the Ministry of the Economy and Trade, by fully computerizing the ministry and linking it to the World Wide Web. He was instrumental in establishing digital databases for the various ministry directorates, including an up-to-date archiving system, and in establishing a document-tracking system within the ministry.

Fuleihan was riding in Rafiq Hariri's motorcade at the time of the prime minister's assassination on February 14, 2005, and he was critically injured in the attack. Ninety-seven percent of his body was covered with third-degree burns. After fighting for his life for more than two months, Basil Fuleihan succumbed to his injuries on April 18, 2005. Many mourned the passing of this dedicated statesman; columnist Peter Grimsditch noted that Fuleihan was "totally devoid of the arrogance that plagues many politicians" and lamented the rarity of his "fluency on matters concerning his ministry."[49]

Emerging Elite Type 4: The Local Representative

Like the previous types of emerging elites, the local representative also has a middle-class background and has studied and worked abroad. In addition to his professional credentials and his innovative civil ideas, he has been able to leverage family connections to assist in his election to a municipal council. His candidacy to municipal elections and his willingness to take a chance on popular support to launch his career—rather than depend on the influence of a political leader—are the main distinguishing factors from other ideal types. The position on the municipal council brought him to the limelight and initiated his political career. The local representative's friendship with one of the leaders of his religious community, or with the son of such a leader, has provided his route into the political elite.

Jean-Louis Qordahi. Jean-Louis Qordahi was born in Jbeil (Byblos) in July 1962, the son of an engineer and entrepreneur who was an active figure in Jbeil's political and cultural life. He graduated with a degree in civil engineering from Switzerland's Polytechnique Lausanne University in 1986 and then returned to Lebanon to work as an entrepreneur and as the chairman and general manager of his family's business. He was elected as president of the Jbeil Municipality in 1998 and in 1999 became the president of the Jbeil Municipalities Union, which brings together the municipalities of Jbeil and its surrounding areas. Qordahi is a founding member of the Louis Qordahi Foundation for the Promotion of Jbeil's Culture and History, a nongovernmental organization named after his father.

Qordahi's national political career was initiated in 2000, when he was appointed as minister of telecommunications, a position that he retained until April 2005. It is widely believed that his position was owing to his relationship with Émile Lahoud. Qordahi ran for the 2005 legislative elections in Jbeil as a representative of the Maronite community, but he received only 10 percent of the vote. He did not run again in 2009, probably because he was aware that he would not be elected. His association with the widely unpopular former president Émile Lahoud and the hold Michel Aoun's list has on the Jbeil district have undoubtedly discouraged him.

Emerging Elite Type 5: The Heir

In contrast to the previous types, the heir is the son of an established member of the elite. He has studied business or management, and he has been prepared as a successor to his father by managing the latter's business, by holding office, or by helping to forge the family's political connections. The heir has excellent relations with regional or international actors, most often in Saudi Arabia, the United States, France, Syria, or a combination of these countries.[50] The heir can be seen as his father's client, one who is particularly favored and encouraged to enter the political sphere. In recent years (2000–2005), heirs who are members of the war generation are beginning to assume positions of responsibility. One example is Elias Murr, the son of former deputy prime minister Michel Murr. Elias Murr came to the head of the Ministry of the Interior starting in 2000, and in 2005 he was appointed as deputy prime minister in the Siniora cabinet. Another example, which merits closer examination, is Saad Hariri, who inherited the mantle of leadership after the assassination of his father in February 2005.

Saadeddine (Saad) Hariri. Born in 1970, Saad is the second son of Rafiq Hariri. He enjoyed a privileged childhood in Saudi Arabia and there initiated a friendship with the Saudi princes. He was educated at Georgetown University, where he received a bachelor's degree in international business in 1992. After graduation, he worked his way up through the ranks in the family's construction, banking, and telecom group, Saudi Oger, ending up as the general manager. He then started diversifying his interests and buying up cell-phone licenses. Saad Hariri was said to have been negotiating the crowning business achievement of his young career, the purchase of Turk Telekom, when his father was assassinated. Very few people in Lebanon knew the emerging businessman at that time, as he had not planned to enter politics.

In the days that followed the assassination, although his brother Baha' became the public face of the family's grief, Saad was the one selected by the Hariri family to take over the political reins, and Baha' chose to continue a career in business. According to Western officials, this decision was heavily influenced by the Saudi royalty, who "already knew Saad from his work in Riyadh and preferred his deferential style over Baha's unpredictable temper."[51] Saad was elected to the parliament in 2005 and in 2009. After the 2005 elections, he expressed a feeling of unpreparedness, and he decided to let his father's old friend and right-hand man Fouad Siniora head the government as prime minister until he could mature politically. After the 2009 elections, he was nominated by the parliamentary majority to head a new government. However, when after nine weeks of negotiations he was unable to form a government, Saad decided to resign as prime minister designate.[52] President Suleiman asked him to continue in his efforts, and in November 2009, a full five months after the elections, Saad was finally able to bring together a new government.[53] He remained Lebanon's prime minister until early in 2011, when Hezbollah and its allies withdrew from the cabinet and caused the administration to collapse. At the time of this writing, it is unclear what the future holds for the heir.

Jeffrey Feltman, the former US ambassador to Lebanon, has declared that "Saad has grown into his job very credibly. . . . I think he's done better than most people thrust into that position could have done. . . . He has had to learn on the job, and I think he has."[54] However, Saad had been under great pressure to deliver, not only from his Lebanese constituency, from the Saudis, and from the White House, but also from his family. There are rumors that his stepmother, Nazik Hariri, has political ambitions and is considering running for office.[55] Saad Hariri's story reveals the centrality of the heir's position in Lebanese politics,[56] but it also showcases the difficulties of the heir's position. Despite the fact that he had accused the Syrian regime of being behind his father's assassination, Saad was forced to make a conciliatory landmark visit to Syria in December 2009. The visit was described by close Hariri ally and former parliamentarian Mustafa Alloush as "very difficult on the personal level" and involving "great sacrifice."[57]

Emerging Elite Type 6: The Hezbollahi

Unlike most of the other political aspirants discussed here, the Hezbollahi comes from the lower middle class or the working class. He has probably studied political science, sociology, history, or philosophy at the Lebanese National University and is politically savvy. He rarely speaks a foreign language, and if he does have some proficiency, he is usually not fluent. He has slowly risen in the ranks of the party, participating in university-level student elections as a Hezbollah representative before being incorporated into the party apparatus after graduation. Throughout his career, he has shown loyalty and commitment to the party's ideology and platform. In this case, it can be argued that class intersects with confessionalism to shape the trajectory of ambitious and talented individuals. Indeed, aspiring Shi'i politicians seem to be the only candidates who are able to overcome their socioeconomic background to enter the political elite.

It is likely that the younger Hezbollahi was first socialized in the al-Mahdi schools run by Hezbollah, then in the Imam al-Mahdi Scouts. The association of the al-Mahdi schools was created in 1993 and includes today fifteen institutions—fourteen in Lebanon and one in Qom, Iran.[58] The objective of these schools is to ensure students are given a high-quality education anchored in Islamic values. By extrapolation, they aim to create an individual able to serve the goals of the Shi'i leadership.[59] The al-Mahdi Scouts were established in 1985 in the southern suburbs of Beirut. As of 1997, they are part of the Lebanese Scouting Federation. According to French scholar Catherine Le Thomas, "The al-Mahdi teams which complement the educational and socialization action of Hezbollah include today about 45,000 youths—boys and girls—from 6 to 18 years old."[60] These scouts are present in most Shi'i villages, and they therefore influence the rural as well as the urban youth. In addition to traditional scouting camps, they promote religious, athletic, and educational activities. The Scouts have also intervened in periods of need, such as during the 2006 summer war, when they were asked by Hezbollah to come to the aid of refugees in southern Lebanon and the Dahiyeh and to help in the cleaning up of rubble.[61]

In an interview with al-Jazeera, al-Mahdi Scouts president Bilal Na'im said that the teenagers are told that "Islamic Resistance is one of the foundations that defends against Israel and that the jihad [struggle] against Israel is one of the concepts of Islam."[62] This statement seems to suggest that these emerging leaders are socialized into Hezbollah's ideology from a young age in the hope that they will grow up and participate in the activities of the party as full members. This notion is corroborated by the unprompted declarations of some of the younger Scouts, who told al-Jazeera that they were already certain of their loyalty to the party.[63] While a bit older than emerging elites socialized in the al-Mahdi Scouts, Ali Fayyad exemplifies the trajectory of the Hezbollahi.

Ali Fayyad. Born in 1962, Ali Fayyad holds a doctorate degree in political sociology from the Lebanese University. His dissertation was published in 2010 under the title "Nazariat al-sulta fi al-fikr al-siyasi al-shi'i al-mu'asir" (Theories of power in contemporary Shi'i political thought). He also specializes in the relations between state and civil society and has authored a book titled *Fragile States: Dilemmas of Stability in Lebanon and the Arab World*. From 1994 to 2009, Fayyad was the director of the Consultative Centre for Studies and Documentation, Hezbollah's main think tank—whose headquarters was completely destroyed by the Israelis during the 2006 war. Fayyad is also a member of Hezbollah's political bureau. He is considered to be an important political ideologue and has represented the organization at international meetings. During the 2006 war, he handled media publicity and international relations for Hezbollah, acting as one of the primary public faces of the party. Fayyad was elected to the Lebanese Parliament in 2009 on Hezbollah's electoral list.

Emerging Elite Type 7: The Nationalist Militant

The nationalist militant is perhaps the most interesting type of emerging political elite in Lebanon in the period under study. He is usually Christian and sympathizes with Michel Aoun's Free Patriotic Movement or with Samir Geagea's Lebanese Forces. The nationalist militant is politically active and participates in demonstrations and sit-ins against the regime. He is dissatisfied with the distribution of power in postwar Lebanon and unhappy with the Christian representation in the political sphere, which he sees as catering to Syrian interests in Lebanon. The nationalist militant rejects Syrian suzerainty over Lebanon and desires that Lebanon become completely free of Syrian influence. He also wants to see the ascension of a new political class that, in his opinion, would be more representative of the Lebanese people's aspirations. He therefore belongs to a group of "rejectionists" who endeavor to radically transform the political system.

As the regional situation changed after the assassination of former prime minister Rafiq Hariri in February 2005 and the withdrawal of Syrian forces in April 2005, the nationalist militant found himself in a unique position as a representative of a large and newly enfranchised segment of Lebanese society. There was a split among members of this group after the 2005 elections, as they aligned themselves in the Lebanese political theater based on their political bosses' positions. Supporters of Samir Geagea's Lebanese Forces became part of the progovernment coalition, while the majority of the supporters of Michel Aoun's Free Patriotic Movement followed their leader in crossing confessional lines to ally themselves with Hezbollah. This striking development, which was formalized in February 2006 with a "Memorandum of Understanding,"[64] can be seen as the result of the convergence of personal interests and pressures of the moment. Hezbollah was seeking national legitimacy beyond its sectarian constituency, while Michel Aoun had returned to Lebanon and was looking for support for his presidential ambitions. This prima facie strange alliance between Hezbollah and the FPM leads to the fact that some of the nationalist militants, associated with the LF, are still perceived as "anti-Syria," while others, associated with the FPM, are seen as newly "pro-Syria."

Not all members of the Aounist FPM followed his lead in allying themselves with Hezbollah—and therefore Syria. In a compilation of several interviews with mostly unnamed former and current Aounists, Lebanese sociologists distinguish two generations of Aounist followers: the "First Awakening Generation," born in the 1960s and early 1970s, who participated in the wars launched by Aoun in the late 1980s, and the "Second Awakening Generation," activists born in the early 1980s, who were inspired by what they perceived as Aoun's message of independence from Syria and were disappointed by the former general's actions upon his return.[65] Indeed, according to these testimonies, the first problem that emerged was Aoun's replacement of the cadres of the FPM who had remained in Lebanon during his years of exile by a group of former exiles. This situation created an insider-outsider dichotomy and led to tensions within the FPM and to the departure of former members from the movement. However, Gebran Basil (Aoun's son-in-law) insists that "those who left the FPM since 1990 left alone and did not take anyone with them."[66] He notes that after the 2005 elections, there were more departures, but dismisses them, affirming that "they are unimportant like their predecessors."[67]

In his sociological study of the FPM, Heiko Wimmen shows that 70 percent of the forty thousand registered members of that organization are under the age of thirty.[68] Wimmen says that "preliminary research into the social composition of the FPM and the Lebanese Forces also suggests that class is a defining difference between the groupings in the Christian camp, adding a dynamic to their frequent clashes."[69] Members of the FPM tend to come from the middle class and tend to be better educated, media savvy, and "endowed with a Westernized veneer." The FPM also has its greatest following in areas where traditional Christian leadership declined during the civil war—in other words, where the notables have lost influence. Wimmen explains the position of the FPM's supporters by linking it to the prevalent clientelism in the Lebanese political system: "The educated middle classes form the backbone of the FPM, whose life chances are hampered by systemic clientelism and sectarian red tape that often extends into the private sector. Barred from many attractive jobs for lack of connections . . . they stand to gain from any change."[70] The fact that FPM members stand to gain from any change in the system helps to explain their alliance with Hezbollah, which had always maintained a reputation of integrity and railed against the corruption and clientelism rife in the political system.

In contrast, members of the LF tend to come from the lower classes and are not as educated. French anthropologist Beltram Dumontier says, "I have encountered more than one family where one brother was with the Aounists and the other with the Lebanese Forces, and always the political preference corresponded to education."[71] It is fascinating that the more educated, middle-class FPM nationalists continue to feel strongly limited by the system, while the more lower-class LF members (whose actual options within the system would appear to be more limited than the opportunities of the FPM members) decide to embrace it. The difference between the two groups can probably be attributed to the political aspirations of the FPM members, who feel more entitled to participate in politics than do the less educated and less affluent LF members.

Ibrahim Kanaan. Born in 1962, Ibrahim Kanaan studied law at the University of St. Joseph in Beirut and then in Paris at the University of Paris II-Assas. As an early supporter of Michel Aoun, he left Lebanon after Aoun's defeat in 1991 and lived in Great Britain, where he was very active in civil society, especially among FPM exiles in Europe. In Great Britain, he established in 1996 an organization called the British-Lebanese Gathering for Freedom in Lebanon. Kanaan was also responsible for organizing a 1996 meeting between Amin Gemayel, Michel Aoun, and Dory Chamoun (the son of Camille Chamoun), in which these leaders called on all Christians in Lebanon to boycott the legislative elections.

Kanaan is very close to Michel Aoun. Although the date of Kanaan's return to Lebanon is unknown, it is probable that he returned with Aoun to help the latter in his political endeavors. It was Aoun himself who announced Kanaan's candidacy for parliament in February 2005. Kanaan ran on Aoun's electoral list and was elected with more than fifty-six thousand votes, the largest number in his electoral district. He was reelected to parliament in June 2009. Kanaan's trajectory shows that many of the Christian rejectionists of the 1990s who initially followed their leaders' call to boycott the settlement achieved at Ta'if have now accepted the rules of the political game and are an integral part of the Lebanese political system. Their acceptance of compromise is perhaps best exemplified in the "understanding" that they have successfully maintained with Hezbollah since February 2006.[72]

Conclusion

The Ta'if Agreement instituted a change *within* the Lebanese regime, not a change *of* the political system. This change resulted in a reinstatement of prewar political behavior in the Second Republic. Clientelism continued unabated, and the new postwar elite imitated the practices of earlier elites in attempting to create political dynasties through policies that reinforced the hold of political bosses and their descendants. The similarities between the prewar and postwar elites are evident: they demonstrate the same attempts to control the political system and the same usage of clientelism with its corollary, corruption. Aspiring elites who wish to enter the system today have to contend with this political legacy and determine how they will negotiate the entrenched system of clientelism.

The majority of elites in power today have been socialized in the prewar era and reproduced the attitudes of previous generations. Although changes might be anticipated with the arrival of the war generation and then the postwar generation into power, it is probable that they too will not attempt to rock the boat. At the time of this writing, the methods by which emerging elites are acceding to power does not appear to presage this kind of change. Emerging elites have mostly adopted a simple and traditional strategy: attaching their political fortunes to an important and established leader. These patron-client relations make emerging elites completely dependent on the political leader who has introduced them into the system. With the exception of the type of emerging elite whom I call the "heir," it is unlikely that these young aspirants will ever become part of the core political elite; many of them will not even succeed in being elected to the parliament. Because their efforts are focused on cultivating the relationship with their patron rather than on building a basis of popular support or gathering financial and symbolic resources, the vast majority of political clients will never be anything other than clients.

One of the most troubling features of the patronage phenomenon is the extension of the patron-client relationship beyond Lebanon's national borders. Indeed, even in the years after the Syrian withdrawal, the majority of Lebanese politicians can still be thought of as either direct or indirect clients of the Syrian regime. This extranational clientelism is a contributor to political stability in Lebanon, but it also creates political stagnation. This situation has grave consequences for the country, as more and more young people are becoming dissatisfied with the system's resistance to change. Those individuals with education and professional skills are emigrating, and the ones who remain are growing restless.

Because there has been no change in the basic arrangement of prewar structures, I have to speculate that the Lebanese political system contains the seeds of its own destruction. The outbreak of a new civil war is not imminent, but such a possibility looms on the horizon if radical changes are not made in the ways that elites are recruited and the political game is played. As long as the confessional formula of power sharing is not abandoned, the door will remain closed against the possibility of new groups, such as women, coming into power. New elites will continue to emerge only through their promotion by an incumbent or by the co-option of dissident leaders into the existing system, reducing the formula of elite circulation to a game of musical chairs.

7

Elite Attitudes on Syria and Sectarianism

With an understanding of the historical trajectory of the Lebanese system and of the characteristics of established and emerging political elites, we can now turn to an examination of the elite discourse on issues of national and strategic interest. In this chapter, I will describe the parameters of recent national debates in Lebanon and identify the most pressing issues for the political future of the country. My fieldwork in Lebanon indicates that the central topics of concern in recent decades can be divided into two main categories: Lebanese-Syrian relations and the deconfessionalization of the political system.

Elite Attitudes Toward Syria

Syria's influence has been both inescapable and controversial since the signing of the Ta'if Agreement in 1989 and the Treaty of Brotherhood and Cooperation in 1991—agreements that the Syrian regime quickly interpreted to further its own interests. By exerting influence over the management of large-scale reconstruction efforts that took place in Lebanon after the war, Syria was able to tie its national economy to Lebanon's. Individual members of the Syrian political and military elite stood to make millions, if not billions, of dollars in personal profit from these endeavors.[1] Such an incentive, combined with the Syrian military presence that had been established in Lebanon since the start of the civil war, led to a postwar situation in which there were serious penalties for any attempt by the Lebanese—and especially by Christians—to shake the

187

Syrian grasp on their country. During this time, the refusal to accept the status quo in the relations between the two countries was mainly limited to the marginalized remnants of the Christian opposition, especially to sympathizers of the exiled general Michel Aoun and to the followers of the jailed leader of the Lebanese Forces, Samir Geagea. The complex economic, political, and military relationship that developed between the two countries in the decade after the Ta'if Agreement has been described by the late Lebanese journalist Samir Qassir as a "Syrian protectorate"— a state of affairs in which the tenuous stability of the Lebanese state was achieved at the cost of obligatory alliances between the Lebanese and Syrian elites.[2]

Syria continued to enforce and legitimize its influence over Lebanese political life throughout the 1990s. During this decade, public discussion of the relationship between the two countries remained taboo. The matter was not a part of the national discourse in either country, nor was it discussed by the press in Lebanon. This situation first began to change in March 2000, when Gebran Tueni published his open letter to Syrian heir Bashar al-Assad. Tueni made it clear that the Lebanese people were questioning the future of their country and the necessity of the Syrian military presence and that they believed Syria had never truly recognized Lebanon's independence. In the name of the Lebanese people, Tueni asked for a redeployment schedule for the Syrian army and for Syria's recognition of Lebanese autonomy in negotiations with Israel.

The discursive opening that Tueni's letter provided was reinforced by two crucial events that occurred in the following months: the Israeli withdrawal from the South of Lebanon in May 2000 and the death of Syrian president Hafez al-Assad in June. The withdrawal of Israeli forces deprived Syria and its allies of a major legitimizing argument for the Syrian presence in Lebanon. With the country no longer occupied, many began to question the basis for Syrian interference in Lebanese affairs. Meanwhile, the death of Hafez al-Assad heralded a period of uncertainty and transition in Syria, which decreased the political and material influence of Syrian political actors in Lebanon. Syria was now ruled by a young and inexperienced leader, who was struggling to maintain a fragile consensus among the various political factions in his country. Further,

Tueni was correct in describing Bashar al-Assad as a relatively progressive voice in Syria: during the first two years of the heir's presidency, he implemented a campaign to promote liberalization and transparency in the Syrian government. This era came to be known as the Damascus Spring, a brief time of political opening in Syria when once-taboo topics such as public freedoms, human rights, and the problem of corruption were openly discussed. This period of opening did not last long—the call for political liberalization and reform was soon replaced by a call for modernization and development, and the democratic aspects of the Damascus Spring were effectively moribund by the end of 2001. Nonetheless, the changes during this time helped to initiate a new era in the relations between Lebanon and Syria, leading to a more open discussion of Lebanon's political future. Since 2000 Lebanese-Syrian relations have become a central topic of Lebanese polemics.

The Declaration of the Maronite Bishops

An important development in the newly emerging discourse came in September 2000, when the Maronite Council of Bishops published a declaration questioning the legitimacy of Lebanon's 2000 legislative elections.[3] The Maronite bishops' declaration maintained that in the decade after the Ta'if Agreement, the Lebanese had begun to lose sovereign control over their nation's governmental institutions. It ascribed the blame for this state of affairs to political corruption and the subversion of the electoral process under the influence of Syrian agents. The bishops argued that certain members of parliament were not truly representative of their electorate, especially since under the Lebanese system the representatives of minority groups are often selected by the majority residing in the area. The bishops also criticized the role of Lebanese and Syrian security agencies in the elections, suggesting that the security agencies were instrumental in coercing local officials to support electoral lists favored by Syria.

Beyond these specific critiques of the electoral process, the bishops' declaration also addressed the broad issues of economics, labor relations, and political corruption. It placed particular emphasis on the favorable access to Lebanese job markets that was at the time allocated to foreign workers (who were mostly Syrian). Syrian workers had been a constant presence in Lebanon prior to the civil war—in the 1972 construction market, for example, Syrians reportedly constituted 90 percent of manual laborers and 70 percent of skilled laborers.[4] Their numbers diminished drastically during the conflict, however, as Syrians were expelled from or fled the country. Some Lebanese interpreted the reappearance of hundreds of thousands of these workers after the end of the war as an "invasion" of the Lebanese job markets by the country's powerful, but economically stagnant, neighbor.[5] The bishops expressed the view that these workers represented a threat to the Lebanese economy and were taking jobs that should be the prerogative of Lebanese citizens. The reality is a bit more complex; Syrian workers were embraced by Lebanese employers because they were willing to work for less pay and because their foreign status resulted in their having fewer social protections. In addition, the evidence seems to indicate that Syrian workers spent the majority of their earnings in Lebanon and that they were instrumental in transferring Lebanese consumption habits to their home country, thereby increasing the demand for Lebanese imports in Syria.[6] The bishops were focused on the wrong group when they criticized the Syrian workers—instead of the Syrian elite—as an economic problem for Lebanon. Nonetheless, the workers were seen as a manifestation of Syrian power in Lebanon. Despite the problematic nature of some of the bishops' arguments, their declaration played a vital role in broadening the public discourse and in propagating the call for a redeployment of Syrian troops.

International Pressure

Another factor that contributed to the expanding discourse on Lebanese-Syrian relations was increasing pressure from the international community. Although the United States had rebuffed Michel Aoun during his 1989 anti-Syria campaigns, the 1990s saw the development of an alliance between right-wing Lebanese Christians and neoconservative scholars and policy makers in the United States. The neoconservatives who took an interest in Lebanon included luminaries such as Richard Perle, former assistant secretary of defense under the Reagan administration;

Jeane Kirkpatrick, former US ambassador to the United Nations; Representative Elliot Engel (D-NY); and others who held positions in the George W. Bush administration. Calling themselves the "Lebanon Study Group," they signed their names in May 2000 to a forty-eight-page document titled "Ending Syria's Occupation of Lebanon: The U.S. Role." The authors of this report were Ziad Abdelnour, a New York financier with dual Lebanese-American citizenship who is the president of a lobbying organization called the United States Committee for a Free Lebanon, and Daniel Pipes, the president of a Philadelphia-based, pro-Israel think tank called the Middle East Forum.[7]

In 2003 Representative Engel introduced the Syria Accountability and Lebanese Sovereignty Restoration Act in the US House of Representatives. The act largely mirrored the language of Abdelnour and Pipes's report, especially in its provisions for sanctions against Syria if the country continued to maintain troops in Lebanon and support the actions of Hezbollah. During the debate on this legislation, the exiled general Michel Aoun was invited to testify before the US Congress. In his testimony, Aoun drew a parallel between the US fight against terrorism and Lebanon's struggle with Syria, which he deemed "a fight for freedom against terrorism and oppression."[8] The bill passed through Congress with minimal opposition and was signed into law by President George W. Bush in December 2003 (US Public Law 108-175). As implemented by the president, the law resulted in a prohibition on the exporting of any US products to Syria, with the exception of food and medicine, and a prohibition on US businesses from investing or operating in Syria.

The success of the Syria Accountability and Lebanese Sovereignty Restoration Act in the United States was followed by the 2004 adoption of United Nations Security Council Resolution 1559, sponsored by the United States and France. This resolution expressed concern for Lebanon's political independence and territorial sovereignty. It called for "all remaining foreign forces to withdraw from Lebanon" and for "the disbanding and disarmament of all Lebanese and non-Lebanese militias" operating in the country.[9] The pro-Syria regime in Lebanon, headed by Émile Lahoud, responded to the UN resolution by stating that the only foreign military presence in Lebanon was the Israeli forces that remained in occupation of the disputed Shebaa Farms region. The Syrian troops, the regime insisted, were allied reinforcements who were present at the request of the Lebanese government. Lebanon also argued that Hezbollah is not a guerrilla organization or militia and that it has no formal security role within the country. Hezbollah was described as a resistance movement directed against Israeli aggression, and according to the Lahoud government, preserving this resistance constituted a Lebanese strategic interest.

In January 2005, after it became apparent that neither the Lebanese nor the Syrian regime was inclined to comply with international pressures, the Security Council issued a new, and more specifically worded, resolution (UNSCR 1583), insisting that the Lebanese government "fully extend and exercise its sole and effective authority throughout the south [of Lebanon], including through the deployment of sufficient numbers of Lebanese armed and security forces, to ensure a calm environment throughout the area . . . and to exert control over the use of force on its territory and from it."[10] The United Nations rejected Lebanon's claim on the Shebaa Farms region as well as the argument that the regime's embrace of Syria and Hezbollah was a matter of national strategic interests.

This international pressure had an effect in Lebanon, lending credence to voices within the country that wanted the Lebanese government to withdraw its support for Hezbollah's operations against Israel. Many Lebanese came to see the Shebaa Farms dispute as a Syrian-backed effort to continue a low-intensity proxy war against the Hebrew state. The Lebanese opposition was further strengthened because of Hezbollah's intermittent inclusion on a number of "terrorist lists," especially in Australia, Canada, and the United Kingdom.[11] Those individuals who were most affected by international pressures were business-oriented Lebanese who were concerned about the country's relationships with donor countries and organizations such as the World Bank and the International Monetary Fund. This locus of opposition largely consolidated around supporters of Rafiq Hariri, who was known for emphasizing international business relations and promoting economic reform in Lebanon (see the more detailed discussion in chapter 4). Hariri was assassinated a couple of weeks after the adoption of UN Security Council Resolution 1583, presumably on the orders of Syrian supporters. Instead of cowing the growing opposition, however, this assassination led to a backlash that completed the process of turning Lebanese public opinion strongly against Syria.

In April 2005, after twenty-nine years on Lebanese soil, the Syrian troops were finally withdrawn. This move did not, however, signal a definitive end to Syrian involvement in the affairs of the Lebanese state. Syria retained a vast patronage network among Lebanese elites, including strong relations with members of the Lebanese security and intelligence apparatuses. It is widely believed that Syria drew on this network over the following years in attempts to destabilize the new status quo in Lebanon (and thereby to show that peace could not be maintained without Syrian arbitration). Syrian involvement was suspected in a series of political assassinations that rocked Lebanon between 2005 and 2008, including the deaths of Samir Qassir, Gebran Tueni, and Pierre Gemayel, among others. By provoking a new round of civil war, the purpose would have been to prove that Lebanon's peace could not survive without the Syrian arbiter.

Researching the Elite Discourse on Bilateral Relations

A cursory glance at the Lebanese political scene might appear to present a simple dichotomy of "pro-Syria" and "anti-Syria" camps. Contrary to expectation, such a straightforward divergence of attitudes was not apparent in the interviews that I conducted between 2001 and 2006 with various members of the Lebanese political elite. The discourse of the elite on the issue of Syrian relations was actually quite nuanced, and the positions of the anti-Syrians and the pro-Syrians were not as divergent as one might expect.

During the interviews, I solicited information about the elites' familial, social, political, and business relations with Syria, before going on to inquire about their opinions on the relations between the two countries. More than a quarter of my informants—including several prominent opponents of Syrian influence in Lebanon—described themselves as having personal relationships with Syrians. Some had Syrian wives or mothers, a rather unsurprising finding considering the close historical relationship between the two countries. Several interviewees, including two who identified as members of the Christian opposition, admitted to having close personal ties with the Syrian regime. Other interviewees admitted to having business relations with Syria. Overall, it was clear from my interviews that personal relationships between the Lebanese and Syrian elites are a systemic part of the country's political culture.

In giving their views on Lebanese-Syrian relations, a large majority of the people I interviewed expressed the opinion that the interaction between the two countries suffered from a "lack of balance." All of my informants, regardless of the degree to which they publicly support or oppose the Syrian regime, were in agreement that Syria interfered too much in Lebanese internal affairs. On the other hand, all of my informants also believed that Lebanon needed to maintain good, if not "special," relations with Syria. Some informants made the argument that Syrian involvement in Lebanon could be justified in times of heightened tension. In a June 5, 2002, interview, for example, an aide of former prime minister Rafiq Hariri went so far as to say, "I believed that Syrian interference was nefarious until the election of Émile Lahoud to the presidency. Since then I understand that without the safeguard that is Syria, Lebanon would have risked total disintegration."[12] This informant mentioned a crisis that occurred shortly before the interview, when the electoral victory of an opposition candidate in the Christian enclave of Metn was challenged by President Lahoud and Minister of the Interior Elias Murr. In the wake of this election, escalating tensions and large youth demonstrations threatened a return to civil violence. In this case, Syrian intervention was instrumental in convincing Lahoud and Murr to accept the electoral victory of the Christian opposition and thereby defuse the situation.

Thus, while the political elite seemed uniformly uncomfortable with the past extent of Syrian interference, the majority understood the relationship between the two countries as a historical constant that at times provides a valuable stabilizing effect in Lebanon. The near-consensus view is that these relations should continue, albeit with a certain degree of "adjustment" to ensure greater parity between the two countries. Interviewees often mentioned that Lebanon should develop a more equitable partnership with Syria around economic and security issues. A significant factor in this outlook was the resilience of the Arab-Israeli conflict and the memory of Israeli invasions of Lebanon. Hariri's aide affirmed, "I don't believe it is in Lebanon's interest to detach its policies from those of Syria regarding strategic security or the Arab-Israeli conflict. Any Arab country that faced Israel alone—be it on the negotiation table or in a military confrontation—has failed. It is in Lebanon's interest to attach itself to Syria and vice versa." Even in my interviews with members of the Christian opposition, who are generally considered to be fiercely anti-Syria, the most commonly expressed view was that Lebanon's position would be stronger in the peace negotiations if the country was in alignment with Syria at the negotiating table.

The interviewees who would generally be classified in the "anti-Syria" camp emphasized that dealings between the two countries needed to become more formal and transparent. In the words of one informant, legitimate international relations "must go through governments, not through people."[13] The tendency for political deals to be arranged through informal or personal channels was seen as a source of corruption and abuse. These informants argued that personalized relations between the Lebanese and Syrian elites often led Lebanese politicians to give preference to Syrian interests rather than the concerns of their own constituents. One of the interviewees alleged that politicians who support Syrian interests receive financial benefits and that "there is a political class of about three hundred persons [in Lebanon] that forms the basis of a Mafia-like regime totally submissive to Syria." He added that Syria's agents in Lebanon "operate on many levels (political, social, and electoral) to eliminate any opposition."[14] The proposed solutions for this state of affairs most often involved a revision of all bilateral agreements between the two countries, changes in Lebanon's electoral laws, the withdrawal of Syrian troops, and the establishment of more formal diplomatic relations through an exchange of ambassadors. It is notable that the interviewees who are seen as speaking for the "pro-Syria" position largely agreed with this discourse. For example, in 2002 a pro-Syria cabinet minister, acknowledging the need for reform, explained to me that "electoral law is part of the reform process. It must be just and must ensure equality among all candidates." Recent years have seen significant steps toward achieving these goals. Syrian troops have not returned to Lebanon since 2005, and in 2008 Syrian president Bashar al-Assad issued a presidential decree that established formal diplomatic ties with Lebanon. It was the first time in the history of the two countries that the Syrian government had formally recognized Lebanon's independence. Among the "pro-Syria" camp, the interviewees who were most open to the idea of Syrian involvement in Lebanese affairs were the older elites who were part of the prewar generation. They were mainly Sunnis, and their perception of Syria was colored by Pan-Arabism, an outlook that they had internalized in their youth. Among these men, Syria is often regarded as the locus and personification of Pan-Arabism.[15] In a 2002 interview, for example, one of my informants admitted that he did not want a Syrian withdrawal, "because that would mean a separation between the two countries." He mentioned the brief unification scheme that brought Syria and Egypt together under the United Arab Republic from 1958 to 1961 and explained that "some are obsessed with obsolete concepts such as independence or sovereignty . . . [while] we should be building a strong national policy that is not based on these symbols." This former adviser to Rafiq Hariri maintained that "we can build a state without insisting on sovereignty or independence." He cited the examples of Hong Kong and Taiwan, both of which are officially part of China—at least according to the Chinese government. Such an outlook, however, was very much a minority view among my informants. In most of the interviews, even supporters of Syria expressed a belief in Lebanese sovereignty and a concern that the current political system was not fully representative of the interests of the Lebanese people.

All told, the discourse of elites in Lebanon seems to show a remarkable degree of convergence in regard to Syrian relations. Whereas the discussion of Syria is a "hot topic" in Lebanese polemics, private interviews with diverse members of the Lebanese elite reveal that their attitudes toward Syria are far from irreconcilable. Only a very small number of older "pro-Syria" elites rejected the idea of an independent Lebanon and the need for reforms. This consensus seems to reveal a widespread acknowledgment of the problematic nature of Syrian interference in Lebanese affairs. Members of the war generation denounced the fact that Syria had allied itself to politicians who do not represent the Lebanese people and parachuted them into important political positions. One of my interviewees said that "Syria should have allied itself to a more representative Lebanon."[16] This complaint was mainly expressed by Christians who were unsatisfied with their representatives in the government. This dissatisfaction with parliamentary representation and with the political elite in general was also noted among the sympathizers of the late prime minister Rafiq Hariri, who felt that his economic reforms were blocked by the Syrian leadership and its Lebanese clients.

Meanwhile, the only "anti-Syria" interviewees who expressed an outright rejection of continuing relations between the two countries were those elites who before 2005 operated outside of the Lebanese political system, such as factions of the Lebanese Forces or members of Aoun's Free Patriotic Movement. The overall willingness to accept an "adjusted" relationship with Syria seemed to reveal a pragmatic recognition of the historical and cultural links between the two countries and of Syria's importance as an economic and strategic ally. Indeed, if Syria were to close its borders to Lebanon, the country's access to Arab countries would be impeded and its commerce significantly disrupted. Given the broad convergence of views on Lebanese-Syrian relations, it can be expected that Syria will continue to have a significant influence in Lebanon, unless the Syrian regime blunders and attempts to force the Lebanese elite into obeisance.

Elite Attitudes on the Future of the Political System

Whereas the discourse of Lebanese elites in the first decade of the twenty-first century shows a convergence on the topic of Syrian relations, the same cannot be said of attitudes toward the future of Lebanon's system of confessional power sharing. In this section I will discuss the history that underlies diverging visions of Lebanon's national identity, as well as the conclusions of my research into current elite perspectives on the Lebanese system.

Lebanese Political Culture

The Lebanese political system is unique in its arrangements for the division of governmental power along religious lines. This governmental structure is a result not only of the confessional cleavages and the strong sense of religious identity that exist in Lebanon, but also of a historically specific political culture. The concept of "political culture" has often been dismissed by political scientists as being inadequately theorized;[17] nonetheless, when properly defined, I believe it to be an invaluable tool for understanding political behavior. Simply put, "political culture consists of assumptions about the political world."[18] It is a socially established pattern of assumptions that tend to define what political behaviors are perceived as being within "the realm of the possible." The collection of attitudes, mind-sets, or habitual approaches that make up the Lebanese political culture can be thought of as the historical background of specific political performances. Although they are not immutable, these ingrained patterns of behavior tend to persist even through institutional changes, and they can thus be regarded as the bedrock of the political system.

Lebanese American historian Ussama Makdisi speaks of a culture of sectarianism that arose in nineteenth-century Lebanon as a response to changes within the Ottoman Empire and as a reaction against European meddling in the region. He argues that disillusionment with the direction of the old (nonsectarian) regime opened a space for "communal reinvention" in the Mount Lebanon area. The pressures of modernization and Westernization were widely perceived as a threat to religious traditions, resulting in a backlash in which public religious identity became the central focus of political representation. As a result, representation by religious community came to be perceived as the only legitimate basis on which democratization and modernization could proceed.[19] This sectarian approach soon permeated the political consciousness of the Mount Lebanon region.

During the creation of the Lebanese state, the overall political culture of sectarianism led to the emergence of power-sharing arrangements and the creation of sub–political cultures along confessional lines. Each of the distinct confessional cultures developed a slightly different concept of Lebanese identity. Although there was a large area of agreement in the overall national discourse,[20] each of the confessional political cultures remained tied to a limited set of interests and to a particular national mythology. Three main subdiscourses of national identity were operative in the formation of the Lebanese state. I will refer to these differing visions as the "Phoenicianist," the "Arabist," and the "Syrianist" discourses. In all three cases, they were tied to specific confessional groups, and today their legacy provides the ongoing basis for imagined political outcomes within and between confessions. Together the three discourses constitute the overlapping and at times contradictory basis of Lebanese political culture.

Phoenicianism. The "Phoenicianist" discourse of Lebanese identity was adopted by Christian (primarily Maronite) intellectuals at the time of the creation of Greater Lebanon. The Maronites' stated goal of establishing a Christian refuge in the Middle East was instrumental in convincing the French authorities to designate Lebanon as a separate nation-state. The origin myth adopted by the Christian advocates involved a purportedly independent cultural legacy that was said to have existed in Lebanon since ancient times. This national discourse was a form of what George Schöpflin calls foundational myths of "ethnogenesis and antiquity," complete with ancestral legends and stories of an original "golden age" followed by a decline and then a national rebirth.[21] This origin myth created an "imagined community" and linked present-day Lebanon to the golden age of Phoenician seafarers, who are credited with establishing a network of colonies throughout the ancient Mediterranean.[22] The narrative suggested that Phoenicians are the founders of Western civilization but that their lands were long ago overrun by Arab occupiers. The coastal inhabitants of historical Phoenicia, wanting to preserve their heritage and virtue, took refuge in the mountains of Lebanon. Their eventual conversion to Christianity, and the influence of the Maronite Church, had only amplified the civilizing nature of Phoenician culture. With the formation of a new Lebanese state, the Phoenician legacy would once again emerge to take on a civilizing role among the nations of the world.[23]

The central point of the Phoenicianist origin myth is its argument that modern Lebanon should not be thought of as "ethnically" Arab. This story of cultural origins functioned as a means for Lebanese Christians to dissociate themselves from their Arab environment and to effect a rapprochement with the West. The idea that national identity is a matter of transhistorical cultural affiliation, rather than actual ethnicity or language, was used to justify the political ascendancy of a minority group who believed in their superiority to their Muslim neighbors. In this regard, Phoenicianism is similar to a number of contemporaneous movements of national (dis)identification. "Pharaonism" in Egypt, for example, also harked back to the ancient world in seeking a national identity disconnected from Arab or Muslim influences.[24]

Phoenicianism exerted a significant influence in the founding of Lebanon, and this outlook was codified in the National Pact by the refusal to describe the new country as an "Arab state." The origin myth held a clearly utilitarian significance for the Christian elite. Michel Chiha, for example, one of the architects of the Lebanese political system and the brother-in-law of Lebanese president Bishara al-Khoury, frequently held forth on the "Mediterranean orientation" of Lebanon. Although Chiha did not personally embrace the story of Phoenician origins, his influential rhetoric invoked the perspectives and terminology of the myth. For Chiha, the accuracy of the myth was not important, but its role in disseminating a sense of Lebanese national destiny was crucial.[25]

Pan-Arabism. The second discourse that was prevalent in Lebanon in the early twentieth century was that of Arab nationalism, or Pan-Arabism. Palestinian American historian Rashid Khalidi explains Arab nationalism as "a revival of old traditions and loyalties and a creation of new myths based on them."[26] Pan-Arabism was marked by a newly consolidated sense of regional pride and a newly self-conscious attention to the importance of Arabic language and tradition. This movement of revival and reinterpretation was a product of the growing exchange between the Islamic world and the West during the nineteenth century, which incited both a cultural renaissance (*Nahda*) in Arabic arts and literature and a rethinking of Islam's role in modern society.[27] Soon this Arabist cultural renaissance led to nationalist movements that sought an end to Western interference in regional affairs. Early luminaries such as Mustafa Kamil, who led the first organized Egyptian nationalist movement, struggled to adapt the Western concept of nationalism to the context of the Arab and Muslim world. This process involved the creation of a new Pan-Arab identity and the adoption of a new Arabic terminology to express unfamiliar political ideas.[28] The premise of an Arab-Muslim past was accepted by all, including some Christians, especially the Greek Orthodox. Arab nationalists saw themselves as the heirs to a great history that belongs to all Arabs, regardless of religion. Hence, all speakers of Arabic were defined as Arabs. These Christians accepted an Arab nationalism that was secular while recognizing the Islamic heritage. Therefore, the lexicon of Islam was often used.[29]

During the early twentieth century, Arabs fought for their independence, first from the Ottoman Empire by asking for decentralization and then from the European colonial systems by demanding control of their own political states. While many diverse national movements existed, the overall tendency was toward a growing sense of regionwide Arab unity.[30] The creation of Greater Lebanon occurred during this era of Arabist rebellion, and the Sunni majority in Lebanon was overwhelmingly influenced by the regional movement toward Arabic national identity. Although the Arabists regarded Lebanese independence from colonial oversight as a good idea, they justifiably felt that the Phoenicianist discourse of the Maronites marginalized the Arab-Muslim community. Lebanese Arabists tended to turn the Phoenicianist origin myth on its head, arguing that all ancient people of the Near East, including the Phoenicians and the Maronites themselves, were the descendants of aboriginal (pre-Islamic) Arab tribes.[31]

When the National Pact consolidated around a rejection of Arabist viewpoints, many Sunnis came to view the newly created Lebanese state as a remnant of Western interference rather than an honest step toward regional independence. The desire for an Arabist national identity in Lebanon continued to motivate the political actions of Sunnis throughout the prewar period, even as the regional cohesion of the Pan-Arabian movement began to give way to more narrow religious and national agendas.

Syrianism. The third discourse that was prevalent in the early history of the Lebanese state is Syrianism. This perspective on the role of Lebanon was tied to the Syrian nationalist movement and particularly to the vision of Antun Sa'adeh, the founder of the Syrian Social Nationalist Party. Resisting the overall trend toward sectarianism, Sa'adeh believed that the temporal power of the clergy was the greatest internal obstacle to the unification of the region. He argued that the basis of the Syrian nation should be secular, grounded primarily in a commitment to regional autonomy rather than in ethnic, religious, or linguistic bonds.[32] Sa'adeh placed a great emphasis on geographical identity, envisioning Greater Syria as one national homeland that he described as extending from "the Taurus range in the north-west and the Zagros mountains in the north-east to the Suez Canal and the Red Sea in the south and include[ing] the Sinai peninsula and the gulf of Aqaba, and from the Syrian sea in the west, including the island of Cyprus to the arch of the Arabia desert and the Persian Gulf in the east."[33] According to Sa'adeh, these natural geographic boundaries provide an appropriate basis for a regional political unity, one that France and Great Britain falsely divided after the fall of the Ottoman Empire. Like the adherents of Phoenicianism and Pan-Arabism, Sa'adeh viewed the ancient inhabitants of this region as the forerunners of civilization. In contrast to the other discourses, however, he saw this accomplishment as a joint effort of multiple ethnic and religious communities.

In Lebanon Syrianism appealed primarily to the Greek Orthodox and other minority communities who felt excluded from the visions of the larger Maronite and Sunni factions. Syrian nationalists held out to these minority groups the promise of full equality in a nonsectarian state.[34] The Syrianists therefore viewed the creation of the Lebanese state as at best a stepping-stone in the trajectory toward a secular unification of the entire region. This point of view did not endear them to the Maronite nationalists, especially after Sa'adeh declared an intention to "seize power in Beirut" so that Lebanon could be "reunited with natural Syria."[35]

The Syrianist discourse was equally unpalatable to the Sunni majority, who preferred to conceptualize the future of the region in Arab-Muslim terms. While Sa'adeh attempted to square this circle by speaking of "the Arabism of Syrian Social Nationalism," his distaste for religious interference in political affairs led some scholars to view this rhetoric as ideological dissimulation (*taqiyya*).[36]

Changing Discourses in the Late Twentieth Century

In the second half of the twentieth century, the Phoenicianist discourse began to mellow into a broader "Lebanist" perspective that sought to incorporate a more representative portion of the country's population in its vision of the Lebanese state. While still insisting on the need for an autonomous and relatively Westernized Lebanon, the Lebanist outlook recognized the diversity of the region's history, and it was far more open to consociational power sharing and collaboration with Lebanon's Arab neighbors. Meanwhile, the decline of radical Pan-Arabism and the failure of the Syrian-Egyptian union in the early 1960s led the Arabist Baath Party to adopt some of the more autocratic principles of Sa'adeh's Syrianism. This move resulted in a composite Syrian regime that many scholars have described as "neo-Baath," and throughout the region Pan-Arabism and Syrianism began to collapse into a single Pan-Syrian outlook.[37] Especially under the influence of Syrian president Hafez al-Assad, the Baathist emphasis on Pan-Arab cultural identity became wedded to the goal of Syrian regional hegemony.

    In Lebanon the end of the twentieth century saw the precarious success of Lebanist discourse over the concept of Syrian hegemony. One of the keys to this victory was the waning of the Phoenicianist origin myth and a series of concessions made by the Maronite community, which helped to encourage Lebanese Muslims (especially Sunnis) to reject Syrian interference and accept Lebanon as an independent country. In the National Pact of 1943, the Christians had abandoned their call for Western military protection and had accepted that there would be a certain degree of collaboration between Lebanon and other Arab countries. Likewise, whereas the Maronites insisted that Lebanon was not an "Arab state," they allowed that it had an "Arab character" and was geographically a part of the Arab world. When the Ta'if Agreement put an end to the civil war, further concessions were made by the Christians, including a full acceptance of Lebanon's "Arabness." This rise of a more inclusive Lebanist discourse, combined with a weariness of aggressive Syrian interference in Lebanon, led to the early-twenty-first-century consensus revealed in my research in which the goal of uniting with Syria was held by only a very small minority of Lebanese elites. The Maronites conceded the Arabness of Lebanon in return for the declaration of the sovereignty and independence of the country.

With the decline of the Pan-Arabist, Pan-Syrianist, and radical Phoenicianist discourses in Lebanon, a somewhat more stable consensus on the national identity was reached. As the idea of an independent, diverse Lebanon has become solidified, the trajectories of the various confessional agendas have begun to center around the governmental structure of the Lebanese state, in particular the confessional division of power. In other words, the often-violent fragmentation of confessional discourses has led toward an interrogation of the overall sectarian nature of Lebanese political culture. The immediate starting point of this debate is the Ta'if Agreement, which endorses sectarianism as a regulating principle of Lebanese political life while simultaneously envisioning the abolition of the system at some unspecified future date. Despite the provisions in the agreement for the eventual obsolescence of sectarianism, most commentators agree that its effect was to give significant momentum to the durability of the system.[38] In addition to maintaining consociational power-sharing arrangements along confessional lines, the Ta'if Agreement redefined the role of religious leaders, giving them an even greater importance in Lebanese political life. For example, the agreement included provisions for the creation of the Constitutional Council, which reviews the constitutionality of new laws and resolves conflicts emerging from parliamentary and presidential elections. The religious leaders of the various sectarian communities are among the few people who are granted the right to petition the Constitutional Council. Their influence is officially limited to matters that affect religion; in practice, however, the religious leaders can use this prerogative to maintain their control of personal status laws (marriage, divorce, custody, and so forth). The right to petition the Constitutional Council also gives religious leaders the ability to block any attempt to secularize education and in general provides them with a vehicle to resist the creation of a secular national identity that would unite all Lebanese citizens.

The confessional formula elaborated in the Ta'if Agreement has become an important topic of debate in Lebanon, especially since the tenth anniversary of the accord, when politicians and intellectuals announced the failure of Ta'if to move Lebanon into the future. It has been pointed out that the 1943 National Pact also included an agreement to end sectarian representation at some unspecified future time, but that neither this declaration nor the Ta'if Agreement has had much of an effect on the resilience of sectarian political culture. In the current debate, there are four main options on the table in regard to the future of Lebanon's political system.

The first option would be to take into consideration the demographic makeup of the country and allow for majority representation, thereby making Lebanon an officially Muslim nation. If this course were to be followed, it is very likely that religious minorities would become or at least feel like second-class citizens. This solution would be totally unacceptable to the large Christian communities living in Lebanon. Given the current power of these communities, the fear of renewed violence, and the effects of Western pressures, it is unlikely that Lebanon will evolve in such a direction.

The second option would be to retain the confessional system more or less in its established form. This alternative is the most currently viable one—or, at least, it is the option with the most inertia. The Ta'if Agreement took this course, reinstating the confessional power-sharing arrangements that had existed before the civil war, with relatively minor adjustments that reflect the contemporary reality of the confessional balance of power. It is a matter of debate as to whether this arrangement has restrained or perpetuated the nation's past difficulties.

The third option would be to gradually reduce the influence of religion in the public sphere, leading toward a more fully democratic system while steadily erecting a divide between religion and state. This option would probably be the most acceptable to Christians and other minorities in Lebanon, especially if it evolves from the basis of the Ta'if Agreement and foresees the changes happening over a long period of time. Former prime minister Salim al-Hoss has emerged as a proponent of this course. Hoss has argued that the collapse of the Lebanese political system during the civil war was owing to a "democracy deficit" in Lebanon and that the division of governmental power along confessional lines creates an unwillingness for the various branches of government to accept "checks and balances" by the other branches.[39] Hoss refers to his vision of a more democratic Lebanese future as the "Third Republic," underlining the fact that this new system would not be a rupture with the past or a refutation of the Ta'if Agreement, but rather a development growing out of the legacy of the first two Lebanese republics. He proposes the following changes to initiate a reduction in sectarianism:

1. Passing a new national electoral law making all of Lebanon into a single electoral district. This change would encourage voters to move away from regionalism, sectarianism, and traditionalism in selecting their national representation.
2. Confining candidacy in legislative elections to members of political parties, thereby strengthening the role of parties in relation to the role of confessions.
3. Opening the presidency to cross-confessional competition. Following the American model, the president would be directly elected, would have clearly delineated powers, and would remain in office for a maximum of two four-year terms.
4. Adopting a system of referendum to consult the public on important issues.
5. Increasing the powers of internal regulatory agencies and taking measures to isolate them from political influence.
6. Implementing the principles of decentralization outlined in the Ta'if Agreement, including the allocation of larger prerogatives to local governors (*muhafiz*) and prefects (*qa'immaqam*). This increase in local autonomy would help the public to be more comfortable with a less sectarian national government.[40]

The fourth option for the future of Lebanon's confessional system would be the immediate transformation of the country into a secular democracy, enforcing a division between religion and state. This more radical approach to deconfessionalization is favored by some intellectuals, such as Daoud Khairallah, who argues that sectarianism is the root cause of all of Lebanon's political and economic woes. Khairallah maintains that resistance to changing the confessional system in Lebanon is near suicidal and that as long as sectarianism is officially sanctioned, it will continue to prevent the emergence of a shared Lebanese identity. In his view, only the rapid adoption of secular democracy can lift Lebanon out of its autodestructive paralysis and prevent a recurrence of the fratricide seen in the civil war. Khairallah also argues that the Ta'if Agreement was not and cannot be the solution to Lebanon's problems. He notes that although the agreement declares deconfessionalization as a national objective, it entrusts the eventual realization of this objective to a vigorously sectarian establishment. Since gradual deconfessionalism would gradually reduce the power of many members of this establishment, Khairallah suggests that it will never be accomplished under the current system.[41]

Khairallah also notes that the inconsistencies in the various personal status laws that regulate members of different confessions in Lebanon are incompatible with democratic practice. He claims that these laws violate three of the articles of the UN's Universal Declaration of Human Rights, since not all Lebanese are treated equally under the laws. For example, Lebanese inheritance laws stipulate that Muslim women receive half as much of their parents' property as is received by their brothers, whereas Christian women get an equal share of the family inheritance. To create a truly democratic national discourse capable of defining shared objectives for all Lebanese, Khairallah argues that religious influence must be totally and rapidly removed from the political sphere. These arguments for democracy and minority rights are supported by advocates both in and beyond Lebanon, but they are rejected by religious leaders and by their practicing flocks, which constitute the majority of the Lebanese people. Thus, it is difficult to see how Khairallah's proposed reforms could be democratically implemented in the near future.

Researching Elite Discourse on the Future of the Political System

In the course of my fieldwork in Lebanon, I asked a diverse selection of Lebanese elites about their views on the durability and viability of the confessional system. Roughly 90 percent of those whom I interviewed agreed that it would be ideal for Lebanon to move toward a nonconfessional government. But how soon can deconfessionalization be implemented, and what would be the optimal results of such a transformation? On these points, there were many diverse suggestions and little convergence in perspective. Referring to the multiple visions of the nation among the Lebanese, one parliamentarian explained to me in October 2001 that "the Lebanese personality is a synthesis of several identities: communitarian, familial, Arab, international. A viable political system must take into consideration this synthesis and ensure the expression of each identity in politics." What kind of system could accomplish this goal?

My interviews found no generational differences regarding the deconfessionalization of the political system, but they revealed a systematic and predictable divergence among the elites of different confessional groups. Although the elites belonging to numerically substantive communities were generally open to the idea of a political system in which parliamentary seats are not allocated according to sect, those elites who belonged to smaller confessional groups were much more hesitant about this idea. Many of them expressed the notion that "the only viable political system is that which takes into consideration these different [sectarian] identities."[42]

Among those interviewees who most strongly supported a rapid deconfessionalization of the political system were Shi'i elites. My Shi'i informants believed themselves to be part of a majority community in postwar Lebanon, and they felt that the deconfessionalization of the system would therefore (perhaps paradoxically) serve their sectarian interests, catapulting Shi'i politicians forward on the political scene. Hence, in my interviews, Shi'i elites most often embraced the idea of "one man, one vote," suggesting that sectarian quotas for political representation were undemocratic. These elites were also the most likely to bring up a desire for direct presidential elections. In contrast, the majority of interviewees from other communities—including Christians and Sunni Muslims—believed that the confessional system plays an important role in ensuring the rights of religious minorities in Lebanon. They argued that deconfessionalization must be gradual and accompanied by initiatives to protect the prerogatives of their communities.

Trepidation regarding the effects of deconfessionalization was particularly notable among the elites of the smaller communities. In 2001, for example, a Druze parliamentarian whom I interviewed expressed skepticism about the prospects for minority representation after deconfessionalization. Explaining his hesitancy about the results of a nonsectarian democracy, he said, "We should build a modern political system, but I am not sure we can build a *secular* and modern system." Likewise, an Armenian parliamentarian whom I interviewed around the same time vehemently refused the idea of political deconfessionalization. He was conscious that his sectarian group would lose its extraproportional political weight in a nonconfessional system, and he feared that the voice of his community would then disappear altogether from the Lebanese political scene. It seems unlikely that these Druze and Armenian elites will support moves toward deconfessionalization until they feel certain that the proposed changes will be a benefit, rather than a detriment, to their political rights. Although the role of minor confessions is limited in the current system, elites of these communities remain unconvinced that deconfessionalization would be an improvement.

The rejection of a nonconfessional system was also particularly prevalent among larger Christian groups. Fearing a divergence of Muslim and Christian interests, these elites were worried about the consequences of making any additional concessions that would reduce their power vis-à-vis other sectarian groups. Although the majority of Christian elites whom I interviewed affirmed the need for a change in the political system, they expressed consternation about the diminishment of Christian privilege that a more democratic system would entail, and they tended to locate the timetable for reform as occurring in a vague and distant future.

Regardless of their enthusiasm or hesitancy about the prospects of deconfessionalization, my interviewees agreed that changing the deep-seated role of sectarianism in the political culture will not be easy. As one

Sunni parliamentarian pointed out, "In the political unconsciousness [of Lebanon], sectarianism always comes back."[43] Some elites suggested that the political culture cannot change until after the Lebanese society as a whole has undergone a transformation toward deconfessionalization. In 2001, for example, one interviewee argued that "political sectarianism does not create a sociological sectarianism in Lebanon." On the contrary, this informant suggested, the confessional political system provides a nonviolent outlet for sectarian tensions, and it would therefore be dangerous to proceed rapidly with deconfessionalization before the necessary shifts in popular notions of Lebanese identity have occurred. Another of my interviewees stated that "sectarianism is a cover for clientelism and for parochial mentalities—we have to break this vicious cycle," but then added the caveat that "change cannot come from inside the system. It is up to civil society and the private sector to push for change."[44]

Other elites were more optimistic about the role of organizational changes in nurturing a new political culture. While also admitting the need for changes in popular identity discourses, they suggested that the political elite should take immediate steps toward a restructuring of the system. These elites frequently pointed to the fact that the provisions of the Ta'if Agreement have not yet been fully implemented. They suggested that moving too quickly toward a fulfillment of the agreement is not as dangerous as is moving too slowly or complete stagnation. In their view, the need and desire for deconfessionalization is too strong to be ignored, and failing to deconfessionalize brings Lebanon closer to renewed confrontation.

One widespread view among the elites (similar to al-Hoss's proposal described above) was that the system could be deconfessionalized in stages, by creating an expanding zone of sectarian-free politics. To this end, some of my interviewees pointed to the Ta'if Agreement's provisions for the eventual establishment of a bicameral system. Whereas the Druze have long supported the idea of a Lebanese Senate as a potential confessional institution for Druze representation, the vision proposed by the Ta'if Agreement is that the senate would be reserved for proportional sectarian representation after the other branches of government have been deconfessionalized. This senate would act as an advisory body to the secular government, and it would focus on "existential questions" (*qadaya masiriyya*) and humanitarian issues.

Beyond the simple inertia of the political culture, the greatest obstacle to deconfessionalization seemed to be concern about the rights of minority religions. In order to assuage these concerns, some proponents of deconfessionalization suggested measures to promote a secular—or, at least, cross-confessional—national identity and to erect barriers between religious communities and the state. Several of my interviewees mentioned the need for a reform in the Lebanese educational system as a vital step in developing the "modern Lebanese citizen," or a more unified, pan-confessional vision of Lebanese national identity. They argued that to create such a citizen, "an emphasis must be put on the education of the youth." A national identity must therefore be created through the public schooling system.[45] Such an attempt was made in the immediate wake of the Ta'if Agreement, when new history and civic-education textbooks were introduced into the Lebanese schools. These revised materials were authored with the express purpose of building a nonsectarian vision of national identity. This movement soon ran into difficulties, however, as the regulating actions of sectarian leaders overwhelmed the efforts of educational reformers.[46]

Other proposals that my interviewees tended to bring up in the context of limiting sectarian agendas in a deconfessionalized Lebanon included the creation of new political parties, the establishment of an independent judiciary, and a revision of the personal status laws. Indeed, an interviewee argued that Lebanon "does not really have a political system. We should build . . . all that makes a state."[47] In regard to political parties, one interviewee pointed out that under the current system, "confessions play the role of political parties."[48] However, this state of affairs was widely perceived as contributing to sectarian tensions. Some elites suggested that new political parties oriented toward explicit national agendas could draw citizens' attention away from alliances based on personal or sectarian ties or both, thus leading to an increase in cross-confessional identifications. In regard to the judiciary, many elites criticized the Lebanese tradition of sectarian influence on court proceedings. The presidency of Émile Lahoud, in particular, was widely associated with interference in judicial affairs, and many interviewees alleged that the presidency had instrumentalized the judicial system for the promotion of its own agenda. Hence, there were widespread calls for the judiciary to be restructured and completely disassociated from executive powers. Finally, a number of my informants brought up the inequalities and sectarian influences that are present in Lebanon's personal status laws. Interviewees suggested that replacing the confession-based laws with secular ones could be vital in establishing a greater separation of religion and state. Some saw this change as important in diminishing the influence of the clergy in the daily lives of Lebanese citizens and thus leading toward the development of a cross-confessional national identity.

In addition to these measures, it is unlikely that the deconfessional-ization of the Lebanese political system can proceed until the memory of the civil war, including its origins and its repercussions, is dealt with. Indeed, there seems to be a general amnesia in Lebanon when it comes to the civil war,[49] which is often euphemistically referred to as "the events," including by my informants, who rarely discussed the war or the need for reconciliation. Although it would be easy to impute the unwilling-ness to deal with the memory of the war to individual political elites, and to the state-sponsored amnesia that followed the 1991 general amnesty law, the issue is far more complicated. The complicity of silence extends deeply into Lebanon's civil discourse.[50] If there is no conflict resolution and reconciliation, if the problems of the past are swept under the carpet, how can Lebanon hope to change its political system and come up with a viable solution for the future?

The confessional system that was adopted in the National Pact of 1943 and then revisited in the Ta'if Agreement of 1989 has shown a disturbing tendency toward instability and outright collapse. The non-sectarian political system that was envisioned in both agreements as an eventual alternative was never implemented, nor does its implementation appear to loom in the near future. During the First Lebanese Repub-lic, sectarian elites who were eager to maintain control over the system helped to ensure that deconfessionalization remained a distant goal. The behaviors and attitudes of many of today's political elites seem to echo the indefinite postponements of the First Republic to a disturbing extent.

This impression of déjà vu is worrisome if it is a predictor for a second breakdown of the Lebanese political system.

Conclusion

Contrary to expectations, the elite's views on Syrian Lebanese relations were nuanced: both those considered pro-Syria and anti-Syria thought the relations between the two countries should remain special but should be recalibrated to ensure parity between the two countries. After Syrian withdrawal, a reevaluation of the Lebanese elite's dependency on Syria was expected but did not take place. Lebanese elite members still went on their weekly pilgrimage to Damascus to receive instructions from the Syrian leadership. With a possible change of regime in Syria on the horizon following the 2011–12 uprising, the relationship between the two countries might enter a new era.

There is no generational difference regarding the deconfessionalization of the political system between the different elite groups; however, there are significant divisions among confessional groups regarding this issue. Whereas numerically important communities are open to the idea of a political system where parliamentary seats are not allocated according to sect, smaller confessional groups are categorically opposed to this idea. Despite their differences on this issue, the majority of the elites whom I interviewed do admit that there is a need for changing the political system. They overtly speak of a deconfessionalized system but place such a fundamental change in the indefinite future. At the same time that they recognized the confessional system as a central locus of strain for Lebanon, these elites were aware the confessional system allows them to monopolize political life. In many ways, their aspiration toward the future stability of Lebanon is balanced against their aspirations for their personal futures and legacies.

Conclusion

The Lebanese civil war led to a renewal and realignment of the Lebanese political elite. Today, that elite is composed of a group of state actors who emerged during the war and consolidated power after the Ta'if Agreement and a strategic elite composed of unelected individuals who influence political debate and help set the national agenda. The appointments to the parliament that followed the Ta'if Agreement in 1991 and the legislative elections of 1992 allowed for the enlargement of the state elite, as the number of parliamentarians was increased to 128. Despite the new institutions created by the Ta'if Agreement and the modification of the power-sharing formula that occurred during this elite settlement, the change of personnel and shifting alliances during the postwar years did not substantially alter elite behavior and attitudes. The underlying cause of this lack of change can be attributed to the continuation of the confessional system and to Syria's opportunistic interference in Lebanon's political affairs. Both of these factors helped to create stability in Lebanon, but at the cost of prospects for any deep-seated change in the country's political culture.

In its composition, the postwar state elite included wealthy businessmen, notables, technocrats, and clients of Syria. The notables, especially those individuals belonging to the Christian community, were originally sidelined after the Ta'if Agreement, but most of these leaders were gradually integrated into the state over the following decade. The postwar strategic elite included religious leaders, influential journalists, and military commanders. Some of these members of the strategic elite made a transition toward becoming more involved in the state in the years after the civil war. A void at the leadership level allowed for greater participation of certain religious leaders and military commanders in the political life of the Second Republic. Although there was a significant circulation of individual elite actors at the end of the civil war, as well as a realignment of the terms of the power-sharing arrangement among the different confessional factions, the same basic form of clientelistic elite recruitment and patronage that had existed before the war continued unabated. If anything, the negative aspects of this personalized system of elite recruitment were exacerbated as the increasing financialization of elite networks led to pervasive corruption and the misappropriation of public funds.

Aspiring Elites and Patronage

Postwar clientelistic practices were not radically different from those practices studied by Michael Johnson in his analysis of Sunni elites in Beirut in the 1970s and 1980s.[1] Johnson notes that in prewar Lebanon, the control of patronage networks was one of the most important assets of a sectarian leader, or *za'im*.[2] He also maintains that the clientelistic system collapsed at the beginning of the war, only to reappear in a different format in a fragmented country.[3] On the basis of my research, it seems clear that these same patterns of clientelism are still prevalent in the postwar era and that they act to the detriment of the inclusion of new forms of political power. Certain groups, such as women, are virtually locked out of the political elite because of these features of the political culture, and the inertia of clientelistic networks is a prohibitive barrier against the modernization and deconfessionalization of the Lebanese system.

Political parties in Lebanon are weak and are not in themselves a reliable basis for elite recruitment or formation, so today's aspiring Lebanese elites still emerge on the political scene almost exclusively through a patronage relationship with an important political leader, generally the leader of the sectarian community to whom the emerging elite belongs. I identified seven different ideals among types of emerging elites: the civil society activist, the technocrat, the academic, the local representative, the heir, the Hezbollahi, and the nationalist militant; however, out of all these groups, only the heir appears to have a solid hope of entering the upper echelons of Lebanese political life. The other emerging elites who rely on clientelism to usher them onto the political scene are likely, at most, to remain indefinitely in the status of client while almost never reaching patronhood. The only type of emerging elite who does not use clientelism as a primary political strategy is the Hezbollahi, as he is a part of an organization that seems prima facie to adhere more closely to the trappings of democracy than does the Lebanese state.

Syrian Guardianship

From 1990 to 2005, Lebanon was under Syrian tutelage. The relationship was institutionalized in a series of agreements signed after the Ta'if Agreement, the most important of which is the Treaty of Brotherhood and Cooperation. Syrian leaders had many reasons for their desire to control Lebanon, including territorial claims going back to the very creation of Greater Lebanon, the need of a buffer against Israel, and the desire for a security valve to assist with Syria's ailing economy. During the period of Syrian guardianship, the Lebanese political system developed a semi-authoritarian tinge because of the "neighborhood" effect. Syrian political elites played the role of mediator among Lebanese factions every time the system became deadlocked. This relationship allowed Syria to claim that its influence on Lebanon was positive and stabilizing and that without Syria, Lebanon would fall back into fratricidal struggle. In the years of the Pax Syriana, having good relations with the Syrian leaders was considered a decisive factor in any bid for political power in Lebanon, and the Syrian leadership had a heavy hand in selecting and shaping the Lebanese political culture.

Future Trends and Prospects

As long as the sectarian formula of power sharing remains in place in Lebanon, only two forms of elite circulation will exist: generational inheritance and co-option. The continual crises in the Lebanese political system cannot be explained by external threats alone; the majority of conflict in Lebanon's history has emerged from sectarian divides that are only exacerbated by international pressures. Most current Lebanese elites agree that the confessional system of political representation is not viable in the long term and that the Lebanese political framework therefore contains the seeds of its own destruction. Radical changes are needed in the Lebanese status quo to promote democratization; unfortunately, these changes are inherently threatening to existing elites and even more so to those individuals whose confessionally mandated power exceeds their demographic standing. Few elites are open to the idea of immediate democratization, especially in the Christian community. Therefore, although nearly all elites recognize the imperative for change, they have a marked tendency to postpone this hypothetical change into the indefinite future. This outlook, which was enshrined in the provisions of the Ta'if Agreement, is disturbingly similar to the conditions that were present in the First Lebanese Republic prior to the outbreak of the civil war.

The Lebanese economy is currently in shambles, mired in clientelism and corruption. Reforms that have been proposed to lift Lebanon out of debt have been consistently gridlocked, not for ideological reasons but simply because of the personal power struggles among the confessional blocs that constitute the "Troika" at the head of the Lebanese state. Those policies that have been established during the postwar years are grounded more on the basis of entrenched corruption than on aspirations for the good of the country. These policies are primarily neoliberal in character: they favor the rich and do not provide social safety nets for the middle class and the poor. These policies have alienated the country's youth, especially the more educated and talented segments of society. These young men and women, who under other circumstances may have cultivated political ambitions and challenged the monopoly of the established elite, are instead disenchanted with the corruption and lack of opportunity that they confront in Lebanon. Since the mid-1990s, Lebanon has witnessed a large outflow of its educated population, a "brain drain" that has emptied the country of its most promising sons and daughters.

The current question for Lebanon is whether the weariness with conflict and the growing consensus toward national unity will outweigh the divisiveness of internal sectarian divides and global geopolitical pressures. The difficulties faced by Lebanon are profound. The country has entered a new era of "political Shi'ism" in which Hezbollah is increasingly flexing its political and demographic muscles. Meanwhile, the return of previously exiled Maronite radicals such as Michel Aoun and the emergence of a new generation of disenchanted youth who have never known the horrors of war portend a possible regression into Christian extremism.

In the international context, the United States' success in ousting Saddam Hussein from Iraq has led to an ongoing project of regional remodeling, primarily with the goals of protecting US and Israeli interests.[4] In the past decade, Syria has increasingly come to the attention of Western powers, as is evidenced by the signing of the Syria Accountability Act and Security Council Resolution 1559 at the United Nations. Even though Syria's military officially left Lebanon in 2005, the influence cultivated during nearly thirty years of occupation will not disappear overnight, especially given the clientelistic nature of the Lebanese system and the close relationship that most Lebanese elites hold with the Syrian leaders.[5]

The elections of Nicolas Sarkozy in France in 2007 and Barack Obama in the United States in 2008 initially provided signs that the international tensions against Syria that all too frequently resound in Lebanon might ease. Sarkozy, who did not share former French president Jacques Chirac's enthusiasm for Lebanon and did not have close personal connections with the Lebanese elite, invited Bashar al-Assad to the Bastille Day parade in July 2008. It was the first signal that Syria had been brought in from the cold and accepted again by the international community. The administration of Barack Obama also has different priorities from its predecessor. In the early months of 2010, the rapprochement between the United States and Syria had culminated with the appointment of a new US ambassador to Syria, Robert Ford. Ford is the first ambassador to Syria since the United States recalled its last representative in 2005 in protest over the assassination of Rafiq Hariri.

However, the American step was preceded by several important landmarks, namely, a Lebanese-Syrian ambassador exchange in January 2009, the first of its kind since the creation of both states; a Saudi-Syrian rapprochement in October 2009 symbolized by King Abdallah's visit to Damascus, the first since his accession to the throne; and, finally, Saad

Hariri's trip to Damascus in December 2009, one month after the Saudi king's visit. Indeed, King Abdallah played an important role in paving the way for this rapprochement. Hariri's visit marks a landmark in the relations between the two countries. He had to accept to let bygones be bygones following the international recognition of Syria and the weakening of the March 14 Coalition formed after the assassination of Rafiq Hariri. Indeed, many of its important stalwarts such as Walid Jumblat had by then reconciled with Syria.

In addition, whereas the investigation into Rafiq Hariri's assassination, led by the United Nations Special Tribunal for Lebanon, indicated in its first two reports that the Syrian government might be linked to the assassination, later reports seemed to walk back this accusation.[6] On June 30, 2011, the STL accused four members of Hezbollah, including a senior military commander, of the assassination.[7] The accusation led to a hardening of the rhetoric between two main elite factions in Lebanon, March 8 and 14, and to attempts by Hezbollah in November 2011 to scuttle Lebanon's participation in the STL. The party does not recognize the legitimacy of the STL, which it considers an American and Israeli tool. Hence, Hezbollah tried to stop Lebanon from paying its share of the tribunal's running costs. However, this action threatened to lead the collapse of the Mikati cabinet, as the Sunni leader, mindful of his community's position on the tribunal, warned his allies of his willingness to resign. The crisis was averted when Mikati paid Lebanon's dues directly from his office's budget without having to hold a cabinet vote.

Syria itself has been undergoing upheavals since March 2011: a popular uprising currently in its second year is endangering Assad's regime. If the regime is to survive the current rebellion, it will be at a very steep price. Its legitimacy will be deeply compromised, and its existence itself is at risk in the long run. Most observers estimate that it is only a question of time before the Assad regime is ousted. During these upheavals, the Lebanese state has maintained a policy of neutrality and nonintervention vis-à-vis events unfolding in Syria. However, Sunni popular mobilization in support of the uprising in Syria is increasing, as evidenced by the fighting between the Alawi minority and the Sunni majority that shook the northern city of Tripoli in May 2012. As Paul Salem notes,

"The mobilization of the Sunni north in support of the Syrian revolution might elicit a response from the Syrian regime. North Lebanon is close to the strategic cities of Homs and Hama and abuts the Alawi heartland in northwest Syria. The Assad regime controlled north Lebanon when its troops and intelligence agents dominated Lebanon between 1976 and 2005. . . . Whether the embattled Assad regime will respond to the growing mobilization in north Lebanon with an escalation of . . . actions is yet to be seen."[8]

Regardless of these recent events, we can expect that political readjustments to the changing status of the Syrian government and the declining fortunes of the Assad dynasty will be resolved in Lebanon through the continued realliance and reconciliation among Lebanese elites that form the foundation of the country's political process. These probable shifts in allegiance direct our attention to the manner in which Lebanese political alliances continue to be affected by the shifting winds of regional conjunctures and international dialogue.

Who's Who of Lebanese Politics

Aoun, Michel. (Maronite.) Lebanese general who was appointed at the end of an interim government at the end of Amin Gemayel's presidential term. He led a military campaign to expel Syria from Lebanon. He attempted to dissolve the parliament in 1989 while the deputies were meeting in Ta'if. Aoun was driven out of the presidential palace by a military campaign on orders of the new president, Elias Hrawi. He went into exile to France and returned only in 2005.

al-Assad, Bashar. (Alawi.) Son of Hafez al-Assad and president of Syria from 2000 to the present.

al-Assad, Hafez. (Alawi.) President of Syria from 1971 until his death in 2000.

Baroud, Ziad. (Maronite.) Lawyer and human rights activist. He served as secretary-general of the Lebanese Association for Democratic Elections in 2004–5 and was appointed as the minister of the interior and municipalities in the cabinet under Prime Minister Fouad Siniora. He has retained his office in the cabinet of Saad Hariri but has not been reappointed in the Mikati cabinet formed in June 2011.

Berri, Nabih. (Shi'i.) A leader of AMAL, one of the important Shi'a militias that fought in the Lebanese civil war. In the mid-1990s, he was one of the "Troika," formed by President Elias Hrawi, Prime Minister Rafiq Hariri, and himself as Speaker of the parliament.

Chamoun, Camille. (Maronite.) President of Lebanon from 1952 to 1958.

Chamoun, Dory. (Maronite.) Son of Camille Chamoun and leader of the National Liberal Party since 1990.

Chidiac, May. (Maronite.) A prominent journalist working as an anchor for LBCI, she was seriously injured in a car bomb in September 2005. After treatment and surgeries, she reappeared on television on May 25, 2006. She published her biography in French in 2007 and in February 2009 announced her resignation from the station.

Chiha, Michel. (Maronite.) One of the architects of the Lebanese political system and the brother-in-law of Lebanese president Bishara al-Khoury.

Fayyad, Ali. (Shi'i.) Former director of the Consultative Centre for Studies and Documentation, Hezbollah's main think tank. He is also a member of Hezbollah's political bureau. Fayyad was elected to the Lebanese Parliament in 2009.

Frangieh, Suleiman. (Maronite.) President of Lebanon from 1970 to 1976. It was during his presidency that the Lebanese civil war erupted.

Fuleihan, Basil. (Protestant.) Elected to the Lebanese Parliament in 2000 and became the minister of economy and trade. Fuleihan was riding in Rafiq Hariri's motorcade at the time of the prime minister's assassination on February 14, 2005, and was critically injured in the attack. He succumbed to his injuries on April 18, 2005.

Geagea, Samir. (Maronite.) Leader of the Christian militia-political party known as the Lebanese Forces. He was the only Lebanese warlord tried for war crimes. In early April 1994, the authorities arrested Geagea in association with several assassinations of political leaders that occurred during the civil war. His death sentence was commuted to life in prison, but he was released after eleven years following the Cedar Revolution in 2005.

Geagea, Setrida. (Maronite.) Wife of Samir Geagea and member of parliament since 2005.

Gemayel, Amin. (Maronite.) President of Lebanon from 1982 to 1988. He succeeded his younger brother, Bashir, as president following Bashir's assassination. He was the leader of the Kata'eb Party until the conclusion of his presidency in 1988, when the party fractured and he left Lebanon. He returned to Lebanon in 2000, and after the Cedar Revolution in 2005 he was able to reunite the Kata'eb Party and resume his leadership role in the organization.

Gemayel, Bashir. (Maronite.) Son of Pierre Gemayel and younger brother of Amin. He emerged as a leader first of the Kata'eb Party and then of the Lebanese Forces. His attack in 1975 against a bus carrying Palestinians in retaliation for an attempted assassination of his father is often regarded as the opening salvo of the Lebanese civil war. Following the Israeli invasion of Lebanon in 1982, he was elected president of Lebanon. He was assassinated before he could assume the office.

Gemayel, Nadim. (Maronite.) Son of Bashir Gemayel, he was elected to the parliament in 2009.

Gemayel, Pierre. (Maronite.) Founder of the Kata'eb (Phalangist) Party and father of Bashir and Amin Gemayel.

Gemayel, Pierre, II. (Maronite.) Son of Amin Gemayel, he became MP for the Metn area after the 2000 parliamentary elections. Siding with the anti-Syria opposition, he was reelected to the parliament in 2005 in the wake of the Cedar Revolution and was subsequently appointed to Fouad Siniora's cabinet. He was assassinated by unknown gunmen in November 2006.

Gemayel, Sami. (Maronite.) Pierre Gemayel II's brother, elected to the parliament in 2009.

Ghaith, Bahjat. (Druze.) Interim religious leader of the Druze until 1995, when Salman Abdul Khaliq was named to the office. Ghaith was then reinstated in 1998. Ghaith's term was supposed to expire in 2001, but he managed to have it extended until 2006, when he was replaced by Na'im Hassan.

Ghazaleh, Rustom. (Sunni.) Succeeded Ghazi Kanaan in 2002 as the head of Syrian intelligence in Lebanon. Ghazaleh was considered the "personal representative" of Bashar al-Assad in Lebanon and was feared, or at least flattered, by the Lebanese elite.

al-Habashi, Abdallah ben Muhammad ben Yousef. (Sunni.) Born in then Abyssinia in 1910. He learned Islamic law at the hands of the grand ulema of Ethiopia; however, because of trouble with the regime of the emperor Haile Selassie, he left for Medina and then Mecca. He also lived in Jerusalem and Damascus before settling in Lebanon in the early 1950s to take advantage of the freedoms available there. He was the force behind the creation of the al-Ahbash movement. Al-Habashi passed away in September 2008.

al-Hajj, Mounir. (Maronite.) Secretary-general of the Kata'eb Party from 1998 to 2002.

Hariri, Bahia. (Sunni.) Sister of Rafiq Hariri. She was elected as a member of parliament in 1992, 1996, 2000, 2005, and 2009. She also served as minister of education.

Hariri, Rafiq. (Sunni.) Dubbed the "merchant prince," he started as a successful businessman who had established close ties with both the French and the Saudi establishments, eventually becoming one of the richest men in the world. He served as prime minister of Lebanon from 1992 to 1998 and from 2000 to 2004. He was assassinated by a car bomb on February 14, 2005; his murder was the immediate impetus that triggered the Cedar Revolution.

Hariri, Saad. (Sunni.) Son of Rafiq Hariri and leader of the Future Movement Party. Saad Hariri was prime minister of Lebanon from November 2009 to the toppling of his government by the opposition in January 2011. He remained as caretaker prime minister until a new government was formed in June 2011.

Helou, Charles. (Maronite.) President of Lebanon from 1964 to 1970. He was one of the founders of the fascist-leaning Kata'eb (Phalangist) Party, but he later parted ways with this group and came under the influence of Michel Chiha, the founder of anti-Arab "Lebanonism."

Hobeiqa, Elie. (Maronite.) A leader of the Lebanese Forces, one of the three main militias that fought in the Lebanese civil war. He was in command of the Lebanese Forces militiamen who entered the Sabra and Shatila refugee camps in September 1982 and massacred the Palestinians who were residing there. Although Hobeiqa denied any personal involvement in the massacres, his claim was refuted by Israel's Kahan Commission. He was ousted from power in 1986 by Samir Gemayel for being pro-Syria, but was rewarded for his allegiance to Syria with important positions in the first decade of the postwar Syrian-influenced government. He was assassinated in 2002 in a bombing attack.

al-Hoss, Salim. (Sunni.) Served as prime minister of Lebanon three times, first from 1976 to 1980. His second and most controversial term was from 1987 to 1990, during which time the negotiations at Ta'if occurred. His third term was from 1998 to 2000, when after losing his parliamentary seat to an unknown candidate, he declared an end to his political career.

Hrawi, Elias. (Maronite.) President of Lebanon from 1989 to 1998, elected after the assassination of René Mouawad. He was effectively the first president of the Second Republic.

Jumblat, Kamal. (Druze.) Founder and leader of the Progressive Socialist Party from 1949 to 1977. He was assassinated in March 1977, leaving the mantle of the party leadership in the hands of his relatively inexperienced son, Walid.

Jumblat, Walid. (Druze.) Leader of the Progressive Socialist Party. He is seen by many as Lebanon's "political weathervane"—he is regarded as one of the smartest politicians in the country, and throughout his career he has been successful in choosing the winning side at the early stages of the contest.

Kanaan, Ghazi. (Alawi.) A close friend of Syria's Assad family, he was one of the two principal Syrian representatives in Lebanon. He served as the head of Syrian intelligence in Lebanon for twenty years, from 1982 until 2002, and was described as a "kingmaker" in the postwar period. Kanaan was recalled to Syria and later appointed as a cabinet minister, holding the interior ministry portfolio. He committed suicide under suspicious circumstances in October 2005.

Kanaan, Ibrahim. (Maronite.) Member of parliament on the Free Patriotic Movement list since 2005. He was reelected in 2009.

Karami, Faisal. (Sunni.) Son of Omar Karami and heir apparent to the Karami political dynasty. Faisal was appointed as minister of youth and sports to the government formed by Najib Mikati in June 2011.

Karami, Omar. (Sunni.) Son of Abdul-Hamid Karami, one of the men of the independence. He inherited leadership when his brother Rashid was assassinated in the late 1980s. He was prime minister of Lebanon from 1990 to 1992. He formed the first government of the Second Republic in December 1990. He also served as prime minister from October 2004 to February 2005.

Karami, Rashid. (Sunni.) He served as prime minister of Lebanon eight times, with his last tenure from 1984 to 1987.

Khaled, Hassan. (Sunni.) Mufti of Lebanon from 1966 to 1989. He was assassinated in May 1989, allegedly by Syrian operatives.

al-Khoury, Bishara. (Maronite.) Part of the first elite coalition in 1943. He helped to organized a cabinet and a parliament that, in accordance with the outlines of the National Pact, incorporated the five largest Lebanese communities. He became the first president of independent Lebanon in 1943.

Lahoud, Émile. (Maronite.) President of Lebanon from 1998 to 2007. Prior to his presidency, he was commander of the Lebanese Armed Forces from 1989 to 1998, during which time he helped to depose Michel Aoun.

Mawlawi, Faisal. (Sunni.) One of the founders of the Jama'a Islamiyyah and its acting leader after Fathi Yakan was elected to the parliament in 1992. He passed away in May 2011.

Mikati, Najib. (Sunni.) Prime minister from April 19 to July 19, 2005. His cabinet was formed to supervise the 2005 elections following the Cedar Revolution. Mikati was reappointed prime minister in January 2011. Because of a gridlock in the system, he was not able to form a government until June 2011.

Mouawad, Nayla. (Maronite.) Widow of President-Elect René Mouawad. First appointed to the postwar parliament in 1991, Nayla Mouawad has since been elected consistently (in 1992, 1996, 2000, and 2005). She retired from politics in 2009 and transferred her parliamentary seat to her son, Michel.

Mouawad, René. (Maronite.) Elected to the presidency of Lebanon in 1989 following the Ta'if Agreement, but on November 22, 1989 (Lebanese Independence Day), he was assassinated in a car bomb before assuming office. Like his successors, Mouawad maintained unusually close ties with Syria.

Murr, Michel. (Maronite.) Dubbed himself a "superminister," as he served in multiple important cabinet positions throughout the Second Republic. He owed his political career to his loyalty to Syria and was rewarded after the Ta'if Agreement with successive elections to parliament from 1992 to 2005. After his son married the daughter of President Émile Lahoud, Murr's access to power became almost unlimited. This situation was especially true in the period between 1998 and 2000, when he shadowed the weak prime minister, Salim al-Hoss.

Nasrallah, Hassan. (Shi'i.) Current secretary-general of Hezbollah. He was not part of the inner circle of the party's founders, and he did not play a prominent role in the organization during the civil war. He gradually became recognized for his leadership qualities, however, and when the previous leader, Musawi, was assassinated in 1992, Nasrallah was elected as Hezbollah's new secretary-general.

Pakradouni, Karim. (Armenian Orthodox.) Succeeded Mounir al-Hajj as secretary-general of the Kata'eb Party in October 2001. From 2001 to 2005, he led the pro-Syria faction of the party and was one of the most eloquent advocates of the Syrian presence and hegemony in Lebanon. He was Armenian and the first non-Maronite leader of the Kata'eb Party.

Qassem, Na'im. (Shi'i.) Current deputy secretary-general of Hezbollah, he is considered a possible future successor to Hassan Nasrallah as the party's secretary-general.

Qassir, Samir. (Greek Orthodox.) Born in Lebanon to a Palestinian father and a Syrian mother, he received a PhD in history from the Sorbonne in 1990 and then came back to Lebanon, where he worked both as a lecturer at the University of St. Joseph and as a columnist for the daily *an-Nahar*. He was assassinated in June 2005.

Qordahi, Jean-Louis. (Maronite.) Elected as president of the Jbeil Municipality in 1998 and in 1999 became the president of the Jbeil Municipalities Union. In 2000 he was appointed as minister of telecommunications, a position that he retained until April 2005. Qordahi ran unsuccessfully for the 2005 legislative elections in Jbeil.

Sa'adeh, Antun. (Greek Orthodox.) Founder of the Syrian Social National Party. In July 1949, the party declared a revolution in Lebanon. The revolt was suppressed, and Sa'adeh took refuge in Syria. He was handed over to the Lebanese authorities, judged by a military tribunal, and then executed on July 8, 1949.

al-Sadr, Musa. (Shi'i.) Of Iranian origin, he arrived in Lebanon in 1959 to assume the leadership of the Shi'a of Tyre. In 1967 al-Sadr managed to obtain parliamentary approval for the creation of the Supreme Shi'a Council, and in 1974, he joined with the Greek Catholic bishop Grégoire Haddad to create the Movement of the Deprived. In July 1975, al-Sadr was obliged to acknowledge the existence of a military branch of his organization known as AMAL.

Sfeir, Mar Nasrallah Boutros. (Maronite.) Patriarch of the Maronite community since the resignation of his predecessor in 1986. In 1994 he was promoted to the rank of cardinal by Pope John Paul II.

Shehab, Fouad. (Maronite.) President of Lebanon from 1958 to 1964. Prior to his presidency, he was the first commander of the Lebanese Armed Forces after Lebanese independence.

Siniora, Fouad. (Sunni.) Prime minister of Lebanon from 2005 to 2009.

al-Solh, Riad. (Sunni.) Part of the first elite coalition in 1943. Helped to organized a cabinet and a parliament that, in accordance with the outlines of the National Pact, incorporated the five largest Lebanese communities. He was appointed the first prime minister of independent Lebanon in 1943.

Suleiman, Michel. (Maronite.) Succeeded Émile Lahoud to the presidency in 2008. Like Lahoud before him, he was also formerly at the head of the Lebanese army.

Tueni, Gebran. (Greek Orthodox.) Former editor and publisher of the daily newspaper *an-Nahar*. He was elected to the parliament in May 2005 and was assassinated in a car bomb in December 2005.

Yakan, Fathi. (Sunni.) A pioneer of the Islamic movement in the 1950s, he was one of the founders of the Jama'a Islamiyyah and its ideologue. He authored more than thirty-five books before passing away in 2009.

Lebanese Political Timeline (1989–2005)

October 22, 1989	Ta'if Agreement signed.
November 4, 1989	Ta'if Agreement ratified.
November 5, 1989	René Mouawad elected president.
November 22, 1989	Mouawad assassinated.
November 24, 1989	Elias Hrawi elected president.
May 1991	"Treaty of Brotherhood and Cooperation" between Syria and Lebanon signed.
June 1991	"Law 88" promulgated, integrating six thousand militiamen into the Lebanese Armed Forces.
September 1991	"Defense and Security Agreement" between Syria and Lebanon signed.
October 1992	First postwar parliamentary elections held. Hezbollah for the first time participated in the elections, while Christian elites boycotted them.
October 1995	President Hrawi's presidential term extended at Syria's behest.
August–September 1996	Parliamentary elections held. Even though the majority of the Christians who ran for office in 1996 were not elected, their participation created a precedent for the return of the Christian community to the political process.
May–June 1998	Municipal elections held.
November 1998	Émile Lahoud elected president.

May 25, 2000	Israel withdraws from Lebanon.
June 10, 2000	Syrian president Hafez al-Assad dies.
August–September 2000	Third postwar parliamentary elections held.
May 2004	Municipal elections held.
September 2, 2004	UN Security Council issues Resolution 1559 calling for the withdrawal of all foreign troops from Lebanon and the disarming of all militias.
September 3, 2004	Syria successfully pushes to extend Émile Lahoud presidential mandate.
February 14, 2005	Former prime minister Rafiq Hariri assassinated by a car bomb.
March 8, 2005	Pro-Syria protesters, including Hezbollah supporters, turn out in Beirut after the announced withdrawal of Syrian troops to express gratitude to Syria for helping end the Lebanese civil war.
March 14, 2005	An estimated one million anti-Syria protesters turn out in Beirut to protest the assassination of former prime minister Rafiq Hariri. This enormous demonstration was heralded the "Cedar Revolution."
April 27, 2005	Syrian troops withdraw from Lebanon.
May–June 2005	The first parliamentary elections after Syrian withdrawal held. The elections saw a high rate of turnover, with new parliamentarians representing 47.66 percent of the deputies.

Notes

Introduction

1. Lebanon's various religious communities are discussed in detail in chapter 5.

2. *Cedar Revolution* is the term used in English, coined by officials in the State Department. In Lebanon it was called the "Independence Intifada." However, the term *Intifada* carries too much baggage in English because it brings to mind the Palestinian-Israeli conflict.

3. Important studies in English of the prewar Lebanese political scene include Leonard Binder, ed., *Politics in Lebanon;* Michael Hudson, *The Precarious Republic: Modernization in Lebanon;* Kamal Salibi, *Crossroads to Civil War;* Michael Johnson, *Class and Client in Beirut: The Sunni Muslim Community and the Lebanese State, 1840–1985;* Samir Khalaf, *Lebanon's Predicament;* and Farid el-Khazen, *The Breakdown of the State in Lebanon, 1967–1976.* Studies that analyze the war years include Charles Winslow, *Lebanon: War and Politics in a Fragmented Society;* Latif Abul-Husn, *The Lebanese Conflict, Looking Inward;* Edgar O'Ballance, *Civil War in Lebanon;* and Elizabeth Picard, *Lebanon: A Shattered Country.* In this book, I also draw from studies of Lebanese electoral politics that were published in Arabic in Beirut, including Farid el-Khazen and Paul Salem, eds., *Al-intikhabat al-ula fi Lubnan ma ba'ad al-harb,* and Fares Abi Saab et al., *Al-intikhabat al-niyabia 1996 wa azmat al-dimuqratiya fi Lubnan* and *Al-intikhabat al-baladiya fi Lubnan 1998.*

4. The term *political elite* is said to have been coined in the nineteenth century by Italian sociologist Vildredo Pareto. The term has been used more recently by political scientists such as Harold Lasswell and Robert Dahl.

5. S. Khalaf, *Lebanon's Predicament,* 94. See also Edward Shils, "The Prospect of Lebanese Civility"; and Arnold Hottinger, "Zu'ama in Historical Perspective."

6. The reputational method involves using the judgment of elite individuals to determine who the most influential people in the system are. For more information on this method, see David Knoke, "Networks of Elite Structure and Decision Making."

7. In some cases, I found that I could not gain access to specific politicians despite my ongoing efforts to arrange an interview. Meanwhile, foreign scholars who were

visiting Lebanon for a week or two were able to obtain an audience with these politicians with apparent ease. A generous interpretation of this difference in treatment would be that Lebanese politicians often view foreign scholars as a conduit to share their ideas with the outside world.

8. Albert Hunter, "Local Knowledge and Local Power: Notes on the Ethnography of Local Community Elites," 65.

9. George Moyser and Margaret Wagstaffe, "Studying Elites: Theoretical and Methodological Issues," 17.

10. Jean Lacouture, "Trois interrogatoires respectifs," 125.

11. Moyser and Wagstaffe, "Studying Elites," 8. For more on the problems and pitfalls of interviewing elites—and the means of avoiding these pitfalls—see Rola el-Husseini, "Insights from the Field: Research Problems and Methodologies."

12. See Brady Sinclair, "Studying Members of the United States Congress," 67.

1. The Lebanese Political System: The Elite Pacts of 1943 and 1989

1. Arend Lijphart, "Consociational Democracy," 217–19; "Typologies of Democratic Systems," 15.

2. Fakhoury Muehlbacher, *Power-Sharing and Democratisation,* 157–58.

3. Similar arguments have been made by Donald Rothchild and Philip Roeder in "Dilemmas of State-Building in Divided Societies" and by Marie-Joëlle Zahar in "Power Sharing in Lebanon: Foreign Protectors, Domestic Peace, and Democratic Failure." My study develops the insights of these authors by providing a more nuanced and in-depth analysis of the functioning of consociational arrangements in postwar Lebanon.

4. Zahar, "Power Sharing in Lebanon," 219.

5. Lijphart, "Consociational Democracy," 216.

6. Arend Lijphart, *Democracy in Plural Societies,* 25.

7. Ibid., 149–50.

8. Lijphart, "Consociational Democracy," 216.

9. See Michael Hudson, "The Problem of Authoritative Power in Lebanese Politics: Why Consociationalism Failed," 227; Joseph Jabbra and Nancy Jabbra, "Consociational Democracy in Lebanon: A Flawed System of Governance," 74–75; and Brenda Seaver, "The Regional Sources of Power-Sharing Failure: The Case of Lebanon," 249.

10. See Theodor Hanf, *Coexistence in Wartime Lebanon,* 70.

11. Bassem Jisr, *Mithaq 1943,* 145–47 (my translation).

12. Ibid., 225.

13. Ibid., 226 (my translation).

14. See Pierre Rondot, "The Political Institutions of Lebanese Democracy," 129–34.

15. Farid el-Khazen, *The Communal Pact of National Identities: The Making and Politics of the 1943 National Pact,* 24.

16. This analysis develops the insights of Richard H. Dekmejian in his article "Consociational Democracy in Crisis: The Case of Lebanon."

17. Eyal Zisser, *Lebanon: The Challenge of Independence,* 51.

18. Ibid., 194.

19. Ibid., 202.

20. Michel Chiha was a Lebanese banker, thinker, and editorialist. He was the brother-in-law of Bishara al-Khoury and one of the architects of the Lebanese Constitution. Believers in his doctrine of "Lebanonism" were eager to identify with Phoenician and Greco-Roman heritage and to reject Arab influences in their culture and society. For more on the ideology of Phoenicianism, see chapter 7.

21. I define state breakdown as the loss of the state's monopoly on violence. It should be noted that throughout the civil war, most Lebanese state institutions continued to operate: the chamber met, presidents were elected, and administrations were confirmed. The government, however, did not have control of the country.

22. See el-Khazen, *Breakdown of the State;* and Seaver, "Regional Sources of Power-Sharing Failure."

23. In most cases, upon the death of a *za'im,* the brother, son, or nephew of that person automatically became the representative of his community.

24. See Dekmejian, "Consociational Democracy in Crisis"; and Judith Harik, *The Public and Social Services of the Lebanese Militias.*

25. Joseph Maila, *The Document of National Understanding: A Commentary,* 14.

26. While the postwar political system was in theory parliamentarian and the Maronite president was formally stripped of his power, in practice (largely because of Syrian support for the president), the new power balance indicated in the Ta'if Agreement was never fully realized. In the following sections, I describe in detail the ways in which the parliamentarianism of the Ta'if Agreement was undermined during the years of Syrian hegemony.

27. These events are discussed in detail in chapter 2. See also Daoud Sayegh, *Al-nizam al-lubnani fi thawabitihi wa tahawulatihi,* 52.

28. Originally, the Ta'if Agreement stipulated that the number of parliamentarians was to be 108, but owing to Syrian pressure (which will be discussed in the following section), the number was increased in practice to 128. Syria wanted to ensure that the parliament would include all of its Lebanese clients and allies.

29. There has been no population census taken in Lebanon since 1932, but as of February 11, 2010, the CIA World Factbook (https://www.cia.gov/library/publications /the-world-factbook/geos/le.html) estimates that Muslims constitute 59.7 percent of the population, while Christians constitute 39 percent.

30. For a further discussion of consociationalism in the Second Republic, see Andrew Rigby, "Lebanon: Patterns of Confessional Politics"; and Michael Hudson, "Trying Again: Power-Sharing in Post–Civil War Lebanon."

31. American scholar Barbara Walter has argued that few civil wars end in implemented peace settlements, and that they do so "only if a third party is willing to enforce or verify demobilization." Walter, *Committing to Peace: The Successful Settlement of Civil Wars,* 5. While Walter was probably referring to international peacekeeping forces, it can be argued that Syria has played the role of the arbiter in postconflict Lebanon.

32. Naomi Weinberger, *Syrian Intervention in Lebanon.*

33. See Eric Thompson, "Will Syria Have to Withdraw from Lebanon?"

34. Daad Bou Melhab-Atallah, "The Treaty of Brotherhood and Cooperation," 89 (my translation).

35. There were two exceptions to this rule in the early 1980s: Bashir Gemayel and then his brother Amin. The former was elected after the Israeli invasion of Lebanon and with covert Israeli support. The latter was elected after his brother's assassination, in part as a sympathy vote and in part because of American support.

36. For more on the postwar elections, see el-Khazen and Salem, *Al-intikhabat al-ula fi Lubnan ma ba'd al-harb;* and Abi Saab et al., *Al-intikhabat al-niyabia 1996 wa azmat al-dimuqratia fi Lubnan.*

37. Bassel F. Salloukh, "The Limits of Electoral Engineering in Divided Societies: Elections in Post-war Lebanon," 641.

38. Michael Young, *The Ghosts of Martyrs Square,* 78–79.

39. Ibid., 69.

40. Ibid., 74–77.

41. Ibid., 70–74.

42. Kanaan was recalled to Syria and was later appointed to the government as minister of the interior. He allegedly committed suicide in October 2005. There was speculation at the time that Kanaan might have been assassinated. Some bloggers and commentators believed that he had been subjected to an "involuntary suicide" as a scapegoat for the 2005 assassination of Lebanese prime minister Rafiq Hariri. Others argued that Kanaan might have been seen as a threat to Syrian president Bashar al-Assad's regime.

43. Mouna Naïm, "Le général qui régnait sur 'Beau Rivage,'" *Le Monde,* Mar. 31, 2005, http://medias.lemonde.fr/mmpub/edt/doc/20050330/633361_sup_liban _050330.pdf.

44. See Augustus R. Norton, *Hezbollah: A Short History,* 127.

45. Mitchell Prothero, "Beirut Bombshell."

46. Nada Bakri, "Lebanese Bank Scandal Linked to Hariri Killing," *Daily Star* (Beirut), Jan. 20, 2006.

47. Mitchell Prothero, "The Money Scandal Behind the Hariri Assassination."

48. See Pippa Norris, *Driving Democracy: Do Power-Sharing Institutions Work?*, 111–12.

49. Nancy Bermeo, "What Democratization Literature Says—or Doesn't Say—about Postwar Democratization," 166.

50. Leonard Wantchekon, "The Paradox of 'Warlord' Democracy: A Theoretical Investigation," 18.

51. Marina Ottaway, "Promoting Democracy after Conflict: The Difficult Choices," 316.

52. Elizabeth Picard, *The Demobilization of Lebanese Militias*, 3–5.

53. See Peter Koekenbier, "Multi-ethnic Armies: Lebanese Lessons and Iraqi Implications."

54. Joanna Spears distinguishes between two types of disarmament, coercive and cooperative, and maintains that cooperative disarmament "is commonly associated with peace settlements where there has been no clear victor in the conflict." Spears, "Disarmament and Demobilization," 142. Spears says that outside monitors play a "crucial role in preventing a backslide into a destructive security dilemma" (147).

55. Terrence Lyons, "The Role of Postsettlement Elections," 217.

56. Charles Call and Susan Cook have argued that peace building involves not only "keeping former enemies from going back to war, but also addressing the root causes of conflict." Call and Cook, "On Democratization and Peacebuilding," 233.

2. Postwar Elite Interaction

1. Michael Burton and John Higley, "Elite Settlements," 295. Burton and Higley are careful to specify that elite settlements "pave the way for, though they do not guarantee, the emergence of democratic politics" (ibid.).

2. Dissident groups and their elites are defined here as those who do not accept the existing "rules of the game."

3. See Michael Burton, Richard Gunther, and John Higley, "Introduction: Elite Transformations and Democratic Regimes," 14–15.

4. George Bacassini, *Asrar al-Ta'if.*

5. The government of Michel Aoun has been the subject of several memoirs, the most important of which are the works of former member of parliament Albert Mansour and former prime minister Salim al-Hoss. Mansour, *Al-inqilab 'ala al-Ta'if* and *Mawt jumhuriyya;* al-Hoss, *'Ahd al-qarar wa al-hawa* and *'Ala tariq al-jumhuriyya al-jadida.*

6. Mansour, *Mawt jumhuriyya*, 221–23.

7. Aref al-Abed, *Lubnan wa al-Ta'if,* 198.

8. Ibid., 199–200.

9. Mansour, *Mawt jumhuriyya*, 224–25.

10. Al-Abed, *Lubnan wa al-Ta'if,* 203.

11. Mansour, *Mawt jumhuriyya,* 321.

12. Al-Abed, *Lubnan wa al-Ta'if,* 204–6.

13. *Accord Libanais d'entente nationale,* 21.

14. Al-Abed, *Lubnan wa al-Ta'if,* 210.

15. Ibid., 233–36.

16. Ibid., 236.

17. Ibid., 237.

18. Marie-Joëlle Zahar, "Lebanon's Ta'if Agreement," 571.

19. Bacassini, *Asrar al-Ta'if,* 86.

20. Ibid., 84.

21. Ibid., 87.

22. European Union Election Observation Mission to Lebanon, 2005, "Final Report on the Parliamentary Elections," 14.

23. Paul Salem, introduction to *Al-intikhabat al-ula fi Lubnan ma ba'd al-harb,* edited by Salem and el-Khazen, 22.

24. Ibid., 22.

25. Nicolas Nassif, "Intikhabat jabal Lubnan al-shamali," 95.

26. Ibid.

27. Ibid., 98.

28. Ibid.

29. Ibid.

30. For example, see Farid el-Khazen, *Intikhabat Lubnan ma ba'd al-harb,* 226.

31. United Nations Programme on Governance in the Arab Region, "Annual Report, 2004: Lebanon," n.p.

32. In an article titled "Lebanese Elections, 2005 Version: Land Liberation or Mind Liberation?," Joseph Ajami notes that "at least 60 new faces became deputies in the new Parliament and a large percentage of those were previously unfamiliar names. By Lebanese standards this is considered bold change, reflecting a desire for a new path" (637). Pertinent analyses of the elections by Lebanese scholars can also be found in Jaafar Abdel-Khaleq, *Intikhabat al-istiqlal 2005;* and Abdo Saad, *Al-intikhabat al-niyabiyya li 'am 2005: Qira'at wa nata'ij.*

33. Aoun's bloc was originally composed of fourteen members, but another parliamentarian named Camille Khoury was added during the by-election of August 2007 (which was held following the assassination of Pierre Gemayel II). Like the other members of Aoun's bloc, Khoury's victory was almost purely a result of his patron's popularity. For more information about Camille Khoury's election, see Andrew Lee Butters, "Hizballah's Christian Soldiers."

34. This appeal for amnesty was successful, and Samir Geagea was released in July 2005.

35. See Gary C. Gambill, "Damascus Co-opts the Phalange."

3. Political Parties

1. Michael W. Suleiman, *Political Parties in Lebanon: The Challenge of a Fragmented Political Culture*, xvi.

2. Exceptions included the Syrian Social Nationalist Party and the Communist Party.

3. Farid el-Khazen, "Political Parties in Postwar Lebanon: Parties in Search of Partisans," 606.

4. Fouad Makhzoumi's al-Hiwar Party, established in 2004, might be seen as a counterexample. However, I subscribe to the view expressed by journalist Taylor Long, who maintains that al-Hiwar is "a one-man show" that was created by Makhzoumi for the purposes of self-aggrandizement. Long, "Visions with No Voice," *NOW Lebanon*, Nov. 18, 2007, http://www.nowlebanon.com/NewsArchiveDetails.aspx?ID=20159.

5. See Khalil A. Khalil, "Ahzab Lubnan: Matha tabaqa minha?," 24.

6. On the definition of *warlord*, see John MacKinlay, "Defining Warlords"; and Anthony Vinci, "'Like Worms in the Entrails of a Natural Man': A Conceptual Analysis of Warlords."

7. Richard Gunther and Larry Diamond, "Species of Political Parties: A New Typology," 176.

8. Ibid., 182–83.

9. Adolf Hitler created the "Brown Shirts" in Germany, while the "Black Shirts" were created by Benito Mussolini in Italy. Other similar groups included the "Green Shirts" in Hungary and the "Blue Shirts" in Ireland.

10. John P. Entelis, *Pluralism and Party Transformation in Lebanon: Al-Kata'ib, 1936–1970*, 46.

11. Ibid., 50–51.

12. Ibid., 63.

13. The Kata'eb elected one member to parliament in the 1959 by-elections, six members in the 1960 elections, four members in the 1964 elections, and nine members in the 1968 elections.

14. Frank Stoakes, "The Supervigilantes: The Lebanese Kata'eb Party as a Builder, Surrogate, and Defender of the State," 215–16; John P. Entelis, "Structural Change and Organizational Development in the Lebanese Kata'ib Party," 21.

15. Ghassan Hage, "Religious Fundamentalism as a Political Strategy: The Evolution of the Lebanese Forces' Religious Discourse During the Lebanese Civil War," 30.

16. Stoakes, "Supervigilantes," 223.

17. Joseph Abou Khalil, *Qissat al-mawarina fi al-harb*, 115.

18. Ibid., 122.

19. Ibid., 137.

20. Ibid., 182–83.

21. Lewis W. Snider, "The Lebanese Forces: Their Origins and Role in Lebanon's Politics," 23.

22. Hage, "Religious Fundamentalism as a Political Strategy," 37–38.

23. Young, *Ghosts of Martyrs Square,* 90.

24. A collection of Pierre Gemayel II's speeches is available on the website of the Kata'eb (http://www.kataeb.org).

25. *An-Nahar.*

26. Sami Moubayed, "Lebanon's Phalange Party: Back from the Grave?," n.p.

27. Ibid.

28. Jessy Chahine, "Divided Phalange Party: Set for Reunification?," *Daily Star* (Beirut), Sept. 3, 2005.

29. Ibid.

30. Hania Taan, "United Phalange Party Is the Only Indicator for Christian Unity," *Daily Star* (Beirut), Sept. 21, 2005, http://www.dailystar.com.lb/News/Politics/Sep /21/United-Phalange-Party-is-the-only-indicator-for-Christian-unity.ashx#axzz1Q58 JO2D6.

31. Pierre Gemayel II's assassination was also symbolic, as it was the 1975 attempt against his grandfather and namesake that triggered the onset of the Lebanese civil war. This time, however, instead of responding violently, an estimated eight hundred thousand people attended Pierre II's funeral, turning it into a political rally against Syria and its supporters. US president George W. Bush also took an active role in condemning the assassination and calling for stability in Lebanon.

32. Political scientist Lewis Snider has disputed this interpretation. Writing in 1984, Snider maintained that "while the Kata'ib [*sic*] party appears to be a dominant component of the Lebanese Forces, the appearance is stronger than the substance. . . . Many of the personnel in positions of responsibility and authority have either weak or no formal ties to the Kata'ib." Snider, "Lebanese Forces," 16. Although Snider may be correct in regard to the foot soldiers and midlevel leaders of the Lebanese Forces, the most important party leaders during the first ten years of the organization's existence were, in fact, drawn primarily from the Kata'eb.

33. Ibid., 12–13.

34. The LF commander ousted by Hobeiqa and Geagea was Fouad Abu Nadir, a nephew and close follower of Amin Gemayel, who had assumed the leadership of the LF in October 1984.

35. Abou Khalil, *Qissat al-mawarina fi al-harb,* 134–35.

36. Israel's Kahan Commission estimated the number of victims at between seven and eight hundred. Yizhak Kahan, Aharon Barak, and Yona Efrat, "Report of the Commission of Inquiry into the Events at the Refugee Camps in Beirut," n.p. The larger number is drawn from the arguments of the French Israeli journalist Amnon Kapeliouk (*Enquête sur un massacre: Sabra et Chatila,* 45–46).

37. Israeli forces had surrounded the Palestinian refugee camps and maintained control of access at the time of the massacre. The Kahan Commission found that Ariel Sharon "bears personal responsibility" for the war crime, and it recommended that he be dismissed as minister of defense and never again allowed to hold public office. Nonetheless, Sharon was elected as prime minister of Israel in March 2001. See Zeev Schiff and Ehud Ya'ari, *Israel's Lebanon War*, 283–84.

38. For more on the CIA's role in this operation, see Bob Woodward, *The Veil*, 397, 516.

39. Abou Khalil, *Qissat al-mawarina fi al-harb*, 369.

40. Despite the fact that he never completed his degree, Geagea's followers often refer to him as "Hakim" ("the Physician").

41. Abou Khalil, *Qissat al-mawarina fi al-harb*, 332.

42. Ghassan Charbel, *Ayna kunta fi al-harb*, 143.

43. Abou Khalil, *Qissat al-mawarina fi al-harb*, 333–34.

44. The *New York Times* reported that the Christian internecine war "killed more than 900 people, wounded 3,000 and forced about 300,000 to flee abroad." Ihsan A. Hijazi, "Lebanese Christians Ravaged, Now by Lebanese Christians," *New York Times*, Apr. 9, 1990, http://www.nytimes.com/1990/04/09/world/lebanese-christians-ravaged -now-by-lebanese-christians.html?scp=6&sq=saadeh%20phalange&st=cse.

45. Joseph Wadi Shartouni, *Inahu Huwa: Samir Geagea, min al-wilada ila al-wilada*, 781.

46. "Lebanon's Cabinet Named, Then Boycotted," *New York Times*, Dec. 25, 1990, http://www.nytimes.com/1990/12/25/world/lebanon-s-cabinet-named-then -boycotted.html.

47. Dany Chamoun, the leader of the National Liberal Party, was assassinated with his wife and two small children on October 21, 1990. This crime outraged the Lebanese public, especially because of the murder of the two children. Geagea was accused of killing Chamoun in order to remove him as a competitor for the leadership of the Maronite community.

48. Amnesty International expressed concern about Geagea's arrest and trial, reporting that the proceedings "fell short of international fair trial standards." Amnesty International, "Samir Gea'gea' and Jirjis al-Khouri: Torture and Unfair Trial," n.p.

49. See ibid.

50. Gary C. Gambill and Ziad K. Abdelnour, "Dossier: Fouad Malek."

51. Ibid.

52. Ibid.

53. *An-Nahar*.

54. This statement was posted on the website of the Lebanese Forces (http://www .lebanese-forces.org/samiegeageabiography/index.shtml).

55. This statement read in part, "I fully apologize for all the mistakes that we committed when we were carrying out our national duties during past civil war years . . . I

ask God to forgive, and so I ask the people whom we hurt in the past." Borzou Daragahi, "An Ex-warlord's Act of Contrition," *Los Angeles Times,* Dec. 15, 2008. http://articles .latimes.com/2008/dec/15/world/fg-warlord15.

56. The other founders of the PSP included Farid Gebran (Catholic), Albert Adeeb (Maronite), Abdallah Alayli (Sunni), Fouad Rizk (Greek Catholic), and George Hanna (Greek Orthodox). These men had much in common: they were all upper-middle-class, college-educated urbanites, and they had all been friends or acquaintances of Kamal Jumblat for some time prior to the founding of the PSP.

57. Farid el-Khazen, "Kamal Jumblatt, the Uncrowned Druze Prince of the Left," 179.

58. Nazih Richani, *Dilemmas of Democracy and Political Parties in Sectarian Societies: The Case of the Progressive Socialist Party of Lebanon (1949–1996),* 36. See also Yusri Hazran, "Between Authenticity and Alienation: The Druzes and Lebanon's History."

59. Richani, *Dilemmas of Democracy,* 87.

60. Most commentators believe that Kamal Jumblat's assassination was carried out on the orders of the Syrian leadership, who viewed the PSP militia as a threat to their plans for Lebanon. See el-Khazen, "Kamal Jumblatt," 184.

61. Judith Harik, "The Effects of the Military Tradition on Lebanon's Assertive Druzes," 54; Richani, *Dilemmas of Democracy,* 97.

62. Judith Harik, "Change and Continuity among the Lebanese Druze Community: The Civil Administration of the Mountain, 1983–1990," 381.

63. Ibid., 383–85.

64. J. Harik, "Effects of the Military Tradition."

65. Ibid., 52.

66. Marwan Rowayheb, "Walid Jumblat and Political Alliances: The Politics of Adaptation," 64.

67. Rowayheb has argued that Jumblat dealt with political changes "pragmatically rather than ideologically" and that "there was no permanent ideological component to his political discourse." Ibid., 48.

68. Charbel, *Ayna kunta fi al-harb,* 310.

69. Ibid.

70. A modified version of this section appeared in *Third World Quarterly* 31, no. 5 (2010), under the title "Hezbollah and the Axis of Refusal."

71. Ervand Abrahamian, *Khomeinism,* 26–27.

72. Michael Fischer, *Iran: From Religious Dispute to Revolution.* See also Kamran S. Aghaie, *The Martyrs of Karbala: Shi'i Symbols and Rituals in Modern Iran,* 13.

73. The spread of the Karbala paradigm in the Shi'i world was also influenced by the work of Ali Shari'ati, an Iranian intellectual who was inspired by the anti-imperialist writings of Jean-Paul Sartre and Frantz Fanon. Fanon's book *The Wretched of the Earth* so excited Shari'ati that he translated it into Persian. Shari'ati was struck by Fanon's idea

of violence as a means of liberation from colonialism, and he restated these liberation-ist themes using Shi'i terms and symbols. Shari'ati's two most important works are *Red Shi'ism vs. Black Shi'ism* and *Fatima Is Fatima*. In more recent years, scholar Fousi Slisli has likewise argued that Islam is naturally affiliated with resistance against colonialism and that this Islamic basis of resistance is a "hidden elephant" in Fanon's work. Slisli maintains that "what *The Wretched of the Earth* actually describes is the combination of two systems of organization—one Marxist, the other Islamic." Slisli, "Islam: The Elephant in Fanon's *The Wretched of the Earth*," 97.

74. An English translation of Hezbollah's "Open Letter" was posted on the web-site of the International Institute of Counter-Terrorism (http://212.150.54.123/articles/articledet.cfm?articleid=409). For further discussion of Hezbollah's ideology, see Norton, *Hezbollah: A Short History.*

75. For more on Hezbollah charities, see Mona Harb and Reinoud Leenders, "Know Thy Enemy: Hizbullah, 'Terrorism,' and the Politics of Perception."

76. "The Middle East Talks: Israel's Planes and Guns Attack Party of God Forces in Lebanon," *New York Times,* Nov. 2, 1991, http://www.nytimes.com/1991/11/02/world/middle-east-talks-israel-s-planes-guns-attack-party-god-forces-lebanon.html.

77. Hezbollah turned Khiam into a museum after the Israeli withdrawal in 2000. It was destroyed by Israel during the summer 2006 war.

78. David Dodge was the president of the American University of Beirut, Terry Waite was the Anglican Church envoy to Lebanon, and Terry Anderson was the chief Middle East correspondent for the Associated Press. In his later writings, Terry Waite referred to his expe-rience of torture at the hands of his kidnappers and decried the use of similar methods by the United States in its "war on terror." See Waite, "Justice or Revenge?" and "Our Loss of the Moral High Ground," *Guardian,* June 21, 2009, http://www.guardian.co.uk/commentisfree/2009/jun/21/iraq-hostages-families.

79. Na'im Qassem, *Hizbullah: The Story from Within,* 187.

80. Ibid., 288.

81. Joseph Alagha, *Shifts in Hizbullah's Ideology,* 150–51.

82. For more on the Qana massacre, see Human Rights Watch, "Operation Grapes of Wrath: The Civilian Victims."

83. Asher Kaufman has argued that the Shebaa Farms situation arose from the way that France originally delineated the Syrian-Lebanese borders. After their independence, both countries avoided taking action to rectify the border anomalies. Since 1920 maps have located the Shebaa Farms area within Syria; however, in all practical matters, the area was considered a part of Lebanon. See Kaufman, "Who Owns the Shebaa Farms? Chronicle of a Territorial Dispute."

84. Hezbollah rejected what is known as the "Blue Line," the border demarcation between Lebanon and Israel that was established by the UN cartography team for the pur-poses of confirming the Israeli withdrawal. The Blue Line is not identical to the original

border between the two countries that was established in the armistice of 1948 following the Arab-Israeli war.

85. See Norton, *Hezbollah: A Short History,* 90.

86. See Claudia Rosett, "Lebanese Staging Rallies Demanding 'the Truth' Behind Hariri Murder," *New York Sun,* Mar. 14, 2005, http://www.nysun.com/foreign/lebanese -staging-rallies-demanding-the-truth/10504/.

87. See Daniel Sobelman, *New Rules of the Game: Israel and Hizbollah after the Withdrawal from Lebanon.*

88. International Crisis Group, "Israel/Hizbollah/Lebanon: Avoiding Renewed Conflict," n.p.

89. Mideast Monitor, "Briefing: Lebanese Public Opinion." (Poll conducted by the Beirut Center for Research and Information.)

90. The term *Divine Victory* is a play on Hezbollah leader Nasrallah's name (*nasr* is the Arabic word for "victory").

91. Amal Saad-Ghorayeb, "Hezbollah's Apocalypse Now," *Washington Post,* July 23, 2006, http://www.washingtonpost.com/wp-dyn/content/article/2006/07/21/AR20 06072101363.html.

92. The full text of the Winograd Commission's report was posted on the website of the US-based Council on Foreign Relations (http://www.cfr.org/israel/winograd -commission-final-report/p15385).

93. The government also dismissed a prominent Hezbollah sympathizer, Brigadier General Wafiq Shuqayr, from his position as head of security at Beirut Airport.

94. Two years before, in a televised interview, Nasrallah had reassured the nation that Hezbollah's weapons would be used only against Israel, and not against Lebanese citizens. See Norton, *Hezbollah: A Short History,* 154.

95. Rola el-Husseini, "Hizbullah and Non-violent Resistance: Delimiting the Boundaries of Peaceful Protest."

96. An English version of the manifesto, translated by Hussein Assi, was posted on the website of the Hezbollah-affiliated broadcasting network al-Manar under the title "Hezbollah New Manifesto." The translation is no longer available from al-Manar, but the English text has been reposted on a number of online blogs (for example, http://realisticbird.wordpress .com/2009/11/30/hezbollah-new-manifesto-we-want-strong-united-lebanon/).

97. Joseph Alagha, *Hizbullah's Documents: From the 1985 Open Letter to the 2009 Manifesto,* 118-22.

98. Hezbollah has cheered for the revolutions in Tunisia, Egypt, and especially in Bahrain, where its coreligionists faced brutal repression by the regime. However, the party has remained closely allied with the regime of Bashar al-Assad in Syria. This apparent contradiction has not been well received by the Arab populations that once adulated Hezbollah and its secretary-general, nor was the Syrian people's reaction to it temperate. Hezbollah flags have been burned in many Syrian cities during the uprising.

99. Max Weber, *Economy and Society*, 241–46.

100. Young, *Ghosts of Martyrs Square*, 96.

101. David Hirst, *Beware of Small States: Lebanon, Battleground of the Middle East*, 243. Note that Nasrallah is not an ayatollah, nor has he reached the position of *mujtahid*. He is sometimes referred to as *Hojat al-Islam*, the lowest rank in the Shi'i religious hierarchy.

102. Ibid., 247.

103. See, for example, Imad Shidiaq, *Al-muqawama wa sayyiduha Hassan Nasrallah;* Rifaat Sayyid Ahmad, *Hassan Nasrallah: Tha'er min al-janub;* and the anonymous *Min al-Sadr ila Nasrallah*.

104. *STRATFOR Global Intelligence,* "Lebanon: Hezbollah's Rising Star."

105. Al-Mourabitoun (the Sentinels) was established in 1967 by Ibrahim Qoleilat, a Sunni opposition leader. The militia members underwent training with the Palestinian Fatah movement and emerged at the outbreak of the civil war as a leftist faction and a central defender of the Sunni community. In the mid-1980s, al-Mourabitoun was decimated by AMAL and Hezbollah fighters at the bequest of Syria, in what became known as the "War of the Camps," and Qoleilat was forced into exile. In recent years, three groups, each espousing different alliances, have emerged to lay claim to the al-Mourabitoun name. None of these groups have been able to cultivate significant support among Lebanon's Sunnis.

106. For more on the PLO in Lebanon, see Rex Brynnen, *Sanctuary and Survival: The PLO in Lebanon*.

107. Since the Future Movement is a personality-based party and did not become fully active until after the period under study, it will not be described in detail in this chapter. A discussion of Rafiq Hariri's influence during the years of Syrian hegemony is provided in chapter 4, while the recent activities of Saad Hariri are mentioned in chapter 6.

108. Abdel-Ghani Imad, *Al-harakat al-islamiyya fi Lubnan*, 31–34.

109. Ibid., 35–40.

110. Ibid., 44.

111. Robert Rabil, *Religion, National Identity, and Confessional Politics in Lebanon*, 37.

112. Sebastian Elsasser, "Between Ideology and Pragmatism: Fathi Yakan's Theory of Islamic Activism," 401.

113. Rabil, *Religion, National Identity, and Confessional Politics*, 33–34.

114. Elsasser, "Between Ideology and Pragmatism," 395.

115. Ibid.

116. Imad, *Al-harakat al-islamiyya fi Lubnan*, 69–70.

117. This manifesto (in Arabic) was posted on the website of the Jama'a (http://www.al-jamaa.org/upload/Wathika_2462010.pdf). The translations here are my own.

118. For more on the al-Ahbash, visit the association's website (in Arabic) (http://www.projectsassociation.org/pages.php?pageid=19).

119. Al-Habashi was born in 1910 in Ethiopia. In the 1960s, he moved to Lebanon, where he died in 2008. See the website dedicated to al-Habashi (http://www.harariyy .org/).

120. A. Nizar Hamzeh and Hrair Dekmejian, "A Sufi Response to Political Islamism: Al-Ahbash of Lebanon," 220.

121. Imad, *Al-harakat al-islamiyya fi Lubnan,* 115.

122. Dominique Avon, "Les Ahbaches: Un movement Libanais Sunnite contesté dans un monde globalisé," n.p.

123. Imad, *Al-harakat al-islamiyya fi Lubnan,* 113; Hamzeh and Dekmejian, "Sufi Response to Political Islamism," 224.

124. The association was originally formed by Sheikh Ahmad al-Ajuz in 1930.

125. Imad, *Al-harakat al-islamiyya fi Lubnan,* 117.

126. Hamzeh and Dekmejian, "Sufi Response to Political Islamism," 224.

127. Daniel Nassif, "Al-Ahbash," n.p.

128. Imad, *Al-harakat al-islamiyya fi Lubnan,* 130.

129. Ibid., 131.

130. See Richani, *Dilemmas of Democracy,* 138.

131. El-Khazen, "Political Parties in Postwar Lebanon," 614.

4. State Elites and the Legacy of Corruption

1. See, for example, Max Weber's discussion of bureaucratic roles in *Economy and Society.*

2. Here, I have in mind the distinction made by Pierre Bourdieu among different "species" of capital: economic, cultural, social, and symbolic. Bourdieu and Loic Wacquant, *An Invitation to Reflexive Sociology,* 119. It is the transformation of these various resources into political capital that allows one to enter the ranks of the state elite. However, if there is a weakness to Bourdieu's analysis, it is in the limited role that he grants to individual agency within the process of structuration. The relative importance of political elites in their relationship to political institutions in Lebanon encourages us to give a greater consideration to this individual agency and transformation. For a theoretical account of the relationship between agency and structural resources, see William H. Sewell Jr., "A Theory of Structure: Duality, Agency, and Transformation."

3. Hariri acknowledged this point in an interview with Ghassan Charbel. Charbel, *La'nat al-qasr: Hiwarat ma' Elias Hrawi, Nabih Berri, Rafiq Hariri, Michel Aoun,* 316.

4. Nicholas Blanford, *Killing Mr. Lebanon,* 121.

5. Shadi K. Abu Issa, *Ru'assa' al-jumhuriyya al-lubnaniyya,* 98.

6. Hrawi admitted to meeting regularly with Syrian president Hafez al-Assad. He maintained that over time, they established a friendly relationship based on trust and

that their contact continued beyond the end of Hrawi's presidency. See Charbel, *La'nat al-qasr,* 41–83.

7. See Fares el-Zein, "Lebanese Administrative Reform Experience from 1992 to 2002."

8. In describing the relationship between Lahoud and Syria, former prime minister Salim al-Hoss carefully explains that "Lahoud believes strongly in common strategic interests between Lebanon and Syria. . . . This is why President Lahoud was excessively sincere, extremely transparent and totally honest in his dealings with Syria. This stemmed from his belief in the Arab character of Lebanon, while being very considerate of Lebanon's independence and sovereignty. . . . This sincerity . . . was sometimes abused by some parties in a way that did not reflect well on the regime, especially when it appeared that in some cases President Lahoud had a tendency to be too considerate of the desires of important Syrian players in Lebanon in issues regarding public administration or the institutions of the state." Al-Hoss, *Li al-haqiqa wa al-tarikh: Tajarub al-hukm ma bayna 1998 wa 2000,* 43–44 (my translation).

9. After the 2005 legislative elections, the late Rafiq Hariri's close friend and adviser Fouad Siniora was entrusted with the task of forming a cabinet. This cabinet lasted until the end of President Lahoud's term in November 2007 and then continued into the following year as an interim administration. Siniora then formed another cabinet in July 2008, after the election of President Michel Suleiman. Following the 2009 legislative elections, a new cabinet was organized by Saad Hariri, Rafiq Hariri's son and political heir. This cabinet was toppled by the opposition in January 2011.

10. Rafiq Hariri, for example, has made a point of stating that an official should "listen to the experts and to those with experience. One should get the right person for the right job." Charbel, *La'nat al-qasr,* 273.

11. See Guilain Denoeux and Robert Springborg, "Hariri's Lebanon: Singapore of the Middle East or Sanaa of the Levant?," 3.

12. Elie A. Salem, *Violence and Diplomacy in Lebanon,* 103.

13. In an interview with Nicholas Blanford, former Lebanese minister of foreign affairs Elie Salem stated that at the peace conferences, "Hariri had real power. When Hariri was talking it was King Fahd talking. He would come up with ideas that were very forceful and say this is what King Fahd wants. And what King Fahd wants is what Hariri tells him." Blanford, *Killing Mr. Lebanon,* 28.

14. Nicholas Blanford states that "money was one of Hariri's most useful assets in his mediation efforts. A few suitcases stuffed with U.S. dollars were often more persuasive and achieved swifter results than patient dialogue. For Hariri money was a tool in negotiations." Ibid., 30. Likewise, former prime minister Salim al-Hoss writes in his memoirs that "the secret of the animosity between . . . [Lahoud] and one of the rich politicians is that this rich man tried to give him a large amount of money after he was appointed chief of

the army." Al-Hoss, *Li al-haqiqa wa al-tarikh,* 43. It is probable that in al-Hoss's writing the phrase "the rich man" is used as a circumlocution to avoid mentioning Hariri's name.

15. Charbel, *La'nat al-qasr,* 268–71.

16. Ibid., 222.

17. See chapter 7 for a more detailed discussion of the circumstance that led to UNSCR 1559 and the resolution's effect on Lebanese-Syrian relations.

18. Muhammad Shmaysani, "Jumblatt: Martyr Hariri Never Supported UNSCR 1559," *Al Manar,* May 25, 2009, http://www.almanar.com.lb/NewsSite/NewsDetails .aspx?id=87605&language=en.

19. Charbel, *La'nat al-qasr,* 199.

20. Albert Hourani, "Ottoman Reform and the Politics of Notables," 87.

21. See Khaled Ziadé, "Tripoli: Famille et politique."

22. Rashid Karami was killed when a bomb was placed under the seat of his helicopter. Samir Geagea and other members of Lebanese Forces were later convicted of the crime. In October 2008, Geagea apologized for the murder, an apology that was rejected by Omar Karami, who replied, "We did not ask for an apology from Geagea . . . we will not forgive and we will not forget." "Hopes for Christian Reconciliation Dashed," NOW Lebanon, Oct. 22, 2008. http://www.nowlebanon.com/NewsArticleDetails.aspx ?ID=63753.

23. Omar Karami boycotted all of the parliamentary sessions after 1996 as a protest against the election of his cousin Ahmed, a competitor from within the family who according to rumor was used by Syria to apply pressure on Omar.

24. Hariri had resigned in October 2004 after the extension of President Lahoud's term.

25. Roderic A. Camp, "The Political Technocrat in Mexico and the Survival of the Political System."

26. Al-Hoss is today the chairman of the board of trustees of the Arab Anti-Corruption Organization.

27. John Kifner, "Lebanese Businessman Once Again Is Premier," *New York Times,* Oct. 24, 2000, http://www.nytimes.com/2000/10/24/world/lebanese-businessman -once-again-is-premier.html.

28. Al-Hoss, *Li al-haqiqa wa al-tarikh,* 51–52.

29. Ibid., 53–62.

30. Ibid., 63.

31. Abdo Baaklini, Guilain Denoeux, and Robert Springborg, *Legislative Politics in the Arab World: The Resurgence of Democratic Institutions,* 92–93.

32. Iliya Harik, "Voting Behavior: Lebanon," 147.

33. El-Khazen, *Intikhabat Lubnan,* 227.

34. The assassination of Rafiq Hariri was termed "a political crime of earthquake magnitude" by the Arab press.

35. El-Khazen, *Intikhabat Lubman*, 228.

36. Ibid., 229.

37. Talal Salman, editor of the Lebanese newspaper *as-Safir*, has stated that he believes the candidates in the 2009 Lebanese elections spent as much as a billion US dollars on buying votes—an average of five million dollars per candidate. Zvi Bar'el, "Would Hezbollah Win in Lebanon Election Lead to War with Israel?" n.p.

38. Vinci, "'Like Worms in the Entrails of a Natural Man,'" 328.

39. See Sasha Lezhnev, *Crafting Peace: Strategies to Deal with Warlords in Collapsing States*, 12.

40. The general amnesty law provided protection against prosecution for crimes perpetrated before March 28, 1991. One important purpose of this law was to garner support for the dissolution of the wartime militias (with the important exception of Hezbollah) and to allow former militia members to pursue civilian, political, or military careers.

41. Berri is discussed here; see chapter 3 for more information on Jumblat.

42. This was acknowledged by Berri. See Charbel, *La'nat al-qasr*, 172.

43. Berri admits that he actively works to bring his supporters into the state institutions; he insists, however, that he did not start this practice but only followed the lead of others. See ibid., 177–78.

44. Omri Nir, *Nabih Berri and Lebanese Politics*, 101–2.

45. This claim is corroborated by a statement made by Jamil al-Sayyed, former head of the Sécurité Générale, who has said that "Berri was one of the political leaders who used to think that state employees 'belong' to them." Quoted in Nir, *Nabih Berri*, 97.

46. *Daily Star* (Beirut), Jan. 31, 2001.

47. Nir, *Nabih Berri*, 111.

48. Ibid., 144.

49. Ibid., 113.

50. Christopher W. Murray, "AMAL Succession: Berri's Bitter, Fruitless Legacy," April 2005, http://wikileaks.org/cable/2005/04/05BEIRUT1123.html#.

51. See George Saliby, *Za'amat wa 'a'ilat*, 43.

52. The animosity was mutual. The Druze leader Walid Jumblat, said, "It is not the cabinet or the head of state which governs, but the almighty Michel Murr, the big boss to whom President Lahoud subcontracted the country." Chantal Rayyes, "Murr, le rempart de Damas" (my translation).

53. Ibid.

54. Ibid.

55. Saliby, *Za'amat wa 'a'ilat*, 44.

56. The cable is not available through WikiLeaks anymore. It is, however, quoted in Angie Nassar, "Secret Admissions from Murr: A WikiLeaks Cable," *Now Lebanon*, December 2, 2010, http://www.nowlebanon.com/BlogDetails.aspx?TID=952.

57. Al-Hoss, *Li al-haqiqa wa al-tarikh*, 71.

58. Ibid.

59. In addition to Prime Minister Rafiq Hariri and Deputy Prime Minister Issam Fares, the cabinet included the following individuals: Abdallah Farhat, minister of the displaced; Abdul-Rahim Murad, minister of state; Ali Hassan Khalil, minister of agriculture; Ali Hussein Abdallah, minister of tourism; Asaad Diab, minister of social affairs; Assad Hardan, minister of labor; Assem Qanso, minister of state; Ayyoub Homayed, minister of energy and water; Bahij Tabbara, minister of justice; Elias al-Murr, minister of the interior and municipalities; Elie Skaff, minister of industry; Fares Boueiz, minister of the environment; Fouad Siniora, minister of finance; Ghazi Aridi, minister of culture; Jean Obeid, minister of foreign affairs and emigrants; Jean-Louis Qordahi, minister of telecommunications; Karam Karam, minister of state; Karim Pakradouni, minister of administrative development; Khalil Hrawi, minister of state; Mahmoud Hammoud, minister of national defense; Marwan Hamadeh, minister of economy and trade; Michel Musa, minister of state; Michel Samaha, minister of information; Najib Mikati, minister of public works and transportation; Samir Jisr, minister of education and higher studies; Sebouh Hovnanian, minister of youth and sports; Suleiman Frangieh, minister of public health; and Talal Arslan, minister of state.

60. The full list of ministers is as follows: Omar Karami, prime minister; Issam Fares, deputy prime minister; Elias Saba, minister of finance; Elie Ferzli, minister of information; Albert Mansour, minister of state; Suleiman Frangieh, minister of the interior; Talal Arslan, minister of the displaced; Sami Minqara, minister of education; Abdel-Rahim Murad, minister of defense; Yassine Jaber, minister of public works and transportation; Ghazi Ze'aiter, minister of social affairs; Karam Karam, minister of state; Sebouh Hovnanian, minister of youth and sports; Mahmoud Hammoud, minister of foreign affairs; Jean-Louis Qordahi, minister of telecommunications; Elie Skaff, minister of agriculture; Assem Qanso, minister of labor; Farid Khazen, minister of tourism; Adnan Qassar, minister of economy and trade; Mahmoud Abdel-Khaleq, minister of state; Adnan Addoum, minister of justice; Naji Bustani, minister of culture; Maurice Sahnawi, minister of energy and water; Leila al-Solh, minister of industry; Ibrahim Daher, minister of state for administrative reforms; Yussef Salameh, minister of state; Muhammad Jawad Khalifeh, minister of public health; Wafa' Hamza, minister of state; Alan Tabourian, minister of state; and Wi'am Wahhab, minister of the environment.

61. Arab Reform Bulletin, "Government Change in Lebanon," n.p.

62. United States Department of the Treasury, "Treasury Designates Individuals Furthering Syrian Regime's Efforts to Undermine Lebanese Democracy," n.p.

63. Mikati was again appointed prime minister in January 2011. He was not able to form a government for close to five months because of disagreements among the different Lebanese factions. A government was finally formed in June 2011. It included thirty ministers, seven of whom were members of the previous cabinet: four were reappointed to their previous positions, and three were asked to change portfolios. See http://www

.ifes.org/Content/Publications/White-Papers/2011/~/media/Files/Publications/White%20PaperReport/2011/Lebanon_New_Cabinet.pdf.

64. Najib Mikati is a Sunni businessman from Tripoli. He is a graduate of the American University of Beirut, and his fortune is estimated at $2.6 billion. The members of the cabinet as it eventually coalesced were: Najib Mikati, prime minister; Elias Murr, deputy prime minister and minister of defense; Mahmoud Hammoud, minister of foreign affairs; Hassan Saba', minister of the interior; Demianos Qattar, minister of finance, economy, and trade; As'ad Rizk, minister of education and culture; Adel Hamiyeh, minister of public works, transportation, and the displaced; Muhammad Khalifeh, minister of health and social affairs; Alain Taburian, minister of telecommunications, youth, and sports; Khaled Qabbani, minister of justice; Bassam Yammin, minister of industry and energy; Charles Rizk, minister of information and tourism; Tareq Mitri, minister of the environment and administrative development; and Trad Hamadeh, minister of labor and agriculture.

65. Manuela Paraipan, "Lebanese PM Najib Mikati Forms a Technocrat Caretaker Government," n.p.

66. "Presidential Dark Horses," NOW Lebanon, Nov. 16, 2007, http://www.now lebanon.com/NewsArticleDetails.aspx?ID=20062.

67. Joseph S. Nye, "Corruption and Political Development: A Cost-Benefit Analysis," 419.

68. See Arvind Jain, "Corruption: A Review," 247.

69. See Michael Johnston, *Syndromes of Corruption: Wealth, Power, and Democracy,* 89.

70. In 2009 Lebanon's graft rating on Transparency International's Corruption Perceptions Index fell to 2.5 out of 10, on a scale where 0 indicates "highly corrupt." Transparency International, "Corruption Perceptions Index, 2009." In addition, the World Bank corruption indicators published in June 2009 ranked Lebanon very poorly in the areas of government efficiency, political stability, and corruption control. Lebanese Transparency Association, "Corruption in Lebanon," n.p.

71. Charles Adwan, "Corruption in Reconstruction," n.p.

72. Examples of this criticism include Najah Wakim, *Al-ayadi al-sood;* Aline Hallaq, *Al-khalawi: Ashhar fada'ih al-'asr;* and Ghada Eid, *Al-khalawi: Akbar al-safaqat* and *Sukleen wa akhawatiha: Al-nifayat, tharwa wa thawra.* For more general works on the role of money in Lebanese politics, see Henry Edde, *Al-mal: In hakam;* and Ghada Eid, *Asas al-mulk.*

73. Mark W. Neal and Richard Tansey, "The Dynamics of Effective Corrupt Leadership: Lessons from Rafik Hariri's Political Career in Lebanon," 36.

74. Tamirace Fakhoury-Muehlbacher, *Power-Sharing and Democratisation in a Stormy Regional Weather: The Case of Lebanon,* 20.

75. Reinoud Leenders, "Nobody Having Too Much to Answer For: Laissez-Faire, Networks, and Postwar Reconstruction in Lebanon," 182.

76. The name Solidere is drawn from the French acronym for Société Libanaise pour le Développement et la Reconstruction du Centre Ville de Beyrouth. For more information about Rafiq Hariri's role in this company, see Wakim, *Al-ayadi al-sood,* 143–56.

77. For more on Elyssar, see Mona Harb, "Urban Governance in Post-war Beirut: Resources, Negotiations, and Contestations in the Elyssar Project."

78. See Rafic Nabaa, *Rafic Hariri: Un homme d'affaires premier ministre,* 44–46; and Wakim, *Al-ayadi al-sood,* 167–72.

79. See George Assaf and Rana al-Fil, "Resolving the Issue of War Displacement in Lebanon."

80. Samir Makdisi, "Rebuilding Without Resolution: The Lebanese Economy and State in the Post–Civil War Period," 109–12.

81. "Salameh Expects Lebanon's Debt," *Daily Star* (Beirut), Jan. 6, 2010, http://www.dailystar.com.lb/Business/Lebanon/Jan/06/Salameh-expects-Lebanons-debt-to-GDP-to-fall-in-2010.ashx#axzz1PtNfTLvc.

82. For more on Horizon 2000 and the reconstruction program, see Tom Najem, "Horizon 2000: Economic Viability and Political Realities" and *Lebanon's Renaissance.*

83. Toufic Gaspard, *A Political Economy of Lebanon, 1948–2002: The Limits of Laissez-Faire,* 212.

84. For more on the controversy surrounding the reconstruction of downtown Beirut, see Aseel Sawalha, *Reconstructing Beirut: Memory and Myth in a Postwar Arab City.*

85. Leenders, "Nobody Having Too Much to Answer For," 183.

86. Ibid., 174.

87. Hallaq, *Al-khalawi,* 60–65.

88. Eid hosts a sensationalist show titled *al-Fassad* (Corruption) on the anti-Hariri television channel New TV.

89. The most important of these collaborators was al-Fadl Chalaq. For the story of the relationship between Hariri and Chalaq, see George Farshakh, *Al-Fadl Chalaq: Tajribati ma'a al-Hariri.*

90. Eid, *Al-khalawi,* 22.

91. Eid, *Sukleen wa akhawatiha,* 268.

92. Ibid., 37.

93. In the 1990s, this financial relationship between Syrian and Lebanese elites was mostly unidirectional. During the first decade of the twenty-first century, however, there was a significant increase in Lebanese investment in Syria. This activity was primarily owing to the growth of new, lucrative markets in Syria following the reforms that took place in that country under the new leadership of Bashar al-Assad. Examples of Lebanese investments in Syria include Najib Mikati's ownership of a large percentage of the Syrian telecommunications market and the extensive involvement of Lebanese banks in Syria's newly privatized financial markets. See *Executive Magazine,* "Syria Banked by Lebanon."

94. Michael Johnston, "The Political Consequences of Corruption: A Reassessment," 466. See also Philippe Le Billon, "Buying Peace or Fueling War? The Role of Corruption in Armed Conflicts."

95. See Leenders, "Nobody Having Too Much to Answer For," 187.

96. Here, I am following a distinction made by Hassan Jouni in his article "Migration circulaire au Liban."

97. See Fadia Kiwan, *La perception de la migration circulaire au Liban.*

98. Anna di Bartolomeo, Tamirace Fakhoury, and Delphine Perrin, "CARIM Migration Profile: Lebanon."

99. Ibid.

100. Choghig Kasparian, "Les migrations irrégulières, au départ, vers et à travers le Liban."

101. *MainGate Magazine,* "Brain Drain," 18.

102. See I. Harik, "Voting Behavior: Lebanon," 147.

5. Strategic Elites

1. Suzanne Keller defines strategic elites as comprising "not only political, economic and military leaders, but also moral, cultural and scientific ones." Keller, *Beyond the Ruling Class,* 20.

2. Samuel Huntington, *The Soldier and the State,* 12.

3. Ibid., 79.

4. Oren Barak, "Commemorating Malikiyya: Political Myth, Multiethnic Identity, and the Making of the Lebanese Army," 69; Michael Gilsenan, "Problems in the Analysis of Violence," 113.

5. For example, army commander Iskandar Ghanem refused the presidency in 1970, and Hanna Sa'id did the same in 1976. See Hubert Dupont, "La nouvelle armée Libanaise: Instrument du pouvoir ou acteur politique."

6. Ronald McLaurin, "Lebanon and Its Army: Past, Present, and Future," 84.

7. Ibid., 83.

8. Ibid., 91.

9. For a more detailed discussion of this reorganization, see Joseph A. Kechichian, "The Lebanese Army: Capabilities and Challenges in the 1980s," 22–23.

10. Ibid., 28.

11. Ronald McLaurin, "From Professional to Political: The Redecline of the Lebanese Army," 546.

12. The military academy began to admit women in 1992, but they are still very much in the minority.

13. See Oren Barak, "Towards a Representative Military? The Transformation of the Lebanese Officer Corps since 1945," 85–87.

14. Nazih Ayubi, *Overstating the Arab State*, 258.

15. Dupont, "La nouvelle armée Libanaise," 60.

16. See Kamal Salibi, "Lebanon under Fuad Chehab, 1958–1964," 216.

17. Hudson, *Precarious Republic*, 304.

18. The name is roughly translated as "International Institute for Research and Training for Development."

19. Salibi, "Lebanon under Fuad Chehab," 220.

20. Ibid., 218.

21. The Central Bank of Lebanon (Banque du Liban) was established on August 1, 1963, and became fully operational on April 1, 1964. From April 1, 1924, until the bank became operational, the Bank of Syria and Great Lebanon, an institution created under French mandatory power, issued legal tender known as the Lebanese-Syrian pound.

22. Roger Owen, *State, Power, and Politics in the Making of the Modern Middle East,* 191.

23. Adel Beshara, *Lebanon, Politics of Frustration: The Failed Coup of 1961,* 97.

24. Hudson, *Precarious Republic*, 304–5.

25. See N. Nassif, *Al-maktab al-thani: Hakim fi al-zul,* 41.

26. Adel Freiha, *L'armée et l'état au Liban (1945–1980),* 153.

27. Ibid., 160.

28. For a detailed biography, see Free Patriotic Movement, "General Michel Aoun."

29. Sarkis Naoum, *Michel Aoun: Hulm am wahem,* 21.

30. Ibid., 51.

31. Oren Barak, *The Lebanese Army: A National Institution in a Divided Society,* 142.

32. Ibid., 142–45.

33. Michel Aoun, *Une certaine vision du Liban,* 161 (my translation).

34. Ibid., 65–66.

35. In an interview with journalist Ghassan Charbel, Samir Geagea also describes Aoun as "pragmatic and authoritarian." Charbel, *Ayna kunta fi al-harb,* 249.

36. Naoum, *Michel Aoun,* 145.

37. Picard, *Lebanon: A Shattered Country,* 161.

38. Mohsen Dalloul, *ʿAhd Lahoud tahta al-muhakama.*

39. Author's interview, Hazmieh, May 2, 2003.

40. See Amnesty International, "Lebanon: Dr. al-Mugraby Must Be Immediately Released."

41. See Amnesty International, "Lebanon: Harassment and Intimidation of Human Rights Defender Must Cease."

42. See Euro-Mediterranean Human Rights Network, "Association Agreement Between the European Union and Lebanon."

43. Article 108 of the Lebanese Penal Code.

44. Ziad K. Abdelnour, "Parliament Reluctantly Caves in to Syrian Pressure," n.p.

45. Amnesty International, "Lebanon: Amnesty International Expresses Concerns at Violations in Pre-trial Detention of Tawfiq al-Hindi and Co-Defendants," n.p.

46. Amnesty International, "Lebanon: Excessive Force and Torture by Security Forces Must Be Investigated," n.p.

47. Ramzi Irani's death is discussed on the website of the Lebanese Forces (http://www.lebaneseforces.com/irani.asp).

48. Edouard Belloncle, "Prospects of SSR in Lebanon," 6–10.

49. Detlev Mehlis, "Report of the International Independent Investigation Commission Established Pursuant to Security Council Resolution 1595."

50. See Belloncle, "Prospects of SSR in Lebanon," 10.

51. Ibid., 9.

52. For a further discussion of the role of the clergy, see Sami Ofeish, "Lebanon's Second Republic: Secular Talk, Sectarian Application."

53. In an article published in 2009, Sami E. Baroudi and Paul Tabar argue that the Maronite patriarch has played a role in Lebanese politics that is inversely related to the presence of strong political leaders. In their words, "Church leadership is brought to the forefront when Maronite political leaders do not manage to properly convey the political feelings of the Maronite community at large (as was the case during the postwar years), while church leadership recedes to the back stage when it fails to tap into those feelings, as during the 1958 Lebanese Crisis and most of the civil war years (1975–1985)." Baroudi and Tabar, "Spiritual Authority vs. Secular Authority: Relations Between the Maronite Church and the State in Post-war Lebanon," 196. I would argue that this phenomenon is not unique to the Maronite community; it seems to be the case for all sectarian groups in Lebanon.

54. The charismatic hierocrat as identified by Max Weber is a relatively rare phenomenon in Lebanon. See Weber, *Economy and Society,* 1147.

55. Thomas Scheffler, "Religion, Violence, and the Civilizing Process," 179.

56. For example, see Fuad Ajami, *The Vanished Imam;* and Sabrina Mervin, "Les yeux de Musa Sadr," 285–86.

57. Augustus R. Norton, "Musa al-Sadr," 195.

58. Mervin, "Les yeux de Musa Sadr," 286.

59. Lebanese nationality is transmitted through the father. A Lebanese woman married to a foreigner cannot transmit her citizenship to her children.

60. For more on AMAL, see chapter 3.

61. In February 2011, al-Arabiya reported, based on sources close to his family, that Musa al-Sadr might still be alive in a Libyan prison. However, in November 2011, Ahmad Ramadan, a former Qaddafi aide, revealed on al-Aan television that Sadr had been liquidated by the Libyan regime after a meeting with Qaddafi. http://www.naharnet.com/stories/en/19874-gadhafi-aide-moussa-al-sadr-was-liquidated-in-libya (accessed Jan. 15, 2011).

62. A mufti is a Sunni scholar who is an interpreter of Islamic law (sharia). In this case, it refers to the highest Sunni religious authority in Lebanon. Mustafa Naja, who was the mufti of Beirut at the beginning of the French Mandate, never accepted the title of mufti of the Lebanese Republic. He insisted on being called the mufti of Beirut until his death in 1932. The following mufti, Muhammad Tawfiq Khaled, is credited with consolidating the voice of the Sunni community in Lebanon and with building the Dar al-Fatwa in Beirut, which still houses the offices of the mufti.

63. See Jakob Skovgaard-Petersen, "A Typology of State Muftis," 89–90.

64. The website of the Hassan Khaled Foundation provides information about Khaled, his speeches, and his political positions (http://www.hasankhaledfoundations.org).

65. Scheffler, "Religion," 180.

66. Nissim Dana, *The Druze in the Middle East: Their Faith, Leadership, Identity, and Status*, 20–21.

67. Robert B. Betts, *The Druze*, 55–56. For additional perspectives, see Philip K. Hitti, *The Origins of the Druze People and Religion;* and Dana, *Druze in the Middle East*.

68. Judith Harik, "Sheikh al-'Aql and the Druze of Mount Lebanon: Conflict and Accommodation," 466 (emphasis added).

69. According to Nissim Dana, the title of "spiritual leader," or *sheikh al-'aql,* was traditionally given to holy men whose modest lifestyles served as models for others in the community. These pious men were part of a united Druze leadership consisting of a prominent head sheikh and four or five senior sheikhs who acted as his assistants. Dana, *Druze in the Middle East,* 67.

70. Jakob Skovgaard-Petersen, "Religious Heads or Civil Servants?," 346–47.

71. See Isabelle Rivoal, "Le poids de l'histoire: Druze du Liban, Druze d'Israël face à l'état," 65.

72. For more on the origins of the Maronites, see Matti Moosa, *The Maronites in History*. For the history of the Maronites in Lebanon, see Iliya Harik, "The Maronite Church and Political Change in Lebanon." For perspectives on the political activities of the Maronite patriarch, see Alexander D. N. Henley, "Politics of a Church at War: Maronite Catholicism in the Lebanese Civil War"; and Fiona McCallum, "The Political Role of the Patriarch in the Contemporary Middle East."

73. For a more detailed discussion of these events, see Sami E. Baroudi, "Divergent Perspectives among Lebanon's Maronites During the 1958 Crisis."

74. Further discussion of Meouchi's political positions can be found in Ephraim Frankel, "The Maronite Patriarch: A Historical View of a Religious Za'im in the 1958 Lebanese Crisis"; and Beshara, *Lebanon,* 112–15.

75. The monks of the Maronite Order were the first warrior-priests to emerge in Lebanon. In this regard, they foreshadowed the rise of leaders such as Hezbollah's Hassan Nasrallah, who combines in his person both religious and military symbolism.

76. See chapter 3 for a more detailed discussion of Bashir Gemayel and the Lebanese Forces.

77. Henley, "Politics of a Church at War," 356–57.

78. Claudia Rosett, "Syria's Tightening Grip on Lebanon," *Wall Street Journal*, Feb. 5, 2003.

79. A transcription of Sfeir's speech was posted on the Middle East Intelligence Bulletin website (http://www.meforum.org/meib/articles/0104_ldoc0307.htm).

80. See Karim Pakradouni, *Sadma wa sumud: ʿAhd Emile Lahoud, 1998–2007*, 223–30; and McCallum, "Political Role of the Patriarch," 934.

81. Beshara Boutros al-Rai became the seventy-seventh Maronite patriarch on March 15, 2011.

82. For more on the history of the Lebanese press, see Nabil Dajani, "The Press in Lebanon."

83. Ziad Majed, "Lebanon: An Overview of the Media," 212.

84. Further biographical information can be found on the website devoted to Samir Qassir (http://www.samirkassir.net).

85. Samir Qassir, *Dimuqratiyat Suria wa istiqlal Lubnan*, 32.

86. Ibid., 41.

87. Ibid., 197.

88. Ibid., 70–71.

89. Samir Qassir, *ʿAskar ʿala meen?*, 42.

90. Ibid., 172.

91. Ibid., 77–78.

92. Ibid., 150–52.

93. Ibid., 175–82.

94. Reporters Without Borders, "Annual Report, 2002: Lebanon," n.p.

95. Robert Fisk, "Who Killed Samir Kassir?," *Independent* (London), June 3, 2005.

96. Adam Shatz, "The Principle of Hope," n.p.

97. Ghassan Tueni, often referred to as "the dean of Lebanese journalism," passed away in June 2012 at age eighty-six. Nadia Hamadeh Tueni was the daughter of a Druze family from Lebanon. She wrote in French, her mother's native language, and won several French awards, including the Prix de l'Académie Française in 1973. She passed away in 1983 after a battle with cancer.

98. An English translation of Tueni's letter was posted on the Middle East Intelligence Bulletin website (http://www.meforum.org/meib/articles/0004_docl.htm).

99. After a seven-year hiatus, Murr TV started broadcasting again on March 31, 2009.

100. See Douglas Boyd, "Lebanese Broadcasting: Unofficial Electronic Media During a Prolonged Civil War."

101. Marwan Kraidy, "State Control of Television News in 1990s Lebanon," 489.

102. May Chidiac and Amal Moghaizel, *Le ciel m'attendra*, 34–43.

103. Prince al-Waleed bin Talal, one of the shareholders of LBCI, sent May Chidiac to Paris for several months, all expenses paid, to receive medical care, prostheses, and physical therapy.

104. Having received a doctoral degree in communication and information sciences from the University of Paris II-Assas in 2008, she turned to academia and started teaching at Notre Dame University of Louayzé in Lebanon.

105. Anthony Mills, "IPI Completes Press Freedom Mission to Lebanon," n.p.

6. Emerging Elites and the Absence of Women from Politics

1. My understanding of "regime change" follows the conception of Alan Richards and John Waterbury, who state that *regime* refers "not only to the type of government but also to ideology, rules of the game and the structuring of the polity in a given nation. Regime change is no mere changing of the guard. . . . [I]t is, rather, profound structural change in all forms of political activity." Richards and Waterbury, *A Political Economy of the Middle East: State Class and Economic Development*, 300.

2. For more on clientelism in Lebanon in the prewar period, see Hottinger, "Zu'ama in Historical Perspective"; Johnson, *Class and Client in Beirut;* and S. Khalaf, *Lebanon's Predicament.*

3. Gero Erdmann and Ulf Engel, "Neopatrimonialism Reconsidered: Critical Review and Elaboration of an Elusive Concept," 105.

4. See S. Khalaf, *Lebanon's Predicament*, 198.

5. Gero Erdmann and Ulf Engel, "Neopatrimonialism Reconsidered: Critical Review and Elaboration of an Elusive Concept," 107. For more on the definition of clientelism, see Rene Lemarchand and Keith Legg, "Political Clientelism and Development," 122–23.

6. S. Khalaf, "Changing Forms of Political Patronage in Lebanon," 185–87.

7. See Johnson, *Class and Client in Beirut,* 97; Shmuel Eisenstadt, *Patrons, Clients, and Friends: Interpersonal Relations and the Structure of Trust in Society,* 94.

8. Johnson, *Class and Client in Beirut,* 159–215.

9. See Marie-Joëlle Zahar, "Fanatics, Mercenaries, Brigands—and Politicians: Militia Decision-Making and Civil Conflict Resolution," 117–19.

10. These institutions are the schools where most French officials are educated, and their alumni retain a quasi monopoly on some of the most prestigious positions in the French government. In his book *The State Nobility: Elite Schools in the Field of Power,* Pierre Bourdieu shows how the dominant classes in France reproduce themselves through elite schooling and how it occurred in the twentieth century.

11. Robert Putnam, *The Comparative Study of Political Elites,* 32.

12. Amal Sabbagh, "Overview of Women's Political Representation in the Arab World," 9.

13. Sheri Kunovich and Pamela Paxton, "Pathways to Power: The Role of Political Parties in Women's National Representation," 506–7.

14. Myrna Boustani was the first woman to enter the Lebanese Parliament; she did so in 1963 to complete her father's term after his death in an airplane crash. This move started a trend whereby women were brought into parliament because of their family connections. In the first postwar elections, three women entered the parliament. It was unsurprising that two of the three were close relatives of important politicians: Bahia Hariri, the sister of Rafiq Hariri, and Nayla Mouawad, the widow of President-Elect René Mouawad.

15. Between 1992 and 2005, there was an average of three women in parliament—2.3 percent of the legislature. After the 2005 elections, the number of women doubled to six. These six parliamentarians were: Setrida Geagea, wife of the Lebanese Forces commander, Samir Geagea; Solange Gemayel, widow of President-Elect Bashir Gemayel; Bahia Hariri, sister of the slain former prime minister Rafiq Hariri; Nayla Mouawad, widow of President-Elect René Mouawad; Gilberte Zoueyn, daughter of former minister Maurice Zoueyn; and Ghinwa Jalloul, who alone of the six women is not a relative of a prominent male political boss. In the 2009 elections, there were thirteen female candidates, but only four were elected. All of the women elected are attached to powerful families or male figures (or both): Nayla Tueni, the daughter of the assassinated *an-Nahar* editor in chief and MP Gebran Tueni, and Solange Gemayel, the widow of President-Elect Bashir Gemayel, in addition to Bahia Hariri and Setrida Geagea, who are mentioned above.

16. Sofia Saadeh, "Women in the Sectarian Politics of Lebanon," 236.

17. None of these portfolios were important ministerial ones. Lebanon has no industry to speak of, and social affairs and education are often considered an extension of a woman's role at home.

18. Joanna Liddle and Elisabeth Michielsens, "Women and Public Power: Class Does Make a Difference," 207–11.

19. Marguerite Helou, "Al-mar'a fi al-intikhabat al-mahaliyya," 418–19.

20. http://www.learningpartnership.org/blog/2010/07/lebanon-women-politics/.

21. Susan J. Caroll, "Political Elites and Sex Differences in Political Ambition: A Reconsideration," 1242.

22. Kunovich and Paxton, "Pathways to Power," 520.

23. Linda Beck, "Democratization and the Hidden Public: The Impact of Patronage on Senegalese Women," 164.

24. Dina Jamali, Yusuf Sidani, and Assem Safieddine, "Constraints Facing Working Women in Lebanon: An Insider View," 583.

25. Arab Reform Initiative, "Women Candidates Sidelined in Lebanon Vote," n.p.

26. Jamali, Sidani, and Safieddine, "Constraints Facing Working Women," 584.

27. Mona Chemali Khalaf, "Women in Post-war Lebanon," 149–50.

28. For more on women's involvement in the Lebanese civil war, see Lamia Rustum Shehadeh, ed., *Women and War in Lebanon*.

29. My use of the term *public sphere* follows the interpretation given by Jürgen Habermas, who wrote that the "public sphere may be conceived above all as the sphere of private people come together as a public; they soon claimed the public sphere regulated from above against the public authorities themselves, to engage them in a debate over the general rules governing relations in the basically privatized but publicly relevant sphere of commodity exchange and social labor. The medium of this political confrontation was peculiar and without historical precedent: people's public use of their reason." Habermas, *The Structural Transformation of the Public Sphere*, 27.

30. For women's experience in Lebanese political parties, see Azza Karam, "Democrats Without Democracy: Challenges to Women in Politics in the Arab World."

31. See Anne Marie Goetz, "Political Cleaners: Women as the New Anti-corruption Force?," 89.

32. Alia Ibrahim, "Few Women Enter Lebanon's Parliament," n.p.

33. Don Duncan, "Women Lose Out in Lebanese Politics," n.p.

34. In response to a question about the role of women in parliament, a male Lebanese parliamentarian whom I interviewed mentioned the politician Ghinwa Jalloul, who is a very attractive woman, and quoted the famous French phrase "Sois belle et tais-toi" (Be beautiful and shut up), despite the fact that Jalloul belonged to his own parliamentary bloc.

35. Hisham Sharabi, *Neo-Patriarchy: A Theory of Distorted Change*, 4. See also Elhum Haghighat, "Neopatriarchy, Islam, and Female Labour Force Participation."

36. Max Weber discussed ideal types as "a conceptual tool with which to approach reality." Richard Swedberg, *The Max Weber Dictionary: Key Words and Central Concepts*, 120. Creating a provisional typology allows us to organize and communicate a complex empirical situation, presenting its most essential aspects as a starting point for analysis. For more on ideal types, see Weber, *Economy and Society*, 20–21, 57.

37. According to one of my interviewees, a Maronite politician from a well-known family, creating a political dynasty is the "goal of every politician" (Beirut, Oct. 15, 2001). This claim is supported by previous scholarship (see S. Khalaf, *Lebanon's Predicament*, 137) and by statistics: Farid el-Khazen, for example, found that after the 1992 elections, a full 38 percent of the elected parliamentarians belonged to political dynasties, while 17 percent had directly "inherited" their seats from their fathers. El-Khazen, *Intikhabat Lubnan*, 111.

38. Karl Mannheim, "On the Problem of Generations."

39. Putnam, *Comparative Study of Political Elites*, 100–102.

40. For example, thousands of young men and women who grew up in the "Christian enclave" of Kisrwan-Metn during the civil war were completely isolated from their Muslim peers.

41. Similar judgments were made by scholars. Lebanese sociologist Samir Khalaf described "the vulgarization of traditional forms of cultural expression and the commodification of kitsch and sleazy consumerism, so rampant in post-war Lebanon." S. Khalaf, *Civil and Uncivil Violence,* 311.

42. For example, several politically inclined activists have emerged from the leadership of an NGO called the Lebanese Association for Democratic Elections. At least two members of the board of this group have tried their luck in legislative elections, and one of them succeeded in gaining a seat in the 2000 and 2005 legislatures. Lebanese political scientist Karam Karam differentiates between traditional Lebanese NGOs, which focus on charity work, and the newer NGOs that appeared in the 1990s. These newer NGOs have directed their attention to "fields of activity that had been previously neglected, such as human rights, ecology, public freedoms, and democracy." Karam Karam, "Civil Associations, Social Movements, and Political Participation in Lebanon in the 1990s," 316. See also Karam Karam, "Les associations au Liban: Entre caritatif et politique," 71.

43. The Saint Cloud Conference was a meeting held at the Chateau de la Celle Saint-Cloud in July 2007. It brought together representatives of the political forces involved in Lebanon's national dialogue, as well as prominent members of Lebanese civil society. The discussions at Saint Cloud focused on the need to strengthen the Lebanese state.

44. This profile is a composite biography drawn from interviews with several civil servants in Beirut who were promised anonymity. I do not offer a specific example of a technocrat because none of the individuals on whom I am basing this portrait have yet emerged as a public figure.

45. Peter Grimsditch, "Basil Fuleihan, 1963–2005," n.p.

46. *Executive Magazine,* "Yasma Fuleihan," n.p.

47. Michael Young, "The Unlikely Quartet," n.p.

48. These donor conferences were organized by Lebanon to raise money for reconstruction efforts. The majority of the participating countries were members of the Gulf Cooperation Council. Saudi Arabia was the largest contributor, donating seven hundred million US dollars for Lebanese reconstruction.

49. Grimsditch, "Basil Fuleihan, 1963–2005," n.p.

50. For example, the sons of Rafiq Hariri hold Saudi citizenship and are close to the Saudi royal family, whereas the relatives of former deputy prime minister Issam Fares are close to the George Bush family. Isam Fares was invited to the presidential inauguration of George W. Bush, to which he and his son Nijad are said to have each contributed one hundred thousand dollars, the maximum legal amount. Leslie Wayne, "Big Companies Picking Up Tab in Inauguration," *New York Times,* Jan. 18, 2001, A1.

51. Kevin Gray, "To Live and Die in Beirut," n.p.

52. Ferry Biedermann, "Hariri Quits as PM-Designate," *Financial Times,* Sept. 10, 2009, http://www.ft.com/cms/s/0/7cd1da10-9e34-11de-b0aa-00144feabdc0.html?cat id=76&SID=google.

53. The new cabinet included fifteen seats for the majority led by Saad Hariri, ten for the Hezbollah-led opposition, and five for President Michel Suleiman, who has struggled to maintain neutrality.

54. Gray, "To Live and Die," n.p.

55. Ibid. I find the rumor that Nazik Hariri might run for office to be rather doubtful. Mrs. Hariri is Paris based and according to a leaked embassy cable is said to bear grudges and looks to get even with those persons who slighted Rafiq Hariri. See the full text of the document posted on the Lebanese newspaper *al-Akhbar* website (http://www.al-akhbar .com/node/9101).

56. The 2009 legislative elections saw the entry of many scions of former politicians into the Lebanese Parliament. They included Sami Gemayel, the son of former president Amin Gemayel; Nadim Gemayel, the son of assassinated president-elect Bashir Gemayel (and cousin of Sami); Samer Sa'adeh, the son of former Kata'eb leader Georges Sa'adeh; Nayla Tueni, the daughter of assassinated journalist and MP Gebran Tueni; Robert Fadel, the son of former Tripoli MP Maurice Fadel; and Alain Aoun, the nephew of Michel Aoun.

57. *Gulf News,* "Lebanon's Saad Hariri Heads to Syria," n.p.

58. Catherine Le Thomas, "Formation et socialisation: Un projet de (contre)-société," 149.

59. Ibid., 151.

60. Catherine Le Thomas, "Les Scouts al-Mahdi: La formation d'une génération résistante," 215.

61. Ibid., 174–75.

62. Andrew Combes, "Hezbollah's Scout Brigade," al-Jazeera, Jan. 9, 2009, http://english.aljazeera.net/news/middleeast/2007/12/20085251919830843.html. The al-Mahdi Scouts received a permit for the organization's activities from the Lebanese Ministry of Education in September 1992. A 2006 report of the Israeli Intelligence and Terrorism Information Center, titled "Hezbollah's Shi'ite Youth Movement," maintains, however, that male al-Mahdi Scouts tend to make their way into Hezbollah's fighting ranks after they turn seventeen. Journalist Thanassis Cambanis concurs, stating that "success in the Scouts led to an invitation to join Hezbollah as a probationary member. The most promising boys were recruited to join the ranks of the fighters. During the summer, scouts spent weeks at camps in the South and the Beqaa, where they practiced fitness and learned survival skills." Cambanis, *A Privilege to Die,* 217. According to Catherine Le Thomas, the al-Mahdi Scouts have published a pamphlet answering these allegations point by point. However, their "reputation as future fighters persists, reinforced by the fact that active members of the Resistance have gone through this structure before engaging a few years later in the Islamic Resistance." Le Thomas, "Les Scouts al-Mahdi," 178.

63. "We want to be good Muslims and defend our land against Israel," fourteen-year-old Adel Ahmar said. His friend Hussein Hamade, also fourteen, said that he shared the same view: "al-Mahdi Scouts told us to be martyrs defending our land from all the

countries that attack us. We should defend our country through the Islamic Resistance in Lebanon." Combes, "Hezbollah's Scout Brigade," n.p.

64. An English translation of the "Memorandum of Understanding" was posted on the Ya Libnan website (http://yalibnan.com/site/archives/2006/02/full_english _te.php).

65. Waddah Charara and Muhammad Abu Samra, *Aqni'at al-mukhallis.*

66. Ibid., 185.

67. Ibid., 186.

68. Heiko Wimmen, "Rallying Around the Renegade," n.p.

69. Ibid.

70. Ibid.

71. Ibid.

72. For more on Kanaan's view of this arrangement, see Manuela Paraipan, "Interview with Ibrahim Kanaan."

7. Elite Attitudes on Syria and Sectarianism

1. See Najem, *Lebanon's Renaissance,* 84.

2. Samir Qassir, "Dix ans après, comment ne pas réconcilier une société divisée?," 13.

3. The full text of the bishops' declaration was posted on the Maronite Heritage website (http://www.maronite-heritage.com/Maronite%20Patriarch.php).

4. John Chalcraft, *The Invisible Cage: Syrian Migrant Workers in Lebanon,* 79.

5. Estimates of the number of Syrian workers in Lebanon vary widely; one 2003 analysis placed the range at anywhere between three hundred and nine hundred thousand. Robert Rabil, *Embattled Neighbors: Syria, Israel, and Lebanon,* 130.

6. Chalcraft, *Invisible Cage,* 141.

7. The full text of the document was posted on the Middle East Forum website (http://www.meforum.org/research/lsg.php).

8. Free Patriotic Movement, "General Michel Aoun," n.p.

9. United Nations Security Council, "Security Council Declares Support for Free, Fair Presidential Election in Lebanon," n.p.

10. United Nations Security Council, "Resolution 1583," 2.

11. See Franklin Lamb, "Why Is Hezbollah on the Terrorism List?"

12. Author's interview, Beirut, June 5, 2002.

13. Author's interview, Beirut, Oct. 2, 2001.

14. Author's interview, Beirut, Oct. 22, 2001.

15. Syria's ruling Baath Party promotes the slogan that Syria is "the beating heart of Pan-Arabism," though many others believe that the party has betrayed the founding principles of the Pan-Arabist movement. See David Hirst, "The Syrian Dilemma."

16. Author's interview, Beirut, May 8, 2002.

17. For a summary of the debate, see Ronald P. Formisano, "The Concept of Political Culture." See also David J. Elkins and Richard E. B. Simeon, "A Cause in Search of Its Effect; or, What Does Political Culture Explain?"; and Robert W. Jackman and Ross A. Miller, "A Renaissance of Political Culture?"

18. Elkins and Simeon, "A Cause in Search of Its Effect," 127.

19. Ussama Makdisi, *The Culture of Sectarianism,* 6–7.

20. See Max Weiss, "The Historiography of Sectarianism in Lebanon," 149.

21. George Schöpflin, "The Function of Myth and the Taxonomy of Myths," 28–35. See also Anthony D. Smith, "The 'Golden Age' and National Renewal."

22. For more on the concept of nations as imagined communities, see Benedict Anderson, *Imagined Communities: Reflections on the Origin and Spread of Nationalism.*

23. The formulation and influence of this myth is discussed in greater detail by Asher Kaufman in his book *Reviving Phoenicia: The Search for Identity in Lebanon* and in his article "Phoenicianism: The Formation of an Identity in Lebanon in 1920."

24. Ankush Sawant, "Nationalism and National Interest in Egypt," 139.

25. Chiha's rhetoric is discussed in Kaufman, *Reviving Phoenicia,* 159–69.

26. Rashid Khalidi, "Arab Nationalism: Historical Problems in the Literature," 1365.

27. See Albert Hourani, *Arabic Thought in the Liberal Age, 1798–1939.*

28. Youssef Choueiri, *Arab Nationalism, a History: Nation and State in the Arab World,* 68.

29. Richard H. Pfaff, "The Function of Arab Nationalism," 151.

30. Youssef Choueiri, *Arab Nationalism, a History,* 83.

31. Kaufman, *Reviving Phoenicia,* 221; Kais Firro, *Inventing Lebanon,* 38.

32. For more on Saadeh and the Syrian Social Nationalist Party, see Adel Beshara, ed., *Antun Sa'adeh: The Man, His Thought;* and Labib Zuwiyya Yamak, *The Syrian Social Nationalist Party: An Ideological Analysis.*

33. Robert D. Sethian, "Sa'adeh and Syrian Nationalism," 99.

34. Daniel Pipes, "Radical Politics and the Syrian Nationalist Party," 307; Beshara, *Antun Sa'adeh,* 3.

35. Pipes, "Radical Politics," 305.

36. Ibid., 309.

37. Ibid., 317; Eyal Zisser, "The Syrian Phoenix: The Revival of the Syrian Social National Party in Syria," 200.

38. Ofeish, "Lebanon's Second Republic," 105.

39. Salim al-Hoss, "Prospective Change in Lebanon," 252.

40. Ibid., 256–58.

41. Daoud L. Khairallah, "Secular Democracy: A Viable Alternative to the Confessional System."

42. Author's interview, Beirut, Oct. 22, 2001.

43. Author's interview, Tripoli, Oct. 6, 2001.

44. Author's interview, Beirut, Apr. 2, 2002.

45. Author's interview, Beirut, Oct. 19, 2001.

46. See Maha Shuayb, "Education: A Means for the Cohesion of Lebanese Society."

47. Author's interview, Beirut, Oct. 22, 2001.

48. Author's interview, Beirut, Apr. 27, 2002.

49. See S. Khalaf, *Civil and Uncivil Violence*, 306–9.

50. See Sune Haugbolle, "Public and Private Memory of the Lebanese Civil War"; and Oren Barak, "Don't Mention the War? The Politics of Remembrance and Forgetfulness in Postwar Lebanon."

Conclusion

1. Johnson, *Class and Client in Beirut*, 97.

2. Ibid., 122.

3. Ibid., 187.

4. American withdrawal from Iraq in December 2011 portended instability for the region, however. It marked the beginning of a new era of struggle in the region, especially as Iran is often perceived as having "won" the Iraq war. This victory might embolden Iran as it continues its support for the embattled Syrian regime.

5. This close relation between the Lebanese and Syrian regimes has, for example, led Lebanon to vote against suspending Syria's membership in the Arab League. It also led Lebanon to abstain from participating in the observer mission the league sent to Syria in late 2011.

6. A report issued by the Special Lebanon Tribunal implied that Rafiq Hariri was killed by a suicide bomber. Indeed a UN commission of inquiry said it had found evidence to implicate Syrian and Lebanese intelligence services, but the four security chiefs who were arrested after the assassination were all released in April 2009. United Nations Special Tribunal for Lebanon, "Annual Report (2009–2010)," 48. The suicide-bomber thesis had originally been offered by then interior minister Suleiman Frangieh, a close personal friend of Bashar al-Assad. *BBC News,* "Beirut Blast 'Was Suicide Attack.'"

7. The indictment of the four Hezbollah members was not unexpected. Analysis of cell-phone communications by a member of the Internal Security Forces (who was then assassinated in January 2008) had already pointed the finger at Hezbollah and seemed to exonerate Syria. Hezbollah tried to discredit these findings by claiming that Israel has infiltrated the Lebanese telecommunication sector. It has also produced what it calls evidence of Israel's role in the assassination.

8. Paul Salem, "Lebanon Edges Closer to Syrian Crisis," *al-Monitor,* May 17, 2012.

Glossary of Arabic Terms

Da'wa. Literally, the "call" (to Islam). It can be translated as "proselytizing."

Fatwa. A religious edict by a Muslim cleric.

Fedayeen. Guerrillas. The term is often used to describe Palestinian militants.

Ijtihad. An independent or innovative interpretation of the Islamic text through reasoning.

Infitah. Opening to the world or to other communities.

Jihad. Literally, "strife" or "struggle." It has been defined in the twentieth century by Islamists as a fight against local regimes declared as *kafir* or against Western powers. It has been translated by some as "holy war."

Kufr. Nonbelief, traditionally used to refer to idolatry.

Mufti. A high-ranking Muslim cleric.

Muhafiz. The governor of a particular province.

Nahda. Literally, "renaissance." A term used to refer to a cultural renaissance that took place in the Arab world in the nineteenth century.

Qada'. Political district.

Qa'immaqam. The representative of the state at the local level.

Sharia. Islamic law. It is based on two main sources, the Qur'an and the Sunna.

Takfir. Excommunication or anathematizing; the act of declaring someone as *kafir,* or nonbeliever (non-Muslim).

Taqiyya. Dissimulation, a practice that was often used by persecuted minorities, especially the Shi'a and the Druze communities. Under duress, these minorities can deny their faith or commit blasphemous acts without being held accountable.

Ulama. Plural of *'alim,* or Muslim religious scholar.

Ummah. Traditionally, the Islamic nation, but the term has also been used to refer to the Arab nation.

Za'ama. Leadership.

Za'im (pl. **zu'ama**). Community leaders who are perceived as intercessors for their clients or followers.

Bibliography

Abdel-Khaleq, Jaafar. *Intikhabat al-istiqlal 2005*. Beirut: Dar an-Nahar, 2006.

Abdelnour, Ziad K. "Parliament Reluctantly Caves in to Syrian Pressure." *Middle East Intelligence Bulletin* 3, no. 8 (2001). http://www.meib.org/articles/0108_l3.htm.

Abed, Aref al-. *Lubnan wa al-Ta'if*. Beirut: Markaz Dirassat al-Wihda al-Arabiya, 2001.

Abi Saab, Fares, et al. *Al-intikhabat al-baladiya fi Lubnan 1998*. Beirut: al-Markaz al-lubnani lil dirasat, 1999.

———, eds. *Al-intikhabat al-niyabia 1996 wa azmat al-dimuqratiya fi Lubnan*. Beirut: al-Markaz al-lubnani lil dirasat, 1998.

Abou Khalil, Joseph. *Qissat al-mawarina fi al-harb*. 6th ed. Beirut: Sharikat al-Matbu'at li al-Tawzi' wa al-Nashr, 2005.

Abrahamian, Ervand. *Khomeinism*. Berkeley and Los Angeles: Univ. of California Press, 1993.

Abu Issa, Shadi K. *Ru'assa' al-jumhuriyya al-lubnaniyya*. Beirut: Sharikat al-Matbu'at li al-Tawzi' wa al-Nashr, 2008.

Abul-Husn, Latif. *The Lebanese Conflict, Looking Inward*. Boulder, CO: Lynne Rienner, 1998.

Accord Libanais d'entente nationale. Lebanon: n.p., 1989.

Adwan, Charles. "Corruption in Reconstruction." Center for International Private Enterprise. http://www.cipe.org/pdf/publications/fs/adwan.pdf. Accessed Feb. 28, 2010.

Aghaie, Kamran S. *The Martyrs of Karbala: Shi'i Symbols and Rituals in Modern Iran*. Seattle: Univ. of Washington Press, 2004.

Ahmad, Rifaat Sayyid. *Hassan Nasrallah: Tha'er min al-janub*. Cairo: Dar al-Kitab al-Arabi, 2006.

Ajami, Fuad. *The Vanished Imam*. Ithaca, NY: Cornell Univ. Press, 1986.

Ajami, Joseph. "Lebanese Elections, 2005 Version: Land Liberation or Mind Liberation?" *American Behavioral Scientist* 49, no. 4 (2005): 634–39.

Alagha, Joseph. *Hizbullah's Documents: From the 1985 Open Letter to the 2009 Manifesto.* Amsterdam: Amsterdam Univ. Press, 2011.

———. *Shifts in Hizbullah's Ideology.* Amsterdam: Amsterdam Univ. Press, 2006.

Amnesty International. "Lebanon: Amnesty International Expresses Concerns at Violations in Pre-trial Detention of Tawfiq al-Hindi and Co-Defendants." Mar. 13, 2002. Amnesty International Index MDE 18/004/2002. http://www.amnesty.org/en/library/info/MDE18/004/2002/en.

———. "Lebanon: Dr. al-Mugraby Must Be Immediately Released." Aug. 13, 2003. Amnesty International Index MDE 18/011/2003. http://www.amnesty.org/en/library/info/MDE18/011/2003/en.

———. "Lebanon: Excessive Force and Torture by Security Forces Must Be Investigated." Jan. 30, 2003. Amnesty International Index MDE 18/004/2003. http://www.amnesty.org/en/library/info/MDE18/004/2003/en.

———. "Lebanon: Harassment and Intimidation of Human Rights Defender Must Cease." Sept. 24, 2003. Amnesty International Index MDE 18/014/2003. https://www.amnesty.org/en/library/info/MDE18/014/2003/en.

———. "Samir Gea'gea' and Jirjis al-Khouri: Torture and Unfair Trial." Nov. 23, 2004. Amnesty International Index MDE 18/003/2004. http://www.amnesty.org/en/library/info/MDE18/003/2004/en.

Anderson, Benedict. *Imagined Communities: Reflections on the Origin and Spread of Nationalism.* London: Verso, 1991.

Aoun, Michel. *Une certaine vision du Liban.* Paris: Fayard, 2007.

Arab Reform Bulletin. "Government Change in Lebanon." Nov. 20, 2004. http://www.carnegieendowment.org/arb/?fa=show&article=21132.

Arab Reform Initiative. "Women Candidates Sidelined in Lebanon Vote." May 29, 2009. http://ari.see-tek.com/spip.php?article2104.

Assaf, George, and Rana al-Fil. "Resolving the Issue of War Displacement in Lebanon." *Forced Migration Review* 7 (Apr. 2000): 31–32.

Avon, Dominique. "Les Ahbaches: Un movement Libanais Sunnite contesté dans un monde globalisé." *Cahiers d'Études du Religieux,* no. 2 (2008). http://cerri.revues.org/331.

Ayubi, Nazih. *Overstating the Arab State.* London: I. B. Tauris, 1996.

Baaklini, Abdo, Guilain Denoeux, and Robert Springborg. *Legislative Politics in the Arab World: The Resurgence of Democratic Institutions.* Boulder, CO: Lynne Rienner, 1999.

Bacassini, George. *Asrar al-Ta'if.* Beirut: Maktabat Bissan, 1993.

Bahous, Dalia. "Michel Sleimane." Centre d'Études et de Recherche sur le Monde Arabe et Méditerranén. http://www.cermam.org/fr/logs/portrait /liban_michel_sleimane_le_gener/. Accessed Feb. 27, 2010.

Barak, Oren. "Commemorating Malikiyya: Political Myth, Multiethnic Identity, and the Making of the Lebanese Army." *History and Memory* 13, no. 1 (2001): 60–84.

———. "Don't Mention the War? The Politics of Remembrance and Forgetfulness in Postwar Lebanon." *Middle East Journal* 61, no. 1 (2007): 49–70.

———. *The Lebanese Army: A National Institution in a Divided Society.* Albany: SUNY Press, 2009.

———. "Towards a Representative Military? The Transformation of the Lebanese Officer Corps since 1945." *Middle East Journal* 60, no. 1 (2006): 75–93.

Bar'el, Zvi. "Would Hezbollah Win in Lebanon Election Lead to War with Israel?" *Haaretz,* June 7, 2009. http://www.haaretz.com/hasen/spages /1090933.html.

Baroudi, Sami E. "Divergent Perspectives among Lebanon's Maronites During the 1958 Crisis." *Critique: Critical Middle Eastern Studies* 15, no. 1 (2006): 5–28.

Baroudi, Sami E., and Paul Tabar. "Spiritual Authority vs. Secular Authority: Relations Between the Maronite Church and the State in Post-war Lebanon." *Middle East Critique* 18, no. 3 (2009): 195–203.

Bartolomeo, Anna di, Tamirace Fakhoury, and Delphine Perrin. "CARIM Migration Profile: Lebanon." Consortium for Applied Research on International Migration. Jan. 2010. http://www.carim.org/public/migrationprofiles/MP _Lebanon_EN.pdf.

BBC News. "Beirut Blast 'Was Suicide Attack.'" Feb. 15, 2005. http://news.bbc. co.uk/2/hi/middle_east/4266587.stm.

Beck, Linda. "Democratization and the Hidden Public: The Impact of Patronage on Senegalese Women." *Comparative Politics* 35, no. 2 (2003): 147–69.

Belloncle, Edouard. "Prospects of SSR in Lebanon." *Journal of Security Management Sector* 4, no. 4 (2006): 1–19.

Bermeo, Nancy. "What Democratization Literature Says—or Doesn't Say—about Postwar Democratization." *Global Governance* 9, no. 2 (2003): 159–78.

Beshara, Adel, ed. *Antun Sa'adeh: The Man, His Thought.* Reading, England: Ithaca Press, 2007.

————. *Lebanon, Politics of Frustration: The Failed Coup of 1961*. New York: Routledge, 2005.

Betts, Robert B. *The Druze*. New Haven, CT: Yale Univ. Press, 1991.

Binder, Leonard, ed. *Politics in Lebanon*. New York: Wiley, 1966.

Blanford, Nicholas. *Killing Mr. Lebanon*. London: I. B. Tauris, 2006.

Bottomore, Tom. *Elites and Society*. 2nd ed. New York: Routledge, 1993.

Bou Melhab-Atallah, Daad. "The Treaty of Brotherhood and Cooperation." In *Al-ʿalaqat al-Lubnaniyya al-Suriyya*, 83–94. Antélias, Lebanon: al-Haraka al-thaqafiya, 2001.

Bourdieu, Pierre. *The State Nobility: Elite Schools in the Field of Power*. Stanford, CA: Stanford Univ. Press, 1996.

Bourdieu, Pierre, and Loic Wacquant. *An Invitation to Reflexive Sociology*. Chicago: Univ. of Chicago Press, 1992.

Boyd, Douglas. "Lebanese Broadcasting: Unofficial Electronic Media During a Prolonged Civil War." *Journal of Broadcasting and Electronic Media* 35, no. 3 (1991): 269–87.

Brynnen, Rex. *Sanctuary and Survival: The PLO in Lebanon*. Boulder, CO: Westview Press, 1990.

Burton, Michael, Richard Gunther, and John Higley. "Introduction: Elite Transformations and Democratic Regimes." In *Elites and Democratic Consolidation in Latin American and Southern Europe*, edited by John Higley and Richard Gunther, 1–37. New York: Cambridge Univ. Press, 1992.

Burton, Michael, and John Higley. "Elite Settlements." *American Sociological Review* 52, no. 3 (1987): 295–307.

Butters, Andrew Lee. "Hizballah's Christian Soldiers." *Time*, Aug. 6, 2007. http://www.time.com/time/world/article/0,8599,1650192,00.html.

Call, Charles, and Susan Cook. "On Democratization and Peacebuilding." *Global Governance* 9, no. 2 (2003): 233–47.

Cambanis, Thanassis. *A Privilege to Die*. New York: Free Press, 2010.

Camp, Roderic A. "The Political Technocrat in Mexico and the Survival of the Political System." *Latin American Research Review* 20, no. 1 (1985): 97–98.

Caroll, Susan J. "Political Elites and Sex Differences in Political Ambition: A Reconsideration." *Journal of Politics* 47, no. 4 (1985): 1231–43.

Chalcraft, John. *The Invisible Cage: Syrian Migrant Workers in Lebanon*. Stanford, CA: Stanford Univ. Press, 2009.

Charara, Waddah, and Muhammad Abu Samra. *Aqniʿat al-mukhallis*. Beirut: Dar an-Nahar, 2009.

Charbel, Ghassan. *Ayna kunta fi al-harb*. Beirut: Riyad el-Rayyes, 2011.

———. *La'nat al-qasr: Hiwarat ma' Elias Hrawi, Nabih Berri, Rafiq Hariri, Michel Aoun*. Beirut: Riyad el-Rayyes, 2008.

Chidiac, May, and Amal Moghaizel. *Le ciel m'attendra*. Paris: J'ai Lu, 2007.

Choueiri, Youssef. *Arab Nationalism, a History: Nation and State in the Arab World*. Oxford: Blackwell, 2000.

Dajani, Nabil. "The Press in Lebanon." *International Communication Gazette* 17, no. 3 (1971): 152–74.

Dalloul, Mohsen. *'Ahd Lahoud tahta al-muhakama*. Beirut: Riad el-Rayyes, 2008.

Dana, Nissim. *The Druze in the Middle East: Their Faith, Leadership, Identity, and Status*. Eastborn, England: Sussex Academic Press, 2003.

Dekmejian, Richard H. "Consociational Democracy in Crisis: The Case of Lebanon." *Comparative Politics* 10, no. 2 (1978): 251–65.

Denoeux, Guilain, and Robert Springborg. "Hariri's Lebanon: Singapore of the Middle East or Sanaa of the Levant?" *Middle East Policy* 6, no. 2 (1998): 158–73.

Duncan, Don. "Women Lose Out in Lebanese Politics." Arab Reform Initiative. July 21, 2009. http://arab-reform.net/spip.php?article2283.

Dupont, Hubert. "La nouvelle armée Libanaise: Instrument du pouvoir ou acteur politique." *Confluences Méditerranée*, no. 29 (1999): 57–71.

Edde, Henry. *Al-mal: In hakam*. Beirut: Sharikat al-Matbu'at li-Tawzi' wa al-Nashr, 1998.

Eid, Ghada. *Asas al-mulk*. Beirut: Sharikat al-Matbu'at lil Tawzi' wal Nashr, 2009.

———. *Al-khalawi: Akbar al-safaqat*. Beirut: Sharikat al-Matbu'at lil Tawzi' wal Nashr, 2008.

———. *Sukleen wa akhawatiha: Al-nifayat, tharwa wa thawra*. Beirut: Sharikat al-Matbu'at lil Tawzi' wal Nashr, 2007.

Eisenstadt, Shmuel. *Patrons, Clients, and Friends: Interpersonal Relations and the Structure of Trust in Society*. Cambridge: Cambridge Univ. Press, 1984.

Elkins, David J., and Richard E. B. Simeon. "A Cause in Search of Its Effect; or, What Does Political Culture Explain?" *Comparative Politics* 11, no. 2 (1979): 127–45.

Elsasser, Sebastian. "Between Ideology and Pragmatism: Fathi Yakan's Theory of Islamic Activism." *Die Welt des Islams* 47, nos. 3–4 (2007): 376–402.

Entelis, John P. *Pluralism and Party Transformation in Lebanon: Al-Kata'ib, 1936–1970*. Leiden, Netherlands: Brill, 1974.

————. "Structural Change and Organizational Development in the Lebanese Kata'ib Party." *Middle East Journal* 27, no. 1 (1973): 21–35.

Erdmann, Gero, and Ulf Engel. "Neopatrimonialism Reconsidered: Critical Review and Elaboration of an Elusive Concept." *Commonwealth and Comparative Politics* 45, no. 1 (2007): 95–119.

Euro-Mediterranean Human Rights Network. "Association Agreement Between the European Union and Lebanon." Oct. 24, 2002. http://www.euromed rights.org/en/news-en/emhrn-releases/emhrn-statements-2002/3380 .html.

European Union Election Observation Mission to Lebanon, 2005. "Final Report on the Parliamentary Elections." http://www.cggl.org/publicdocs /EU%20Final%20Report.pdf. Accessed June 23, 2011.

Executive Magazine. "Syria Banked by Lebanon." Apr. 2008. http://www .executive-magazine.com/getarticle.php?article=10501.

————. "Yasma Fuleihan." May 2006. http://www.executive-magazine.com /getarticle.php?article=8204.

Fakhoury-Muehlbacher, Tamirace. *Power-Sharing and Democratisation in a Stormy Regional Weather: The Case of Lebanon.* Wiesbaden, Germany: VS Research, 2009.

Farshakh, George. *Al-Fadl Chalaq: Tajribati ma'a al-Hariri.* Beirut: Dar al-'Arabiyya li al-'Ulum, 2006.

Firro, Kais. *Inventing Lebanon.* London: I. B. Tauris, 2003.

Fischer, Michael. *Iran: From Religious Dispute to Revolution.* Cambridge, MA: Harvard Univ. Press, 1980.

Formisano, Ronald P. "The Concept of Political Culture." *Journal of Interdisciplinary History* 31, no. 3 (2001): 393–426.

Frankel, Ephraim. "The Maronite Patriarch: A Historical View of a Religious Za'im in the 1958 Lebanese Crisis." *Muslim World* 66, no. 3 (1976): 213–25.

Free Patriotic Movement [al-Tayyar al-Watani al-Hur]. "General Michel Aoun." http://www.tayyar.org/Tayyar/FPMParty/GMA/Biography.htm. Accessed June 23, 2011.

Freiha, Adel. *L'armée et l'état au Liban (1945–1980).* Paris: Librairie Générale de Droit et de Jurisprudence, 1980.

Gambill, Gary C. "Damascus Co-opts the Phalange." Christian Falangist Party of America. http://falangist.net/kataeb.htm. Accessed July 23, 2011.

Gambill, Gary C., and Ziad K. Abdelnour. "Dossier: Fouad Malek." *Middle East Intelligence Bulletin* 4, nos. 11–12 (2002). http://www.meforum.org/meib/articles/0211_ld.htm.

Gaspard, Toufic. *A Political Economy of Lebanon, 1948–2002: The Limits of Laissez-Faire*. Leiden, Netherlands: Brill, 2004.

Gilsenan, Michael. "Problems in the Analysis of Violence." In *Guerres civiles: Economies de la violence, dimensions de la civilité*, edited by Jean Hannoyer, 105–22. Paris: Karthala, 1999.

Goetz, Anne Marie. "Political Cleaners: Women as the New Anti-corruption Force?" *Development and Change* 38, no. 1 (2003): 2–24.

Gray, Kevin. "To Live and Die in Beirut." *Portfolio.com*, Aug. 13, 2007. http://www.portfolio.com/careers/features/2007/08/13/Saad-Hariri-Profile/.

Grimsditch, Peter. "Basil Fuleihan, 1963–2005." *Executive Magazine*, May 2005. http://www.executive-magazine.com/getarticle.php?article=7106.

Gulf News. "Lebanon's Saad Hariri Heads to Syria." Dec. 19, 2009. http://gulfnews.com/news/region/lebanon/lebanon-s-saad-hariri-heads-to-syria-1.555493.

Gunther, Richard, and Larry Diamond. "Species of Political Parties: A New Typology." *Party Politics* 9, no. 2 (2003): 167–99.

Habermas, Jürgen. *The Structural Transformation of the Public Sphere*. Cambridge: MIT Press, 1991.

Hage, Ghassan. "Religious Fundamentalism as a Political Strategy: The Evolution of the Lebanese Forces' Religious Discourse During the Lebanese Civil War." *Cultural Anthropology* 12, no. 1 (1992): 27–45.

Haghighat, Elhum. "Neopatriarchy, Islam, and Female Labour Force Participation." *International Journal of Sociology and Social Policy* 25, nos. 10–11 (2005): 84–105.

Hajj, Hanna al-. "Al-intikhabat al-baladiyya wa al-ikhtiyariyya." In *Al-intikhabat al-baladiya fi lubnan 1998*, edited by Fares Abi Saab et al., 107–99. Beirut: al-Markaz al-Lubnani li al-Dirasat, 1999.

Hallaq, Aline. *Al-khalawi: Ashhar fada'ih al-'asr*. Beirut: Sharikat al-Matbu'at li al-Tawzi' wa al-Nashr, 2003.

Hamzeh, A. Nizar, and Hrair Dekmejian. "A Sufi Response to Political Islamism: Al-Ahbash of Lebanon." *International Journal of Middle East Studies* 28, no. 2 (1996): 217–29.

Hanf, Theodor. *Coexistence in Wartime Lebanon*. London: I. B. Tauris, 1993.

Harb, Mona. "Urban Governance in Post-war Beirut: Resources, Negotiations, and Contestations in the Elyssar Project." In *Capital Cities: Ethnographies of Urban Governance in the Middle East*, edited by Seteney Shami, 111–33. Toronto: Univ. of Toronto Press, 2001.

Harb, Mona, and Reinoud Leenders. "Know Thy Enemy: Hizbullah, 'Terrorism,' and the Politics of Perception." *Third World Quarterly* 26, no. 1 (2005): 173–97.

Harik, Iliya. "The Maronite Church and Political Change in Lebanon." In *Politics in Lebanon*, edited by Leonard Binder, 31–55. New York: Wiley, 1966.

———. "Voting Behavior: Lebanon." In *Electoral Politics in the Middle East*, edited by Jacob Landau, Ergun Özbudun, and Frank Tachau, 145–72. Stanford, CA: Hoover Institute Press, 1980.

Harik, Judith. "Change and Continuity among the Lebanese Druze Community: The Civil Administration of the Mountain, 1983–1990." *Middle Eastern Studies* 29, no. 3 (1993): 377–98.

———. "The Effects of the Military Tradition on Lebanon's Assertive Druzes." *International Sociology* 10, no. 1 (1995): 51–70.

———. *The Public and Social Services of the Lebanese Militias*. Papers on Lebanon 14. Oxford: Centre for Lebanese Studies, 1994.

———. "Sheikh al-'Aql and the Druze of Mount Lebanon: Conflict and Accommodation." *Middle Eastern Studies* 30, no. 3 (2004): 461–85.

Hatem, Robert. *From Israel to Damascus: The Painful Road of Blood, Betrayal, and Deception*. La Mesa, CA: Vanderblumen, 1999.

Haugbolle, Sune. "Public and Private Memory of the Lebanese Civil War." *Comparative Studies of South Asia, Africa, and the Middle East* 25, no. 1 (2005): 191–203.

Hazran, Yusri. "Between Authenticity and Alienation: The Druzes and Lebanon's History." *Bulletin of the School of Oriental and African Studies* 72 (2009): 459–87.

Helou, Marguerite. "Al-mar'a fi al-intikhabat al-mahaliyya." In *Al-intikhabat al-niyabia 1996 wa azmat al-dimuqratiya fi Lubnan*, edited by Fares Abi Saab et al., 403–50. Beirut: al-Markaz al-lubnani lil dirasat, 1998

Henley, Alexander D. N. "Politics of a Church at War: Maronite Catholicism in the Lebanese Civil War." *Mediterranean Politics* 13, no. 3 (2008): 353–69.

Hirst, David. *Beware of Small States: Lebanon, Battleground of the Middle East*. New York: Nation Books, 2010.

———. "The Syrian Dilemma." *Nation*, May 2, 2005. http://www.thenation
.com/article/syrian-dilemma.

Hitti, Philip K. *The Origins of the Druze People and Religion*. London: Saqi
Books, 2008.

Hoss, Salim al-. *'Ahd al-qarar wa al-hawa*. Beirut: Sharikat al-Matbu'at li al-
Tawzi' wa al-Nashr, 1991.

———. *'Ala tariq al-jumhuriyya al-jadida*. Beirut: Sharikat al-Matbu'at lil
Tawzi' wa al-Nashr. 1999.

———. *Lil haqiqa wa al-tarikh: Tajarub al-hukm ma bayna 1998 wa 2000*. Beirut: Sharikat al-Matbu'at lil Tawzi' wa al-Nashr, 2001.

———. "Prospective Change in Lebanon." In *Peace for Lebanon*, edited by
Deirdre Collings. Boulder, CO: Lynne Rienner, 1994.

Hottinger, Arnold. "Zu'ama in Historical Perspective." In *Politics in Lebanon*,
edited by Leonard Binder, 85–105. New York: Wiley, 1966.

Hourani, Albert. *Arabic Thought in the Liberal Age, 1798–1939*. Cambridge:
Cambridge Univ. Press, 1983.

———. "Ottoman Reform and the Politics of Notables." In *The Modern Middle East*, edited by Albert Hourani, Philip Khoury, and Mary C. Wilson,
83–110. London: I. B. Tauris, 2004.

Hudson, Michael. *The Precarious Republic: Modernization in Lebanon*. New
York: Random House, 1968.

———. "The Problem of Authoritative Power in Lebanese Politics: Why Consociationalism Failed." In *Lebanon: A History of Conflict and Consensus*,
edited by Nadim Shehadi and Dana Haffar-Mills, 224–39. London: I. B.
Tauris, 1988.

———. "Trying Again: Power-Sharing in Post–Civil War Lebanon." *International Negotiations* 2, no. 1 (1997): 103–22.

Human Rights Watch. "Operation Grapes of Wrath: The Civilian Victims."
Sept. 1997. http://www.hrw.org/legacy/reports/1997/isrleb/Isrleb.htm.

Hunter, Albert. "Local Knowledge and Local Power: Notes on the Ethnography of Local Community Elites." In *Studying Elites using Qualitative Methods*, edited by Rosanna Hertz and Jonathan Imber, 151–70. London: Sage,
1995.

Huntington, Samuel. *The Soldier and the State*. Cambridge, MA: Belknap, 1981.

Husseini, Rola el-. "Hezbollah and the Axis of Refusal." *Third World Quarterly*
31, no. 5 (2010): 803–15.

———. "Hizbullah and Non-violent Resistance: Delimiting the Boundaries of Peaceful Protest." In *Civilian Jihad,* edited by Maria Stephan, 235–52. New York: Palgrave Macmillan, 2009.

———. "Insights from the Field: Research Problems and Methodologies." *Orient* 44, no. 4 (2003): 607–22.

Ibrahim, Alia. "Few Women Enter Lebanon's Parliament." *Women's eNews,* Dec. 19, 2003. http://www.womensenews.org/story/the-world/031219/few-women-enter-lebanons-parliament.

Imad, Abdel-Ghani. *Al-harakat al-islamiyya fi Lubnan.* Beirut: Dar al-Tali'a, 2006.

International Crisis Group. "Israel/Hizbollah/Lebanon: Avoiding Renewed Conflict." Middle East Report no. 59. Nov. 1, 2006. http://www.crisis group.org/home/index.cfm?id=4480.

Israeli Intelligence and Terrorism Information Center. "Hezbollah's Shi'ite Youth Movement." Sept. 11, 2006. http://www.terrorism-info.org.il/malam _multimedia/English/eng_n/html/hezbollah_scouts_e.htm.

Jabbra, Joseph, and Nancy Jabbra. "Consociational Democracy in Lebanon: A Flawed System of Governance." *Journal of Developing Societies* 17, no. 2 (2001): 71–90.

Jackman, Robert W., and Ross A. Miller. "A Renaissance of Political Culture?" *American Journal of Political Science* 40, no. 3 (1996): 632–59.

Jain, Arvind. "Corruption: A Review." In *Issues in New Political Economy,* edited by Stuart Sayer, 241–92. Oxford: Wiley-Blackwell, 2002.

Jamali, Dima, Yusuf Sidani, and Assem Safieddine. "Constraints Facing Working Women in Lebanon: An Insider View." *Women in Management Review* 20, no. 8 (2005): 581–94.

Jisr, Bassem. *Mithaq 1943.* 2nd ed. Beirut: Dar an-Nahar, 1997.

Johnson, Michael. *Class and Client in Beirut: The Sunni Muslim Community and the Lebanese State, 1840–1985.* Reading, England: Ithaca Press, 1986.

Johnston, Michael. "The Political Consequences of Corruption: A Reassessment." *Comparative Politics* 18, no. 4 (1986): 459–77.

———. *Syndromes of Corruption: Wealth, Power, and Democracy.* New York: Cambridge Univ. Press, 2005.

Jouni, Hassan. "Migration circulaire au Liban." Consortium for Applied Research on International Migration. http://cadmus.eui.eu/handle/1814 /12256. Accessed June 23, 2011.

Kahan, Yizhak, Aharon Barak, and Yona Efrat. "Report of the Commission of Inquiry into the Events at the Refugee Camps in Beirut." Israel Ministry of Foreign Affairs. Feb. 8, 1983. http://www.mfa.gov.il/MFA/Foreign%20 Relations/Israels%20Foreign%20Relations%20since%201947/1982-1984 /104%20Report%20of%20the%20Commission%20of%20Inquiry%20 into%20the%20e.

Kapeliouk, Amnon. *Enquête sur un massacre: Sabra et Chatila.* Paris: Seuil, 1982.

Karam, Azza. "Democrats Without Democracy: Challenges to Women in Politics in the Arab World." In *International Perspectives on Gender and Democratization,* edited by Shirin Rai, 64–83. New York: Palgrave Macmillan, 2000.

Karam, Karam. "Les associations au Liban: Entre caritatif et politique." In *Pouvoirs et Associations dans le Monde Arabe,* edited by Sarah Ben Nefissa, 311–36. Paris: Centre National de la Recherche Scientifique, 2002.

———. "Civil Associations, Social Movements, and Political Participation in Lebanon in the 1990s." In *NGOs and Governance in the Arab World,* edited by Ben Nefissa, 311–36. Cairo: American Univ. in Cairo Press, 2005.

Kasparian, Choghig. "Les migrations irrégulières, au départ, vers et à travers le Liban." Consortium for Applied Research on International Migration, Notes d'Analyse et de Synthèse 2008/54. http://cadmus.eui.eu/dspace /bitstream/1814/10099/1/CARIM_AS%26N_2008_54.pdf. Accessed Feb. 26, 2010.

Kaufman, Asher. "Phoenicianism: The Formation of an Identity in Lebanon in 1920." *Middle Eastern Studies* 37, no. 1 (2001): 173–94.

———. *Reviving Phoenicia: The Search for Identity in Lebanon.* London: I. B. Tauris, 2004.

———. "Who Owns the Shebaa Farms? Chronicle of a Territorial Dispute." *Middle East Journal* 56, no. 4 (2002): 576–96.

Kechichian, Joseph A. "The Lebanese Army: Capabilities and Challenges in the 1980s." *Conflict Quarterly* 5, no. 1 (1985): 15–39.

Keller, Suzanne. *Beyond the Ruling Class.* Edison, NJ: Transaction, 1991.

Khairallah, Daoud L. "Secular Democracy: A Viable Alternative to the Confessional System." In *Peace for Lebanon,* edited by Deirdre Collings, 259–72. Boulder, CO: Lynne Rienner, 1994.

Khalaf, Mona Chemali. "Women in Post-war Lebanon." In *Lebanon's Second Republic,* edited by Kail C. Ellis, 146–58. Gainesville: Univ. Press of Florida, 2002.

Khalaf, Samir. "Changing Forms of Political Patronage in Lebanon." In *Patrons and Clients*, edited by Ernest Gellner, 185–206. London: Duckworth, 1977.

———. *Civil and Uncivil Violence*. New York: Columbia Univ. Press, 2002.

———. *Lebanon's Predicament*. New York: Columbia Univ. Press, 1987.

Khalidi, Rashid. "Arab Nationalism: Historical Problems in the Literature." *American Historical Review* 96, no. 5 (1991): 1363–73.

Khalil, Khalil A. "Ahzab Lubnan: Matha tabaqa minha?" *al-Massir* (Beirut), Apr.–May 1999.

Khazen, Farid el-. *The Breakdown of the State in Lebanon, 1967–1976*. Cambridge, MA: Harvard Univ. Press, 2000.

———. *The Communal Pact of National Identities: The Making and Politics of the 1943 National Pact*. Papers on Lebanon 12. Oxford: Centre for Lebanese Studies, 1991.

———. *Intikhabat Lubnan ma ba'ad al-harb*. Beirut: Dar an-Nahar, 2000.

———. "Kamal Jumblatt, the Uncrowned Druze Prince of the Left." *Middle Eastern Studies* 24, no. 2 (1988): 178–205.

———. "Political Parties in Postwar Lebanon: Parties in Search of Partisans." *Middle East Journal* 57, no. 4 (2003): 605–24.

Khazen, Farid el-, and Paul Salem, eds. *Al-intikhabat al-ula fi Lubnan ma ba'd al-harb*. Beirut: al-Markaz al-lubnani li dirasat, 1993.

Kiwan, Fadia. *La perception de la migration circulaire au Liban*. Consortium for Applied Research on International Migration, Notes d'Analyse et de Synthèse 2008/14. http://cadmus.eui.eu/dspace/bitstream/1814/8335/1/CARIM_AS%26N_2008_14.pdf. Accessed Feb. 26, 2010.

Knoke, David. "Networks of Elite Structure and Decision Making." *Sociological Methods and Research* 22, no. 1 (1993): 22–45.

Koekenbier, Pieter. "Multi-ethnic Armies: Lebanese Lessons and Iraqi Implications." Conflict Studies Research Centre. June 2005. http://www.comw.org/warreport/fulltext/0506koekenbier.pdf.

Kraidy, Marwan. "State Control of Television News in 1990s Lebanon." *Journalism and Mass Communication Quarterly* 76, no. 3 (1999): 485–98.

Kunovich, Sheri, and Pamela Paxton. "Pathways to Power: The Role of Political Parties in Women's National Representation." *American Journal of Sociology* 111, no. 2 (2005): 505–22.

Lacouture, Jean. "Trois interrogatoires respectifs." In *L'art d'interviewer les dirigeants*, edited by Sammy Cohen, 125–32. Paris: Presses Universitaires de France, 1999

Lamb, Franklin. "Why Is Hezbollah on the Terrorism List?" *CounterPunch*, Apr. 6, 2007. http://www.counterpunch.org/lamb04062007.html.

Lebanese Transparency Association. "Corruption in Lebanon." http://www .transparency-lebanon.org/index.php?option=com_content&view=article &id=22&Itemid=10&lang=en. Accessed June 23, 2011.

Le Billon, Philippe. "Buying Peace or Fueling War? The Role of Corruption in Armed Conflicts." *Journal of International Development* 15, no. 4 (2003): 413–26.

Leenders, Reinoud. "Nobody Having Too Much to Answer For: Laissez-Faire, Networks, and Postwar Reconstruction in Lebanon." In *Networks of Privilege in the Middle East: The Politics of Economic Reform Revisited*, edited by Steven Heydemann, 169–200. New York: Palgrave Macmillan, 2004.

Lemarchand, Rene, and Keith Legg. "Political Clientelism and Development." In *Analyzing the Third World: Essays from Comparative Politics*, edited by Norman W. Provizer, 120–49. Cambridge, MA: Schenkman, 1978.

Lerner, Robert, Althea K. Nagai, and Stanley Rothman. *American Elites*. New Haven, CT: Yale Univ. Press, 1996.

Le Thomas, Catherine. "Formation et socialisation: Un projet de (contre)-société." In *Le Hezbollah, état des lieux*, edited by Sabrina Mervin, 147–72. Paris: Actes Sud, 2008.

———. "Les Scouts al-Mahdi: La formation d'une génération résistante." In *Le Hezbollah, état des lieux*, edited by Sabrina Mervin, 173–79. Paris: Actes Sud, 2008.

Lezhnev, Sasha. *Crafting Peace: Strategies to Deal with Warlords in Collapsing States*. Lanham, MD: Lexington Books, 2006.

Liddle, Joanna, and Elisabeth Michielsens. "Women and Public Power: Class Does Make a Difference." *International Review of Sociology* 10, no. 2 (2000): 207–22.

Lijphart, Arend. "Consociational Democracy." *World Politics* 21, no. 2 (1969): 207–25.

———. *Democracy in Plural Societies*. New Haven, CT: Yale Univ. Press, 1977.

———. "Typologies of Democratic Systems." *Comparative Political Studies* 1, no. 1 (1968): 3–44.

Lyons, Terrence. "The Role of Postsettlement Elections." In *Ending Civil Wars: The Implementation of Peace Agreements*, edited by Stephen J. Stedman, Donald S. Rothchild, and Elizabeth M. Cousens, 215–36. Boulder, CO: Lynne Rienner, 2002.

MacKinlay, John. "Defining Warlords." *International Peacekeeping* 7, no. 1 (2000): 48–62.

Maila, Joseph. *The Document of National Understanding: A Commentary.* Prospects for Lebanon 4. Oxford: Centre for Lebanese Studies, 1992.

MainGate Magazine (American Univ. of Beirut). "Brain Drain." Fall 2009. http://viewer.zmags.com/publication/2e67a8ed#/2e67a8ed/20.

Majed, Ziad. "Lebanon: An Overview of the Media." In *Information and Public Choice: From Media Markets to Policymaking,* edited by Roumeen Islam, 209–14. Washington, DC: World Bank, 2008.

Makdisi, Samir. "Rebuilding Without Resolution: The Lebanese Economy and State in the Post–Civil War Period." In *Rebuilding of Devastated Economies in the Middle East,* edited by Leonard Binder, 95–126. New York: Palgrave Macmillan, 2007.

Makdisi, Ussama. *The Culture of Sectarianism.* Berkeley and Los Angeles: Univ. of California Press, 2000.

Mannheim, Karl. "On the Problem of Generations." In *Essays on the Sociology of Knowledge,* edited by Karl Mannheim, 276–322. London: Oxford Univ. Press, 1952.

Mansour, Albert. *Al-inqilab ʿala al-Taʾif.* Beirut: Dar al-Jadid, 1993.

———. *Mawt jumhuriyya.* Beirut: Dar al-Jadid, 1994.

McCallum, Fiona. "The Political Role of the Patriarch in the Contemporary Middle East." *Middle Eastern Studies* 43, no. 6 (2007): 923–40.

McLaurin, Ronald. "From Professional to Political: The Redecline of the Lebanese Army." *Armed Forces and Society* 17, no. 4 (1991): 545–68.

———. "Lebanon and Its Army: Past, Present, and Future." In *The Emergence of a New Lebanon: Fantasy or Reality?,* edited by Edward Azar, 79–114. New York: Praeger, 1984.

Mehlis, Detlev. "Report of the International Independent Investigation Commission Established Pursuant to Security Council Resolution 1595." United Nations. Oct. 19, 2005. http://www.un.org/News/dh/docs/mehlis report/.

Mervin, Sabrina. "Les yeux de Musa Sadr." In *Saints et héros du Moyen-Orient contemporain,* edited by Catherine Mayeur-Jaouen, 285–319. Paris: Maisonneuve et Larose, 2002.

Mideast Monitor. "Briefing: Lebanese Public Opinion." *Mideast Monitor* 1, no. 3 (2006). http://www.mideastmonitor.org/issues/0609/0609_6.htm.

Mills, Anthony. "IPI Completes Press Freedom Mission to Lebanon." International Press Institute. Oct. 23, 2009. http://www.freemedia.at/our -activities/missions/singleview/4582/.

Min al-Sadr ila Nasrallah. Beirut: Manshurat al-Rida, 2007.

Moosa, Matti. *The Maronites in History.* Syracuse, NY: Syracuse Univ. Press, 1986.

Moubayed, Sami. "Lebanon's Phalange Party: Back from the Grave?" *Washington Report on Middle East Affairs* (Jan.–Feb. 2002). http://www.wrmea .com/archives/janfeb2002/0201032.html.

Moyser, George, and Margaret Wagstaffe. "Studying Elites: Theoretical and Methodological Issues." In *Research Methods for Elite Studies,* edited by George Moyser and Margaret Wagstaffe, 3–23. London: Allen and Unwin, 1987.

Nabaa, Rafic. *Rafic Hariri: Un homme d'affaires premier ministre.* Paris: L'Harmattan, 1999.

Najem, Tom. "Horizon 2000: Economic Viability and Political Realities." *Mediterranean Politics* 3, no. 1 (1998): 29–56.

———. *Lebanon's Renaissance.* Reading, England: Ithaca Press, 2000.

Naoum, Sarkis. *Michel Aoun: Hulm am wahem.* Beirut: Matba'at al-Mutawasit, 1992.

Nassif, Daniel. "Al-Ahbash." *Middle East Intelligence Bulletin* 3, no. 4 (2001). http://www.meforum.org/meib/articles/0104_ld1.htm.

Nassif, Nicolas. "Intikhabat jabal Lubnan al-shamali." In *Al-intikhabat al-niyabiya 1996 wa azmat al-dimuqratiyya,* edited by Fares Abi Saab et al. Beirut: al-Markaz al-Lubnani lil Dirasat, 1998.

———. *Al-maktab al-thani: Hakim fi al-zul.* Beirut: Mukhtarat, 2005.

Neal, Mark W., and Richard Tansey. "The Dynamics of Effective Corrupt Leadership: Lessons from Rafik Hariri's Political Career in Lebanon." *Leadership Quarterly* 21 (2010): 33–49.

Nir, Omri. *Nabih Berri and Lebanese Politics.* New York: Palgrave Macmillan, 2011.

Norris, Pippa. *Driving Democracy: Do Power-Sharing Institutions Work?* New York: Cambridge Univ. Press, 2008.

Norton, Augustus R. *Hezbollah: A Short History.* Princeton, NJ: Princeton Univ. Press, 2007.

———. "Musa al-Sadr." In *Pioneers of Islamic Revival,* edited by Ali Rahnema, 184–207. London: Zed Books, 1994.

Nye, Joseph S. "Corruption and Political Development: A Cost-Benefit Analysis." *American Political Science Review* 61, no. 2 (1967): 417–27.

O'Ballance, Edgar. *Civil War in Lebanon*. New York: Palgrave Macmillan, 1998.

Ofeish, Sami. "Lebanon's Second Republic: Secular Talk, Sectarian Application." *Arab Studies Quarterly* 21, no. 1 (1999): 97–99.

Ottaway, Marina. "Promoting Democracy after Conflict: The Difficult Choices." *Perspectives* 4, no. 3 (2003): 314–22.

Owen, Roger. *State, Power, and Politics in the Making of the Modern Middle East*. New York: Routledge, 2004.

Pakradouni, Karim. *Sadma wa sumud: ʿAhd Emile Lahoud, 1998–2007*. Beirut: Sharikat al-Matbuʿat li al-Tawziʿ wa al-Nashr, 2009.

Paraipan, Manuela. "Interview with Ibrahim Kanaan." World Security Network. http://www.worldsecuritynetwork.com/showArticle3.cfm?article_id=14915. Accessed June 23, 2011.

———. "Lebanese PM Najib Mikati Forms a Technocrat Caretaker Government." *Global Politician*, Apr. 19, 2005. http://www.globalpolitician.com/2634-lebanon.

Pfaff, Richard H. "The Function of Arab Nationalism." *Comparative Politics* 2, no. 2 (1970): 147–67.

Picard, Elizabeth. *The Demobilization of Lebanese Militias*. Prospects for Lebanon 9. Oxford: Centre for Lebanese Studies, 1999.

———. *Lebanon: A Shattered Country*. Teaneck, NJ: Holmes and Meier, 2002.

Pipes, Daniel. "Radical Politics and the Syrian Nationalist Party." *International Journal of Middle East Studies* 20, no. 3 (1988): 303–24.

Prothero, Mitchell. "Beirut Bombshell." *Fortune*, May 4, 2006.

———. "The Money Scandal Behind the Hariri Assassination." *Time*, Oct. 2005. http://www.time.com/time/world/article/0,8599,1123483,00.html.

Putnam, Robert. *The Comparative Study of Political Elites*. Englewood Cliffs, NJ: Prentice-Hall, 1976.

Qassem, Naʿim. *Hizbullah: The Story from Within*. London: Saqi Books, 2005.

Qassir, Samir. *ʿAskar ʿala meen?* Beirut: Dar an-Nahar, 2004.

———. *Dimuqratiyat Suria wa istiqlal Lubnan*. Beirut: Dar an-Nahar, 2004.

———. "Dix ans après, comment ne pas réconcilier une société divisée?" *Mahreb-Machrek* (Paris) (July–Sept. 2000).

Rabil, Robert. *Embattled Neighbors: Syria, Israel, and Lebanon*. Boulder, CO: Lynne Rienner, 2003.

————. *Religion, National Identity, and Confessional Politics in Lebanon.* New York: Palgrave Macmillan, 2011.

Rayyes, Chantal. "Murr, le rempart de Damas." *Libération* (Paris), Aug. 28, 2000. http://www.liberation.fr/monde/0101344633-murr-le-rempart-de-damas.

Reporters Without Borders. "Annual Report, 2002: Lebanon." May 3, 2002. http://www.unhcr.org/refworld/docid/487c5262c.html.

Richani, Nazih. *Dilemmas of Democracy and Political Parties in Sectarian Societies: The Case of the Progressive Socialist Party of Lebanon (1949–1996).* New York: St. Martin's, 1998.

Richards, Alan, and John Waterbury. *A Political Economy of the Middle East: State Class and Economic Development.* Boulder, CO: Westview Press, 1990.

Rigby, Andrew. "Lebanon: Patterns of Confessional Politics." *Parliamentary Affairs* 53, no. 1 (2000): 169–80.

Rivoal, Isabelle. "Le poids de l'histoire: Druze du Liban, Druze d'Israël face à l'état." *Annales, Histoire, Sciences Sociales,* no. 1 (2002): 46–69.

Rondot, Pierre. "The Political Institutions of Lebanese Democracy." In *Politics in Lebanon,* edited by Leonard Binder, 127–41. New York: Wiley, 1966.

Rothchild, Donald, and Philip Roeder. "Dilemmas of State-Building in Divided Societies." In *Sustainable Peace: Power and Democracy after Civil Wars,* edited by Donald Rothchild and Philip Roeder, 1–26. Ithaca, NY: Cornell Univ. Press, 2005.

Rowayheb, Marwan. "Walid Jumblat and Political Alliances: The Politics of Adaptation." *Middle East Critique* 20, no. 1 (2011): 47–66.

Saad, Abdo. *Al-intikhabat al-niyabiyya li 'am 2005: Qira'at wa nata'ij.* Beirut: Markaz Beirut li al-Abhath wa al-Ma'lumat, 2005.

Saadeh, Sofia. "Women in the Sectarian Politics of Lebanon." In *Views from the Edge: Essays in Honor of Richard W. Bulliet,* edited by Richard W. Bulliet, Neguin Yavari, Lawrence G. Potter, and Jean-Marc Ran Oppenheim, 230–39. New York: Columbia Univ. Press, 2004.

Sabbagh, Amal. "Overview of Women's Political Representation in the Arab World." In *The Arab Quota Report: Selected Case Studies,* 7–18. Stockholm: International Institute for Democracy and Electoral Assistance, 2004.

Salem, Elie A. *Violence and Diplomacy in Lebanon.* London: I. B. Tauris, 1995.

Salem, Paul. Introduction to *Al-intikhabat al-ula fi Lubnan ma ba'd al-harb,* edited by Paul Salem and Farid el-Khazen, 11–28. Beirut: Dar an-Nahar, 1993.

Salibi, Kamal. *Crossroads to Civil War.* Ann Arbor, MI: Caravan Books, 1976.

————. "Lebanon under Fuad Chehab, 1958–1964." *Middle Eastern Studies* 2, no. 3 (1966): 211–26.

Saliby, George. *Za'amat wa 'a'ilat.* Beirut: Dar al-Nahda al-Arabiyya, 2001.

Salloukh, Bassel F. "The Limits of Electoral Engineering in Divided Societies: Elections in Post-war Lebanon." *Canadian Journal of Political Science* 39 (2006): 635–55.

Sawalha, Aseel. *Reconstructing Beirut: Memory and Myth in a Postwar Arab City.* Austin: Univ. of Texas Press, 2010.

Sawant, Ankush. "Nationalism and National Interest in Egypt." *International Studies* 22, no. 2 (1985): 135–51.

Sayegh, Daoud. *Al-nizam al-lubnani fi thawabitihi wa tahawulatihi.* Beirut: Dar an-Nahar, 2000.

Scheffler, Thomas. "Religion, Violence, and the Civilizing Process." In *Guerres civiles: Économies de la violence, dimensions de la civilité,* edited by Jean Hannoyer, 163–86. Paris: Karthala, 1999.

Schiff, Zeev, and Ehud Ya'ari. *Israel's Lebanon War.* New York: Simon and Schuster, 1984.

Schöpflin, George. "The Function of Myth and the Taxonomy of Myths." In *Myths and Nationhood,* edited by Geoffrey A. Hosking and George Schöpflin, 19–35. New York: Routledge, 1997.

Seaver, Brenda. "The Regional Sources of Power-Sharing Failure: The Case of Lebanon." *Political Science Quarterly* 115, no. 2 (2000): 247–71.

Sethian, Robert D. "Sa'adeh and Syrian Nationalism." In *Antun Sa'adeh: The Man, His Thought,* edited by Adel Beshara, 81–120. Reading, England: Ithaca Press, 2007.

Sewell, William H., Jr. "A Theory of Structure: Duality, Agency, and Transformation." *American Journal of Sociology* 98, no. 1 (1992): 1–29.

Sharabi, Hisham. *Neo-Patriarchy: A Theory of Distorted Change.* Oxford: Oxford Univ. Press, 1992.

Shari'ati, Ali. *Fatimah Is Fatima.* http://www.al-islam.org/fatimaisfatima/. Accessed June 29, 2011.

————. *Red Shi'ism vs. Black Shi'ism.* http://www.iranchamber.com/personalities/ashariati/works/red_black_shiism.php. Accessed June 29, 2011.

Shartouni, Joseph Wadi. *Inahu Huwa: Samir Geagea, min al-wilada ila al-wilada.* N.p, 2007.

Shatz, Adam. "The Principle of Hope." *Nation,* June 14, 2005. http://www.thenation.com/doc/20050704/shatz.

Shehadeh, Lamia Rustum, ed. *Women and War in Lebanon.* Gainesville: Univ. Press of Florida, 1999.

Shidiaq, Imad. *Al-muqawama wa sayyiduha Hassan Nasrallah.* Beirut: al-Maktaba al-Haditha, n.d.

Shils, Edward. "The Prospect of Lebanese Civility." In *Politics in Lebanon,* edited by Leonard Binder, 1–12. New York: Wiley, 1966.

Shuayb, Maha. "Education: A Means for the Cohesion of Lebanese Society." In *Breaking the Cycle: Civil Wars in Lebanon,* edited by Youssef Choueiri, 167–95. London: Stacey International, 2007.

Sinclair, Brady. "Studying Members of the United States Congress." In *Research Methods for Elite Studies,* edited by George Moyser and Margaret Wagstaffe, 48–71. London: Allen and Unwin, 1987.

Skovgaard-Petersen, Jakob. "Religious Heads or Civil Servants?" *Mediterranean Politics* 1, no. 3 (1996): 337–52.

———. "A Typology of State Muftis." In *Islamic Law and the Challenges of Modernity,* edited by Yvonne Haddad and Barbara Stowasser, 81–98. Walnut Creek, CA: AltaMira Press, 2004.

Slisli, Fousi. "Islam: The Elephant in Fanon's *The Wretched of the Earth.*" *Critique: Critical Middle Eastern Studies* 17, no. 1 (2008): 97–108.

Smith, Anthony D. "The 'Golden Age' and National Renewal." In *Myths and Nationhood,* edited by Geoffrey A. Hosking and George Schöpflin, 36–59. New York: Routledge, 1997.

Snider, Lewis W. "The Lebanese Forces: Their Origins and Role in Lebanon's Politics." *Middle East Journal* 38, no. 1 (1984): 1–33.

Sobelman, Daniel. *New Rules of the Game: Israel and Hizbollah after the Withdrawal from Lebanon.* Tel Aviv, Israel: Jaffee Center for Strategic Studies, 2004. http://www.isn.ethz.ch/isn/Digital-Library/Publications/.

Spears, Joanna. "Disarmament and Demobilization." In *Ending Civil Wars: The Implementation of Peace Agreements,* edited by Stephen J. Stedman, Donald S. Rothchild, and Elizabeth M. Cousens, 141–82. Boulder, CO: Lynne Rienner, 2002.

Stoakes, Frank. "The Supervigilantes: The Lebanese Kata'eb Party as a Builder, Surrogate, and Defender of the State." *Middle Eastern Studies* 11, no. 3 (1975): 215–36.

STRATFOR Global Intelligence. "Lebanon: Hezbollah's Rising Star." Nov. 16, 2009. http://www.stratfor.com/analysis/20091116_hezbollahs_rising_star.

Suleiman, Michael W. *Political Parties in Lebanon: The Challenge of a Fragmented Political Culture.* Ithaca, NY: Cornell Univ. Press, 1967.

Swedberg, Richard. *The Max Weber Dictionary: Key Words and Central Concepts.* Stanford, CA: Stanford Univ. Press, 2005.

Thompson, Eric. "Will Syria Have to Withdraw from Lebanon?" *Middle East Journal* 56, no. 1 (2002): 72–93.

Transparency International. "Corruption Perceptions Index, 2009." http://www.transparency.org/policy_research/surveys_indices/cpi/2009/cpi_2009_table. Accessed Feb. 28, 2010.

United Nations Programme on Governance in the Arab Region. "Annual Report, 2004: Lebanon." http://www.pogar.org/arabic/govnews/2004/elections/lebanon.html. Accessed Apr. 28, 2011.

United Nations Security Council. "Resolution 1583." Jan. 28, 2005. http://daccess-ods.un.org/TMP/1343547.10578918.html.

———. "Security Council Declares Support for Free, Fair Presidential Election in Lebanon." Feb. 9, 2004. http://www.un.org/News/Press/docs/2004/sc8181.doc.htm.

United Nations Special Tribunal for Lebanon. "Annual Report (2009–2010)." http://www.stl-tsl.org/x/file/TheRegistry/Library/presidents_reports/Annual_report_March_2010_EN.pdf. Accessed Mar. 11, 2010.

United States Department of the Treasury. "Treasury Designates Individuals Furthering Syrian Regime's Efforts to Undermine Lebanese Democracy." Nov. 5, 2007. http://lebanon.usembassy.gov/latest_embassy_news/press-releases/prtreasury110507.html.

Vinci, Anthony. "'Like Worms in the Entrails of a Natural Man': A Conceptual Analysis of Warlords." *Review of African Political Economy* 34, no. 112 (2007): 313–31.

Waite, Terry. "Justice or Revenge?" *Counterpunch,* Jan. 23, 2002. http://www.counterpunch.org/waite1.html.

Wakim, Najah. *Al-ayadi al-sood.* Beirut: Sharikat al-Matbu'at li al-Tawzi' wa al-Nashr, 2000.

Walter, Barbara. *Committing to Peace: The Successful Settlement of Civil Wars.* Princeton, NJ: Princeton Univ. Press, 2002.

Wantchekon, Leonard. "The Paradox of 'Warlord' Democracy: A Theoretical Investigation." *American Political Science Review* 98, no. 1 (2004): 17–33.

Weber, Max. *Economy and Society.* Berkeley and Los Angeles: Univ. of California Press, 1978.

Weinberger, Naomi. *Syrian Intervention in Lebanon.* Oxford: Oxford Univ. Press, 1986.

Weiss, Max. "The Historiography of Sectarianism in Lebanon." *History Compass* 7, no. 1 (2009): 141–54.

Wimmen, Heiko. "Rallying Around the Renegade." Middle East Research and Information Project. Aug. 27, 2007. http://www.merip.org/mero /mero082707.html.

Winslow, Charles. *Lebanon: War and Politics in a Fragmented Society.* London: Routledge, 1996.

Woodward, Bob. *The Veil.* New York: Simon and Schuster, 2005.

Yamak, Labib Zuwiyya. *The Syrian Social Nationalist Party: An Ideological Analysis.* Cambridge, MA: Harvard Univ. Press, 1966.

Young, Michael. *The Ghosts of Martyrs Square.* New York: Simon and Schuster, 2010.

———. "The Unlikely Quartet." *Executive Magazine,* Dec. 2005. http://www .executive-magazine.com/getarticle.php?article=7825.

Zahar, Marie-Joëlle. "Fanatics, Mercenaries, Brigands—and Politicians: Militia Decision-Making and Civil Conflict Resolution." PhD diss., McGill Univ., 2000.

———. "Lebanon's Ta'if Agreement." In *Ending Civil Wars,* edited by Stephen John Stedman, Donald S. Rothchild, and Elizabeth M. Cousens, 567–98. Boulder, CO: Lynne Rienner, 2002.

———. "Power Sharing in Lebanon: Foreign Protectors, Domestic Peace, and Democratic Failure." In *Sustainable Peace: Power and Democracy after Civil Wars,* edited by Philip Roeder and Donald Rothchild, 219–40. Ithaca, NY: Cornell Univ. Press, 2005.

Zein, Fares el-. "Lebanese Administrative Reform Experience from 1992 to 2002." Lebanese Army. Mar. 1, 2004. http://www.lebarmy.gov.lb/article .asp?ln=en&id=3204.

Ziadé, Khaled. "Tripoli: Famille et politique." In *La vie publique au Liban,* edited by Joseph Bahout and Chaoul Douayhi, 274–41. Beirut: Centre d'Études et de Recherches du Moyen-Orient Contemporain, 1997.

Zisser, Eyal. *Lebanon: The Challenge of Independence.* London: I. B. Tauris, 2000.

———. "The Syrian Phoenix: The Revival of the Syrian Social National Party in Syria." *Die Welt des Islam* 17, no. 2 (2007): 188–206.

Index

sociological study of, 183–84; student arrests and, 135

French mandate: Bank of Syria and Great Lebanon under, 254n21; Rafiq Hariri and, 94; Kata'eb Party and, 41; Bishara al-Khoury and, 7; mufti and, 144, 256n62; origins of, 15; Phoenicianism and, 199; press during, 152–53; Resolution 1559 and, 96; Syrianism and, 202; Troupes Spéciales du Levant and, 123

fromagistes (cheese eaters), 128–29

From Israel to Damascus (Hatem), 52–53

Frontiers Center, 135

Fuleihan, Basil, xi, 175–77, 224

Fuleihan, Yasma, 176

Future Movement, 39, 77, 245n107

Future TV, 156, 157

Gaspard, Toufic, 116

Geagea, Samir: Aoun and, 28, 254n35; apology by, 58, 241–42n55; arrest and imprisonment of, 30–31, 55, 56, 103, 188, 241n48; assassination of Rashid Karami and, 248n22; Battle of the Mountain and, 61; brief biography of, 224; Bsharri district and, 34; education of, 53, 241n40; Lebanese Forces and, 50–51, 52, 53–55, 240n34; legislative elections of 1992 and, 31; Malek and, 57–58; on Mouawad, 27; Ta'if Agreement and, 55–56. *See also* Lebanese Forces

Geagea, Setrida: brief biography of, 224; election of, 58; Samir Geagea's arrest and, 56; on gender quotas, 170;

marginalization of, 57; marriage of, 54; in Parliament, 259n15

Gemayel, Amin: Fouad Abu Nadir and, 240n34; anti-Syrian faction and, 47; Aoun's appointment by, 24, 46, 54, 125, 131; brief biography of, 224; heirs of, 262n56; Salim al-Hoss on, 100; Ibrahim Kanaan and, 184; Kata'eb Party and, 48, 49, 50, 51; Lebanese Armed Forces and, 124–25; legislative elections of 1992 and, 31; Michel Murr and, 107; "National Union" of, 33; as president, 45–46, 236n35; on presidential terms, 90–91

Gemayel, Bashir: assassination of, 44–45, 50, 51, 53; brief biography of, 224; election of, 236n35; Samir Geagea and, 53; heirs of, 262n56; leadership of, 43–45; Lebanese Forces and, 43–44, 49; Maronite monks and, 150; son of, 49

Gemayel, Nadim, 49, 224, 262n56

Gemayel, Pierre: arrest of, 41; brief biography of, 225; dynasty of, 42–43, 54; Kata'eb Party and, 40, 41, 51; Michel Murr and, 106; as parliamentarian, 42

Gemayel, Pierre, II: assassination of, 43, 49, 193, 240n31; career of, 46–47, 225; on Pakradouni, 48

Gemayel, Sami, 49, 225, 262n56

Gemayel, Solange, 259n15

gender inequality, 167, 170

gender quotas, 167, 169–70

general amnesty law, 56, 103, 249n40

General Directorate for State Security (Direction Générale de la Sécurité de l'État), 138